Religion and Society in Modern Europe

THE MAKING OF EUROPE

Series Editor: Jacques Le Goff

The *Making of Europe* series is the result of a unique collaboration between five European publishers – Beck in Germany, Blackwell in Great Britain and the United States, Critica in Spain, Laterza in Italy and le Seuil in France. Each book will be published in all five languages. The scope of the series is broad, encompassing the history of ideas as well as of societies, nations and states to produce informative, readable, and provocative treatments of central themes in the history of the European peoples and their cultures.

*Religion and Society in
Modern Europe*

René Rémond

Translated by Antonia Nevill

Copyright © René Rémond 1999
English translation copyright © Blackwell Publishers Ltd, 1999

First published in 1999 by Blackwell Publishers and by four other publishers: © 1999
Beck, Munich (German); © 1999 Critica, Barcelona (Spanish); © 1999 Editions du Seuil,
Paris (French); © 1999 Laterza, Rome and Bari (Italian).

2 4 6 8 10 9 7 5 3 1

Blackwell Publishers Ltd
108 Cowley Road
Oxford OX4 1JF
UK

Blackwell Publishers Inc.
350 Main Street
Malden, Massachusetts 02148
USA

British Library Cataloguing in Publication Data

A CIP catalogue record for this book is available from the British Library.

Library of Congress Cataloging-in-Publication Data

Rémond, René.
[Religion et société en Europe.   English]
Religion and society in modern Europe/René Rémond; translated by Antonia Nevill.
p.   cm. — (The making of Europe)
Includes bibliographical references and index.
ISBN 0–631–20817–8 (alk. paper). — ISBN 0–631–20818–6 (pbk.: alk. paper)
1. Church and state—Europe—History—19th century. 2. Church and state—Europe
—History—20th century. I. Title. II. Series.
BR735.R45613 1999
322'.1'09409034—dc21   99–19777
                                                  CIP

Typeset in 11 on 12.5pt Sabon
by Grahame & Grahame Editorial, Brighton.
Printed in Great Britain by MPG Books Ltd, Bodmin, Cornwall

This book is printed on acid-free paper

Contents

Contents

Series Editor's Preface

Europe is in the making. It is our great hope. But it will not be achieved unless it takes account of history: a Europe without a history would be a sad orphan, for today is born of yesterday, and tomorrow rises from the past. A past that must not paralyse the present but help it to be different in its loyalty and new in its progress. Our Europe, between the Atlantic, Asia and Africa, has indeed existed for a very long time, mapped out by geography, modelled by history, from the time when the ancient Greeks gave it the name which has been used ever since. The future must rely on those legacies which, since antiquity or even prehistory, have made Europe a world of exceptional richness and extraordinary creativity in both its unity and diversity.

It is the aim of the series The Making of Europe, which came into being on the initiative of five publishers of different languages and nationalities – Beck in Munich, Basil Blackwell in Oxford, Critica in Barcelona, Laterza in Rome and Le Seuil in Paris – to throw light on the building of Europe and its unforgettable assets, without disguising its inherited difficulties. In striving towards unity, the continent has lived through internal dissensions, conflicts, divisions and arguments. This series will make no attempt to conceal them. Commitment to the European undertaking must be made in the full knowledge of the entire past and in the perspective of the future; hence the active title of the series. The time does not seem to have arrived yet to write a synthesized history of Europe. The studies we offer are the work of the best present-day historians, European or not, already well known or not. They will tackle the essential themes of European history in the economic, political, social, religious and cultural fields, using both the long historiographic tradition that stemmed from Herodotus and the new ideas which, developed in Europe, have profoundly transformed historical science in the twentieth century, notably in the last few decades. Because their avowed aim is clarity, these studies are accessible to a wide readership.

Our ambition is to present some of the answers to the great questions asked by those who are building and will build Europe, and all those throughout the world who are taking an interest in it: 'Who are we? Where did we come from? Where are we going?'

Jacques Le Goff

Introduction: Religion and Society

Singular or Plural?

Religion and society: two entities, two abstract ideas that we do not ordinarily have occasion to encounter directly. Society is a creation of the mind; we belong to a social category, are members of a family, citizens of a nation, but where can we grasp the flesh and blood evidence of society? The same may be said of religion: we are acquainted with various churches, states maintain relations with the differing denominations, there is concern about the increasing number of sects, but what about religion as a tangible reality? For a time, therefore, I wavered between singular and plural: religion or religions? The hesitation was not merely a matter of whether or not to add an 's', any more than my uncertainty rested on a point of grammar. The choice involved the very direction of the subject and the angle of approach. If I chose the plural, I would inevitably take the path of a fragmented study of the different types of relationships that have been established, or broken, between the various religious denominations and society in each of the nations which make up the diversity of the European continent. This was not at all my intention. If my preference was finally for the singular, as this book's title shows, it was because it corresponded better with my wish to embrace religion overall, and with my original argument that through the particular features of all kinds, dogmatic as well as institutional and disciplinary, which create the differences between religions, a unique social phenomenon is at work posing common problems to all societies. I mean that I use the term 'religion' as it was understood at the beginning of the nineteenth century, and as it was depicted in painting or sculpture, as an allegorical figure, or as politicians spoke of it when paying homage and praising its social usefulness. It was the antithesis of impiety, the mother of charity, personified, usually adorned with a capital letter as befits a virtue. In their rhetorical language they were thus describing something probably not far removed from what our own day, using a less ambitious and less solemn expression, though more inelegant, would call the religious factor or phenomenon. Is this a transfer from the noble style to the sociological comment? Or is it, rather, a sign of our difficulty in finding a relevant term that will satisfy an intellectual requirement without being clumsy?

Which Religions?

At all events, my intention is to study the part played by this great social phenomenon in the life of European societies, and to measure the place it has occupied in people's minds, institutions, laws, customs, collective behaviour and exchanges of ideas. Although this study has a wider backdrop, its field of observation will be confined to religions in a stricter sense: only those which profess a belief in a personal God, present people with a way of salvation, teach a dogma and have produced stable communities, organized in institutions. I shall not include haphazard forms of belief in the supernatural, or those expressions of the search for the fantastic which flourish all the more as the great organized faiths wane, or any manifestations of the irrational. There is a good example of the criteria applied. The body calling itself the Church of Scientology will receive no consideration, even though its activities and very existence are a cause for concern to the public authorities. Should its exclusion be judged arbitrary because some of its members probably find that for them it answers what might be described as a religious aspiration? In France, under the ministry responsible for managing social affairs and, in particular, defining the categories with a right to the rules of social protection, there is a commission which examines requests from organizations which themselves claim to be religious, and gives a decision on their merits. This board rejected the petition of the Church of Scientology on the grounds that it offered no characteristics which could allow it to be considered religious, and especially the absence of any reference to a personal transcendence. One may note, in passing, the curious paradox of a state which declares itself unqualified in religious matters yet which is obliged by necessity to decide what is religious and what is not. I shall return to this peculiarity, because it is an excellent illustration of the complexity of the subject and also of the way in which practices have evolved.

For the same reason – concern for an exact definition of religion – my field of study will not include those religions which, in the wake of Jules Monnerot and Raymond Aron, it has become customary to call secular; in other words, the great contemporary ideologies, of which Marxism and its application, communism, are the most perfect expressions. Certainly, they offer more than one analogy with the classic religions, chiefly in the motivation and behaviour of their followers. Many joined the communist party as one joins a church, with the same fervour, and with all their heart and soul expected the same satisfaction.

Similarities abound in their organization, too. The political machinery of these ideologies employed excommunication, and demanded of those who were found wanting a self-criticism that was devilishly like confession. The parallel could be extended. But the term 'secular' that was applied to them draws attention to their insurmountable differences from religions properly speaking. One is dissuaded from making comparisons, not so much because, in the case of Marxism, their philosophy is materialistic, but because they rule out the existence of a next world or affect to have no interest in it, and this fact removes at the very outset the problem which will be the fundamental subject for observation and reflection: the relations, cordial or conflicting, of co-operation, submission or opposition, that can be established between religions whose prime aim is personal salvation with a view to a future life, and political societies busy with resolving the difficulties of the moment and devoted to organizing existence in this world.

Religion, Not Faith

This is not a book of religious history, or only indirectly so. It does not propose to measure the degree of adherence of populations to the faith taught by the churches, or the observance of rules of worship or even conformity to precepts concerning individual morality. If there is a direction to the distinction between faith and religion sketched out by theologians for some decades, between the internal nature of personal choice and obedience to social imperatives, my research does not lie in the act of faith but in the religious factor which is its corollary. In setting forth this duality as obvious and, even more, in affirming it to be self-evident that every religious conviction has a social dimension, I am well aware that I have already plunged into the controversies inherent in the subject. The social character is in fact one element for discussion and an issue in these debates. Obvious and quite legitimate for some, it is rejected by others as an undue pretension. Without going into the matter too deeply for the moment, let us note that the question lies at the heart of the dispute and arouses impassioned argument. That, alone, would be enough to justify a historical approach. In any case, and whatever one may think of the legitimacy of a public expression of the religious factor and its presence in the community, it is an unchallengeable historical fact that in Europe religion has for centuries had a collective dimension, and that its various confessional expressions have entertained all kinds of relationships with society.

As this book is not a study of religious history, it will not deal with individual convictions, yet it is impossible not to take them into account. Society's religion is not unrelated to the sincerity and fervour of personal faith; if there were no believers, there would be no problem of relations between society and religion. On the other hand, history teaches us that the fervour of the faithful, even if few in number, can break down a tyrannical regime. In any case, the two aspects do not merge; there may be a wide gap between the degree of people's religious feeling and the nature of relations between the churches and the state. In England and the Scandinavian countries the proportion of faithful who regularly attend services is minimal – 1 or 2 per cent – yet the state church enjoys a status which earns it the regard of the authorities and public opinion. Abiding by judicial criteria, these countries are still in the situation of being a confessional state and a Christian society. On the contrary, in nineteenth-century France and a number of catholic countries, Bavaria, Belgium, Italy and Portugal, governments practised a policy of hostility to religion and adopted a legislation intended to weaken it, while the majority of the population continued to observe religiously – that's the right word for it – the church's commandments. Today it would be the reverse; relations have relaxed between governments and religious authorities; disputes have found an amicable settlement, while the vast majority of individuals are indifferent to religion and no longer consider themselves duty bound to observe the rules laid down by the church, whether for forms of worship or private morality. This reversal of the situation is not illogical. The catholic church, having lost a great part of its influence, no longer gives the political power cause for anxiety; it no longer represents a threat to the independence of civil society or personal behaviour. The reader will have understood that my subject is the religiousness, no matter whether sincere or feigned, of the collective group and not of individuals.

Religion and Civil Society

Leaving aside individual religious convictions and feelings, and without in any way neglecting what the researches of religious history have to teach, the subject is not reduced to the never-ending story of the often stormy relations between the machinery of politics and ecclesiastical hierarchies, marching to the rhythm of surges of anticlerical fever and periods of clerical revenge. Nor is this book a study of juridical regimes, although it cannot do without an analysis of the statutes and legal matters that have occupied such an important place in the political history of the religious issue, between states and churches.

Though the well-known vicissitudes of this history are obviously not without a bearing on the relations between religion and society, more is involved; they do not necessarily follow the same curve on the graph. Between the level of political and juridical relations at the summit between the authorities of the two sorts of society and, at the other extreme, that of the convictions, feelings and behaviour of hundreds of millions of Europeans who are simultaneously the subjects or citizens of a country and followers of a church, there lies an intermediate level: the religiousness of civil society, its explicit references to religion, the latter's regulation of collective activities and the life of the national community. Contrary to an over-simplified representation, relations between religion and society do not lie entirely in a head-on confrontation between the political and the religious. The relationship is triangular; alongside state and religion is the society known today as civil. It is an area of principal interest to me and will receive my special attention. Let us pause for a moment at this term 'civil society'. Its recent usage is not without relevance to my topic. Formerly, civil was defined by contrast with religious, and some traces linger in current vocabulary: civil status, civil marriage, civil funerals as a display of the rejection of religion. Civil is also the opposite of military. Today it is most often used as the antonym of political; civil society is the opposite of the political class.

For all that they are distinct, political and legal relations between states and churches and those between religion and civil society are not totally out of tune. It would be absurd to think that measures taken by a government do not reflect the state of mind of a proportion of the population, even more so to imagine that they could have no effect on the religion of the civil society; as if the war waged against catholicism by Bismarck in Prussia at the time of the *Kulturkampf* (1873–5), or the secularization undertaken by the republicans in France on their coming to power in 1879 had not had some influence on individual behaviour and thinking, even though these two policies bear less responsibility for the progress of religion's detachment than the churches impute to them.

Nevertheless, they are different areas, and developments were not necessarily parallel or synchronous. The examples already quoted of countries in northern Europe have suggested that the two things were not always connected. Taking a casual view of the history of the nineteenth and twentieth centuries, one might even venture the theory that they developed in opposite directions. In the nineteenth century, relations between the authorities of the two societies were often execrable, although the majority of the population remained religious; in the twentieth century, disputes abated, a *modus vivendi* was gradually established, but large sections of the population had become alienated from religious practice. Some will perhaps argue that this was merely the result of the passing of time. But was this alienation, which concerns religious history, accompanied by civil society's abandoning all religious reference in its legislation and the organization of its activities? I intend to consider to what extent religion continued, and continues today, to exert an influence, either determinant or limited, on the conduct of society; in particular, whether civil law is still inspired by moral law as defined by the churches.

The Religious Era

Whatever today's response, there is no doubt that religion did hold an eminent position everywhere in Europe; and in a still recent past. Argument about it lay at the heart of philosophical debates and political controversies. At certain periods in the history of the continent its influence was almost unequalled. Not to take account of religion would be to prevent oneself from understanding a fundamental part of people's preoccupations, reactions and behaviour. It was an intrinsic feature of general history, which it affected on more than one count – political, religious, intellectual and cultural. There is hardly a country in Europe where it has not contributed to the making of history and influencing the course of events.

Present throughout all Europe, even if the terms and conditions in which it was set out vary to quite an extent from one country to another according to their particular histories, the issue also travels through time and spans generations. It comes from a distant past, almost from the mists of antiquity, and though it has become less urgent nowadays, questions about it have not entirely vanished, and we shall find plenty of proof when we approach the present. At one time it was believed that this long history had finally reached its conclusion with the definitive settlement of contentious points. For example, that was the intention and certain belief of the French members of parliament who passed a law in 1905 severing the last links connecting the churches to the state. What happened subsequently revealed the illusory nature of that conviction. In the first place, there is the enduring quality peculiar to religions. If every category of social happening has a specific duration, religions probably have the longest of all. They are part of the longevity peculiar to those cultural and intellectual matters which endure. Ideologies, too, outlive their founders as they do the circumstances of their origins. Religions do this even more; every religion is attached to a tradition, is defined by its faithfulness to the words and example of its founder and refers to sacred scriptures on which its followers meditate generation after generation. Relations between religion and society naturally reap the consequences of this capacity for survival. Governments, for their part, do not easily relinquish acquired habits, so even those most won over to liberal ideas arguing for a separation of churches from government are tempted to preserve the practices of the old regimes which regulated the religious life of their subjects. Moreover, without anticipating the lessons that will emerge from a historical study of situations and developments, it is possible that the idea of an absolute separation of religion from society may be a utopia that could not withstand the force of reality. At all events, in the majority of European countries the matter has for some years been topical again. But is this merely an anachronistic resurgence of archaic problems or the emergence of a new set of difficulties? History will have to provide the answer.

The perspective of this long timescale alone enables the dominant tendencies to be distinguished. It also endows singular events with their true significance. Otherwise it would be impossible to understand how these controversies have gone on for so long. It would be difficult, for instance, to gain an insight into those bitter struggles in the political history of nineteenth- and twentieth-century France without returning to 1790, and the passing by the Constituent Assembly of the bill named the Civil Constitution of the Clergy (a title which by itself defined a certain concept of the relations between religion and society). It was at the roots of the division of national conscience over the act of the revolution; even today its consequences are not all exhausted. Similarly, the sort of problems which the reunified Germany has experienced since 1989 would not be comprehensible if one took no account of the Reformation which, some four hundred and fifty years ago, introduced confessional plurality into the Germanic world.

The Starting Point

It remains to choose a starting point somewhere in this long history, and this must be the French Revolution. Not from Gallocentrism, but because the decisions taken at that time, the Declaration of the Rights of Man and the Citizen and the Civil Constitution, inaugurated a new era – our own. Even though the protagonists were not clearly aware of it for, if their initiatives were the prelude to relations within the law between churches and states, their views remained among the most traditional; they were the heirs of the Gallican monarchy.

The objection may be raised to this point of departure that the roots of state secularization are far older. To stay within the frontiers of the kingdom of France, the state had freed itself from clerical domination as early as the time of Philip the Fair. In the empire, one can go even further back in time to the dispute over the Investitures and the confrontation of Guelphs and Ghibellines. G. de Lagarde devoted a number of books to the birth of secular thinking in the middle ages. However, on the eve of the Revolution all European societies were still confessional; everywhere religion was intimately interwoven with the life of society, allied with the ruling power and legitimizing it, a presence in all collective activities, governing social existence as well as private conduct.

We shall begin, therefore, in 1790, but just how far shall we travel in time? Right up to the present day. Current events invite us to do so, and show increasing signs that the matter is reactivated and controversies relaunched. The undertaking is not without risk, not because of the passions it arouses: for it is the historian's profession and a matter of honour to tackle the most burning and controversial topics objectively and try to introduce a little reasoning; but because by anticipating, one risks crediting this or that happening with an influence which subsequent events will prove wrong. It is difficult to assess with any certainty the relative importance and fundamental significance of events which have not yet emerged from the circumstances surrounding them. On the other hand, there would be no social usefulness in the historian who abandoned the present and failed to integrate it into an overall perspective.

Two Centuries of Change: Where Do They Lead?

The boundaries of the timespan are therefore set: a little over two hundred years, from the last decade of the eighteenth century to the very end of the twentieth. Though the question of relations between religion and society continued to be posed throughout this period, its terms changed a great deal. Political regimes evolved. Religion itself was transformed. Catholicism experienced a succession of periods: after the revolutionary turmoil came the triumph of ultramontanism over national particularisms, setting up a system that was both centralized and intransigent; then there was a recent development in the opposite direction.

Protestant churches have changed no less; the divergence is no smaller between the liberal protestantism of the nineteenth century and the thinking of Karl Barth in this century. The boundary which used to form the demarcation line of mutual interference has shifted. No state today would assume the right to intervene in the internal organization of churches to alter their discipline or liturgy. In return, the churches acknowledge that they have fewer rights to dictate the life of the community. Areas of friction are no longer the same; governments generally have ceased to interfere in epis- copal appointments. In France, the ringing of bells and the routes of religious processions scarcely give rise any more to a resort to administrative jurisdiction. With the few exceptions of countries that have remained in Christendom until the recent past (Italy, Ireland or Poland), the catholic hierarchy no longer goes to war against the legalization of divorce. Not that the Vatican has in the least modified its position on the indissolubility of the conjugal bond; it is the illusion of certain leaders of opinion that one day the Vatican will be obliged to change its view in order to adapt to the development of behaviour that has made divorce common- place. On the other hand, it is not inconceivable that it should ponder the attitude to be taken regarding the remarriage of divorcees and become more flexible for pastoral reasons. But if the catholic hierarchy no longer campaigns for the abrogation of divorce, today it fights against the legalization of abortion and for an unconditional defence of life against certain consequences of scientific progress.

Is it possible to find a direction in these changes in relations between religion and society? Do they obey a sort of logic and, if so, what? In the same way that by joining disconnected and apparently random dots on a surface one sometimes reveals an ordered pattern, by arranging all these changes in the order in which they took place and comparing them from one country to another, may they not reveal a general direction in which the whole of Europe has been travelling since the end of the eight- eenth century? These are the theories which inspired the concept of this book.

But the supposition is not entirely original. It is even a common- place of religious historiography; the growing separation between religion and society is a widely acknowledged paradigm. It is one of the aims of this book, therefore, to examine its relevance. What grounds are there for the idea that our societies, formerly governed by religion, are today emancipated from it; and, similarly, that reli- gion has less and less influence on individuals? In other words, is the whole religious history of Europe leading to the decline and ulti- mate disappearance of religion itself?

The Choice of Words

In setting forth this interpretation, all kinds of expressions are used, such as dechristianization, laicization, secularization, deconfessionalization and even, for England, disestablishment. Oddly enough, the word 'dereligionization' does not exist, probably because it is too clumsy and virtually unpronounceable. They are sometimes used indiscriminately, but these words are not interchangeable. They must therefore be distinguished from one another – a precaution that is particularly necessary on such a delicate and controversial subject. To give a name to a happening is at once to characterize it; words translate concepts. So let me be precise about those I prefer to use and those I shall leave aside.

Dechristianization is out; all present-day historians banish it after having made much use of it in the past. To use it implies that the country under consideration was previously christianized. Apart from the fact that yardsticks for the degree of christianization in former times are unreliable, how can it be said of a population that it attained such a stage of religious fervour that it could be called Christian? I can hardly use the word *laïcisation*;[1] it suffers from the inconvenience of being too exclusively French and too stamped by a singular history. The proof is that no true equivalent exists in other languages, and one is forced to resort to paraphrase. With a use that is already questionable for France, it could not serve in a perspective intended to be comparative. It has another failing: its ambiguity. The prolonged confusion between laicity and laicism, sometimes deliberately kept up by both partisans of laicity and its adversaries, gives it a hybrid status, straddling the opinions of reality, referring to a law-based regime – the laicity of the state, education or other institutions – and the reference to laicism, the ideology which inspired it but set itself up as a counter-religion. Disestablishment would not present the same drawbacks; it indicates the process by which a denomination is deprived of the prestige which made it a component of the state, a pillar of society.

---

[1]   The French word *laïcité* (laicity) means the system that excludes churches from the exercise of political or administrative power, especially with regard to the organization of education. *Laïcisme* (laicism) refers to the doctrine of the supporters of total *laïcisation* (laicization) of education, that is, the replacement of religious personnel with lay personnel. (*Trans. note*)

Rarely used in France, it is commonly employed in England, but its range is confined to a single aspect of the phenomenon that I shall consider in its entirety. All in all, it is the word secularization that receives my vote. Less equivocal than 'laicization', it embraces the entire field of relations between religion and society, civil as well as political. In addition, it has enjoyed international currency for a long time. It would be better to acclimatize it to France, where it was slower to penetrate. This, then, is the term it will be easiest to use, and the general intention of this book is to retrace the history of the process of secularization over the last two hundred years.

While I am on the subject of semantics, allow me to use two further instances which are closely connected with my theme and are a good illustration of the responsibility incumbent on words, which can be at the root of certain misunderstandings. People often contrast the actual relations that have been established between the public authorities and the religious authorities in France during this century, with article 2 of the Law of Separation, which stipulates that the Republic recognizes no system of religious belief. From this it is inferred that these contacts contravene the law, through a confusion between two interpretations of the word 'recognize'. It is one thing for a state to acknowledge a church as an institution that is the custodian of a truth, and quite another to take note of the existence in a country of communities to which a number of citizens belong and to establish relations with them. It is the simple recognition of a factual state, a sociological and not a philosophical or ideological reality. In truth, the French state had made an early start along the path of this distinction when the preamble to the Concordat agreed in 1801 between the Consulate and the Holy See stated that catholicism was the religion of the majority of French people as well as of the three Consuls. This was a statistical truth and not a dogmatic assertion.

The same observation obtains for the idea of separation. Because the law that instituted it was passed in a context of dispute, separation was interpreted as synonymous with the absence of any kind of relations. But there can be a distinct separation without antagonism. The separation of the two powers does not imply the absence of all relations between them. Quite the opposite, and it was the task of the constitutional documents to organize their co-operation. When husband and wife separate, it does not mean that they no longer have any contact, if only to decide on the upbringing of the children born to them when they were married. That is why the breach brought into force in France in 1905 was unable to put a definitive end to all relations between religion and society.

The Whole of Europe

After placing the subject in a timeframe, I must now define its area, which will be nothing less than the European continent in its entirety. This is an ambitious plan, but it is dictated by an assumption of the relative unity of Europe and a certain similarity in its problems, and is justified by the theory that the choice of a perspective on the scale of the continent will provide a more fundamental understanding and explanation than making separate and individual studies.

Generally speaking, relations between religion and society, whether cordial or stormy, close or loose, are dealt with in the framework of state entities. I mention the crisis of the *Kulturkampf* in Prussia, which set Bismarck against the catholic church, and consequently pay major attention to its political implications, the conflict between the Chancellor and the leader of the Zentrum, Windthorst, which seemed at the time to be an episode in the process of building the Reich and a vicissitude of the party system. Similarly, the dispute between Piedmont and the papacy is seen in relation to the unification of Italy. What is referred to in the classic account of France's history as the religious question, which is only one aspect – and the most superficial – of religious history, the ups and downs of relations between governments and the catholic church, is a chapter in political history. Though it is obvious that these conflicts certainly form part of the internal history of the peoples under consideration, and offer special features connected with their particular history and proceeding from the conditions peculiar to each country, these confrontations still had a bearing on common points at issue and arose from similar demands and revealed general problems. One senses the existence of forces that crossed frontiers and spread throughout the continent. Certain events had European repercussions and their immediate or deferred results made themselves felt in countries other than those where they had taken place. It was so for the French Revolution, and we shall see its implications and consequences for the whole of Europe. By assembling these separate histories in a synthesized view, we have some chance of grasping the essence of the problem of fundamental relations between religion and society. That is the gamble we take by treating the subject in a European perspective.

It is a real gamble, for we may well wonder if in all Europe's history there are other fields in which there is such a great variety of examples to draw on. Not only are there as many histories as there are peoples, but the diversity of denominations adds an extra differentiating factor, each religious faith having its own kind of organization and also its own particular concept of what should be the ideal relationship between religion and society. Moreover, the nations do not all keep in step. Time lapses between the countries touched first by secularization and those reached last may span more than a century. Since this study aims to pick out what is commonly at stake, to reveal points of convergence, it will not go into a detailed account of the particular developments of some twenty national entities which coexist on the surface of the smallest, but also the most history laden, continent on earth. It will favour the long term, and its first concern will be to extricate the main threads from the complex tangle of situations. It will attempt to throw light on the motives and considerations that inspired the process of secularization, for there is scarcely any other happening which has been so guided by ideas.

Part I

The Heritage and the Break

1

An All-Christian Europe

Even though it is agreed that the field of study will be confined to the last two centuries, it would be unthinkable not to look farther back in history. In no other sector of social activity has the weight of the past, which is always important, been so determinant as in religion and its relations with society. For some, it is a point of reference and source of authority, others challenge or dispute it, but all, consciously or unconsciously, are greatly dependent upon it. Even the most deliberate and radical breaks do not entirely sever links with the past; nor do they completely abolish its legacy or manage to erase its memory totally. It is still perceptible today even in those societies who believe themselves to be the most liberated from it. On the threshold of a study devoted to the relations between religion and society, it is therefore necessary to take stock of the situation on the eve of the event that was to turn traditional order upside down, and to recall some facts which remain constant.

The Special Feature of Europe

In the matter of religion, of all the continents Europe presents one original feature which is a point of major importance: it is the only one to have been totally christianized, although it was not the first to be evangelized. Christianity was born in the near east and the first churches were founded in Asia, but they later disappeared like those in Egypt and North Africa, submerged by Islam, and now survive in the titles of prelacies known as *in partibus infidelium*. The Gospel was not far behind in reaching Europe. In St Paul's lifetime there were churches in Corinth and Thessalonica, as witness the epistles addressed to them by the one who was known specifically as the Apostle of the Gentiles. In Gaul, the first Christian communities were formed probably as early as the second century in Provence and the Rhône valley. The presence of a bishop is attested at Lyons in 177 at the time of the persecution that struck this church. The Edict of Milan (313) made the existence of Christianity official throughout the Roman Empire, and at the end of the fourth century Theodosius made it the state religion, suspending the imperial cult and proscribing pagan forms of worship. In Gaul, the number of villages, amounting to several hundred, which today bear the name of St Martin, who died in 395, proclaim the antiquity of the evangelization of rural areas. That of the British Isles would come a little later, but by the sixth century Christianity had touched all the territories formerly incorporated in the Roman Empire.

The christianization of the rest of Europe took place in a second wave, four or five hundred years later in the ninth and tenth centuries. Around the year 1000 the Polish, Hungarian, Russian and Scandinavian monarchs by their conversion brought about the baptism of their subjects. The entry of these nations into Christian Europe completed the christianization of the continent. Although their conversion was belated in comparison with the first peoples to receive the Gospel, there is today no European country whose adherence to Christianity dates from fewer than a thousand years or so. Europe is certainly the oldest Christian continent.

For several of these peoples conversion was the founding event of their nation. Birth and baptism merged, as they did for individuals, whose baptism once marked their entry into existence. Even today they date the birth of their nation from the conversion of their sovereign. Hungary, annually celebrating the feast of St Stephen on 20 August, provides a memorial to the founder of the state and commemorates the birth of the nation. Even the soviet leaders celebrated with great splendour the thousandth anniversary of the baptism of Vladimir (987), regarded as the birth certificate of Russia. This concomitance established one of the most powerful bonds between national identity and religion, which would play a leading role in the nineteenth century in the movement through which nations would work towards their emancipation. Even today this identification remains a geopolitical factor and a key to understanding international relations in part of the continent.

Common adherence to the Christian faith was a component of European identity. It created an initial distinction from the other continents, which dwindled as Europe's missionary movement carried its faith to other lands. Christianity left its mark on the continent. Europe became covered by a great white mantle of churches. Monasteries were founded everywhere, and their monks helped to clear and cultivate the land. Terrain was marked out in grids, signs of the faith erected, ranging from humble crosses at intersections to the loftiest cathedrals and basilicas. With its liturgical calendar, Christianity left its imprint on time as well.

Breaks in the Unity

The religion of the whole of Europe, Christianity could have been a unifying agent, the cement of a community on the scale of the continent, and perhaps it was for a while. But, far from bringing people closer, religion became a cause of discord; Christianity divided into rival denominations, each jealously challenging the others for the honour of being the sole authentic expression of the Christian truth. The breach in Europe's religious unity occurred in two distinct phases.

The first closely followed the completion of the continent's evangelization; it was the consummation of the split between the western church, grouped around Peter's successor, situated in Rome near the tomb of the Prince of Apostles, and the eastern church, which recognized the absolute primacy of the Patriarch of Constantinople. The schism was the extension of the division of the Roman Empire. After the fall of Byzantium, which in 1453 succumbed to Turkish attacks, Moscow took over and claimed the honour of being the third Rome. This rupture between the Latin and Greek churches was perpetuated to the present day and is an element of the tensions which are now tearing apart the eastern side of the continent since the collapse of communism. The second split is more recent, and dates from the sixteenth century. This was caused by the Reformation in the sixteenth century, which completed the break-up of Christian Europe. Henceforward there were several religious Europes, fighting one another with the ferocity inspired by the certainty of being the sole custodians of the truth, the desire to propagate it and a zeal to win souls, apparently disinterested motives which were added to all the other reasons that heads of state and peoples derive from ambition or covetousness. The consequences of those divisions are still making themselves felt; religious wars are not all extinguished, and this distinct category of conflict does not yet belong in the 'outmoded' list. In Ulster, confrontation between catholics and protestants remains. As for the continuation of the first split, now over a thousand years old, the wounds are still raw. In former Yugoslavia the religious difference between orthodox and catholic adds one more element to the other reasons that Serbs and Croatians have for hating one another.

It is strange that, in a Europe described as having become vastly indifferent to religion, opposing camps continue to be designated, as in Northern Ireland, by their confessional denomination. Might the reciprocal lack of understanding and resentment of persecutions be the last flames of the fanaticisms of yesteryear? But is religion really the prime cause of today's conflicts? It may simply be a pretext for confrontation. These issues need to be included in any reflection on the present state of relations between religion and society.

Several Religious Europes

Owing to these huge fractures, on the eve of the Revolution which, having started out in France, went on to upset relations between religion and society and plant the seeds of a decisive development, Europe presented the picture of a continent that was religiously disunited and divided into enemy denominations. At least three, and possibly even four or five, entangled religious Europes can be distinguished.

One Europe stayed catholic, although the term leads to confusion, for this Europe was scarcely less transformed by the catholic Reformation than the other was by the Reformation. It made up a territorial whole that was relatively compact and almost in a continuous bloc, grouping the Iberian peninsula, with Spain (the bastion of the Counter-Reformation, where being catholic became identified with being Spanish), and Portugal, the entire Italian peninsula, the kingdom of France, from which the religion known as Reformed had been officially eradicated since the Edict of Fontainebleau (1685), annulling that of Nantes, putting an end to one of the rare experiments in confessional plurality; the Austrian Netherlands (today's Belgium), a few Swiss cantons, the western and southern regions of the Germanic world, chiefly the Rhineland and Bavaria, the patrimonial states of the Habsburgs, most of Hungary and, as the isolated sentinel, the republic of Poland.

A second Europe was that of the Reformation, or rather, Reformations, for it was not homogeneous and was shared among several denominations. Therein lies its difference from catholic Europe, and the Counter-Reformation's apologia did not fail to draw its argument from this fact, contrasting its own unity with the divisions of protestantism. The centre of gravity in this Europe lay in the north of the continent. The Scandinavian countries, Sweden, Denmark and part of the Germanic world immediately embraced Lutheran reform. The Reformation of Calvinist inspiration burgeoned in Switzerland, Hungary, Scotland and more than one German principality. As for England, which was among the first to separate from Rome, it finally adopted a middle road, preserving the fundamentals of the common heritage, dogma, liturgy and episcopal hierarchy. The United Provinces, which had escaped from Spanish domination, opted for a Reformation of democratic inspiration, repudiating the hierarchical structure.

The rift between these two Europes passed right through the middle of the Germanies, which mirrored the religious division. The western Rhineland and Bavarian south sided with the catholic Counter-Reformation, while Prussia, Brandenburg, Saxony and others chose the Reformation, but the dividing line was not clear-cut. After decades of advances and retreats following the fortunes of wars and the choices of rulers, the fronts were established in the mid-sixteenth century. Two hundred years later, the religious geography of the Germanic world perpetuated on a long-term basis the consequences of the choices, which were sometimes quite arbitrary, depending on the mood or ambition of a ruler, drifting along with a sovereign's spiritual itinerary, and central Europe presented a mottled appearance, like a panther-skin, in its juxtaposition of denominations. Going from one principality to its neighbour, one changed religion. The Augsburg Interim of 1555 having settled the religious problem on the principle of the unity of faith, and elevated the maxim *Cuius regio, eius religio* to a political principle, their locality determined the faith of subjects who perforce embraced the religion of their monarch. Germany, which at that time comprised a multiplicity of entities, free towns, principalities, bishoprics, some secularized, also combined the unity of faith of each element and the diversity of the empire's denominations. To the east of this nebula, the republic of Poland took a reverse position against the world of the Reformation, and prided itself on being the bulwark of catholicism in the face of orthodoxy. On the front line between the Latin church and the eastern church since the end of the sixteenth century, in the Ukraine and Belorussia the Uniate minorities combined loyalty to Rome with eastern tradition. As a general rule, the more eastern countries of Europe were more open to a plurality of denominations and more tolerant than western Europe. Whereas Spain and France imposed unity of faith by coercion, and expelled or forcibly converted dissidents, in the east denominations coexisted, in Poland or in Hungary.

The third Europe was, in fact, that of orthodoxy, looking towards Constantinople and Moscow. It covered the south-eastern quarter of the continent, but had been under the yoke of the infidel since the Turks set foot in Europe in the early fifteenth century. One after another, they subdued the populations of the Balkans and Danubian Europe, successively destroying the Christian kingdoms. The Ottoman tide flowed on, penetrating ever deeper into central Europe, to lap the walls of Vienna, where the siege in 1683 marked the farthest limit of Islam's advance on Europe. The ebb began almost at once; a century later, Hungary had recovered its freedom, but Serbia, Greece, Albania, Bulgaria and the Romanian provinces remained under Turkish domination. Because of this, Islam was a fourth component of religious Europe. The sultans never sought to convert the conquered populations; they left them to practise their religion, even negotiating with their religious leaders, being content to levy a tribute and ensure the people's docility. It was by staying faithful to their Christian religion that Greeks, Bulgars, Serbs, Romanians and Macedonians managed to preserve their identity. Nevertheless, in some regions, particularly Bosnia and Hercegovina, sections of the native populations converted to Islam. This religious difference lies at the roots of some of the antagonisms currently rending the states which used to be Yugoslavia.

Such a picture of the plurality of religions in Europe on the eve of the French Revolution would not be complete without mention of the Jewish diaspora. It was very unevenly spread over the continent, as there were few Jews in the west, from which they had been driven out, expelled from France by St Louis, from Spain by the catholic kings, from Portugal after its annexation by Spain in 1640. They sought refuge eastwards. The Ottoman Empire made them welcome. Jews were more numerous in central and eastern Europe, in Germany, Hungary and Poland, where they lived in communities, withdrawn into themselves, carefully preserving their own particular doctrine. In catholic Europe there was one exception; in his lands in the Comtat and in Rome the pope admitted a small Jewish community which would always be tolerated. There was thus a pronounced contrast between an intolerant western Europe, except for the United Provinces, and a more kindly disposed central and eastern Europe. This explains the unequal geographical distribution which foreshadowed the tragedy of Jewish communities in the twentieth century.

The official unity of faith in each territory and the apparent conformity of all subjects to the rules of the state churches must create no illusions or conceal the resistance of certain non-conformist spirits, those who were called free-thinkers, or make us overlook the existence of dissident minorities who affirmed their singularity against the world in general and were more or less tolerated by the authorities. Tolerated is the right word – provided it is allowed to retain the restrictive sense it had in those days.

The religious panorama of eighteenth-century Europe is thus the outcome of an extremely complex history. It was completely, or almost, Christian, but with a great diversity containing many divisions. The homogeneity to which the majority of states inclined was matched only by the variety of churches, their dogmatic pronouncements, liturgical expressions and disciplinary organizations.

Different Ecclesiological Traditions

The situation contains an additional complicating element with the great variety of answers given by the various denominations to the question of their relations with society and the political powers. If the question were put to all of them, they would give far from similar responses. Their diversity extended to the field of relations with society. The churches did not all deduce the same answers from the distinction set forth in the Gospel between what belongs to Caesar and what to God. There were nearly as many interpretations and definitions of what should be the relations between church and government as there were denominations.

If we consider the respective shares of circumstances and theologies in these differences, then the answer, even today, is not obvious and probably varies from one church to another. One may well think, for instance, that the heritage of Byzantium, taken up by tsarist Russia practising Caesaro-papism, partly explains the tradition of the eastern churches' submission to the will of the sovereign. In none of the nations in which orthodoxy was the religion did the churches ever enjoy true independence. To this specifically historical fact may perhaps be added a spiritual tradition turned more towards union with God than to sustaining the body of society, thereby implying a passive acceptance of temporal events.

The principle of the churches' internal organization was a further differentiating factor, depending on whether it was rather hierarchical or made room for a certain democratic expression. As well as leading to a conception of the organization of civil society, the type of discipline shaped behaviours, created customs, moulded sensibilities. In this regard Roman catholicism, Anglicanism and Lutheranism, which all preserved the episcopal hierarchy, differed profoundly from the Presbyterian denominations, Calvinist or Scottish, whose functioning relies on the participation of their followers in the faith's administration. The first group were more naturally disposed to accept all higher authority and to show it reverence and submission; the second, who practised collective deliberation, were predisposed to accept democratic operation, and more likely to challenge the decisions of authority. To that difference must be added their relative situation within the state, according to whether they were associated with the ruling power and enjoyed a privileged position or, if in the minority, whether they were persecuted or merely tolerated. Thus the Church of England had close links with the crown and its sympathies lay with the Tories, whereas the Whigs, Radicals and, later, Labour always recruited from the dissenters, among the Methodists or Baptists.

While acknowledging that all generalizations of this kind err by over-simplifying and reference will inevitably have to be made to exceptions, the divergences between the various confessional expressions of Christianity were clear-cut.

Of them all, in the matter of relations with state and society, the Roman catholic church indubitably made the greatest demands, even if it frequently had to come to terms with the powers that be and agree to compromises that restricted its freedom of speech and action. It also possessed the firmest and clearest doctrine. Not only did it expect the secular powers to recognize it as the perfect society, but it also made it their duty to support the faith in the exercise of its spiritual mission. In the churches that emerged from the Reformation there was not always a similar demand for official recognition; it was from their ranks that voices were often raised advocating a separation of the religious and the political in an era when alliance seemed the norm. The catholic church did not refrain from intervening in politics in the name of the morality which it drew from revealed religion and the Gospel. Though the papal institution sincerely repudiated the theocratic pretensions of men like Innocent III or Boniface VIII, and no longer upheld the theory of indirect power that justified the papacy's interference in government matters, the symbol of which was the triple crown worn by the supreme pontiffs until Paul VI set it aside, the pope deemed it to be his responsibility to define the Christian position on all problems of morality, private and public. This tendency has become even more pronounced since the end of the nineteenth century. Of course, the catholic church has always defined individual ethical conduct, especially for what has come to be called 'morals'. In the face of their liberalization, it has by no means relaxed its vigilance. The reverse is the case; the possibilities thrown open by the advances in scientific knowledge posed unprecedented questions to which the pope had every intention of providing an answer. Chiefly since the initiative of Leo XIII in 1891, devoting an encyclical to workers' conditions brought about by the industrial revolution, the church of Rome has increasingly intervened, building up a coherent doctrinal corpus on almost all the major problems presented to human society by the organization of social relations and those between peoples. For these reasons, for the catholic church relations between religion and society were especially close, and ran counter to the idea of a total separation between the two.

Since the split between the ideas of the Revolution and the principles of catholicism, it is usual to think that the latter was drawn by a natural inclination towards the unconditional defence of established order and the affirmation of conservative values: submission to authority, the cult of tradition, respect for the hierarchy, acceptance of inequalities. This tough line, undeniable in the nineteenth century, must not make us forget that catholicism had other potentialities which blossomed in different eras. Most French electoral practices – the rules followed by deliberative assemblies in France – were invented and applied by religious orders which acted as 'laboratories' for parliamentary institutions. In the very heart of catholicism runs a vein, which notably found its noblest expression in Franciscan spirituality, which dreams of a world where Isaiah's prophecy will be fulfilled and where all wars and conflicts will disappear, once and for all liberated from inequality and domination. From Joachim de Flore to certain groups of 1968 protesters, by way of the Jesuit conquests in South America, a vision of a Christian utopia has counterbalanced inclinations to alliance with governments. But in all instances, catholicism is always characterized in its relations with society by its attitude of maintaining an active presence.

It was not the same for all the churches of the Reformation, some of which were plainly less anxious to intervene in the public arena and were more willing to accept a certain reduction of the religious factor to a matter of personal conscience and confinement within a private area. Not all derived from reference to revealed religion such a precise conception of social order as did the church of Rome; in any case they did not seek to work out such a coherent social doctrine. In view of the positions adopted by certain churches today regarding demands for the autonomy of individuals and the liberating of everyday behaviour, demonstrating great liberalism, it would be tempting to think that they allowed personal responsibility a greater freedom than catholicism, which was accustomed to surrounding individual conduct with a network of obligations and constraints, if history did not remind us that no society went as far as protestant societies in the desire to dictate behaviour and impose a moral order. Puritanism is more the affair of protestant than of catholic societies. What could be more restrictive in the observance of morality than the communities of New England, Calvin's Geneva, Cromwell's England, Dreyer's Denmark or Bergman's Sweden?

In German history, some people believe they can explain why so many Christians unprotestingly accepted the policies of the Third Reich by reference to the theory formulated by Luther, at the time of the peasant wars, of two kingdoms or two rules. It sets forth a distinction, which is not only conceptual but governs behaviour, between the realm of conscience where the freedom of the believer is total, and the one where the ruler's authority is exercised, to which the Christian submits without in any way alienating his inner freedom. This idea certainly played a part in the formation of German political culture, but the schism that took place in 1934 in the heart of the German evangelical church, specifically on the attitude to adopt regarding national socialism, between German Christians, their allegiance pledged to the system, and the confessing church, like the sacrifice of Dietrich Bonhoeffer, suggest that Christians could infer opposing conclusions from the tradition of their church.

In the universe of the Reformation there is another tradition; one which inspired social Christianity, and which from 1925 was expressed in Life and Work within the ecumenical movement, to apply the spirit of Christianity to the problems of contemporary society, in the conviction that God has a plan for the world from which the church and Christians derive the duty to act in the society of mankind.

Anyhow, was it the logical application of their interpretation of Christianity or the result of persecution that shaped an attitude of subversive minority in French protestantism? At all events, it naturally tended to be anti-establishment and its sympathies went spontaneously to the downtrodden, more rarely to the established authorities.

If there is a conclusion to be drawn from this over-rapid inventory, then on the one hand it is undeniable that the various denominations derived differing ideas of relations with society from their theological tradition, and that this aspect must therefore be considered; on the other, great care must be taken not to generalize, as particular features of local histories can add special nuances to general outlines.

Catholicism's Special Features

In the range of denominations there is at least one institution that creates a major difference between the catholic church and the other expressions of Christianity in its relations with society: the existence of a pontiff whose supreme authority is recognized by the faithful in every country. Of course, in other churches there are institutions which enjoy exceptional regard, possess great moral authority and a certain influential power. The Patriarch of Constantinople is acknowledged by the whole of orthodoxy and holds an honoured primacy; his name is mentioned in prayers in all the churches in communion with the patriarchate. The Archbishop of Canterbury, the primate of the Church of England, enjoys the respect of all the churches throughout the world that are linked to it, but neither one nor the other has effective power over the functioning of the sister churches or the appointment of their officials. The recent controversies over the ordination of women showed the various Episcopalian churches taking opposite sides without anyone being able to arbitrate between them or impose a decision. The Lutheran alliance is just one instance of meeting and agreement without the power to act.

It is a very different matter for the church of Rome. The pope is the outward sign of the communion of faith and a respected personage. One would, of course, be wary of projecting on to the Europe of the *ancien régime* the picture that a combination of the strengthening of ecclesiastical centralization, the tightening of the links between the Holy See and the churches, and the proclamation of papal infallibility elevated to the status of dogma have all helped to produce. On the eve of the Revolution the papacy exerted only a distant and very loose supervision over the day-to-day life of churches that might be termed national. The catholic church in Europe was more a federation of churches than a centralized body; each had its own institutions, its rules of operation, its customs. The pope only rarely gave any teaching and the Curia intervened even less in choices for the episcopate since it had generally handed over appointments to the rulers who commanded the allocation of benefices and consequently possessed unopposed power over the churches. Governments meddled in their life in order to keep it under their thumb. Sovereigns appropriated this right with a clear conscience, since by virtue of the sacred rite of their crowning they themselves were part of the ecclesiastical establishment. In the eighteenth century, they intervened with the intention of bringing churches into line with the spirit of the age; thus Joseph II boldly reformed the liturgy, and in France the Regular Clergy Commission effected all kinds of regroupings of monasteries.

Nevertheless, the original feature created by the presence of a supreme authority had a major consequence for relations between religion and society. Whereas for all other Christian denominations, orthodox and reformed alike, dialogue was established directly between the political power and the various national churches, with catholicism relations were always more complicated by the intervention of a third partner: the Holy See, which negotiated with governments. The relationship was thus triangular. When disputes arose, the Holy See did not necessarily blame governments and did not always espouse the viewpoint of local episcopates. It was more inclined to look for an amicable solution, and on more than one occasion it would disappoint the expectations of the faithful. The result of the existence of the Holy See was that, instead of being decreed unilaterally by the state, the catholic church's status was the subject of negotiations of a diplomatic nature between the states and the Holy See, and the measures adopted were consigned to documents that bear all the characteristics of a treaty between one power and another. When disagreements occurred, the points at issue assumed an international dimension.

Catholicism presented another feature which further accentuated its difference from other Christian denominations: the existence of the Papal States. The name is a good indication of the oddness of the situation; the pope was not only the spiritual leader of a church that stretched throughout the continent, he was also the ruler of an extensive territory which cut the Italian peninsula in two, from one sea to the other and from the banks of the Po to the kingdom of Naples, taking in Emilia, Romagna, the Marches, Umbria and Latium. Over this state the pope exercised absolute power. It was the only territory in Europe where theocracy persisted. The pope combined the two sovereignties, temporal and spiritual, religious and secular. This fusion was justified by the need to guarantee the pope's independence and harked back to historical arguments of questionable value. Though this mixture of the spiritual and temporal seems strange to us, it appeared less so to contemporaries in a Europe where, even after the secularizations of the Reformation, a number of bishop-princes survived, not only in Salzburg, exerting over their subjects an authority that had nothing to do with purely spiritual authority, perpetuating a medieval situation.

2

The Traditional Regime

To characterize the relationship of societies with religion under the *ancien régime*, and to describe the closeness of their union, the expression usually employed is the 'alliance of the throne and the altar'. It is not a satisfactory one; it became used in the nineteenth century after the revolutionary split and in the context of a restoration of the traditional order that had been overthrown. It is not a suitable term to convey the earlier state, for to speak of alliance implies a prior distinction starting from which agreements are struck between two clearly individualized powers who each stand to gain advantages thereby. For the *ancien régime* it is an anachronistic view, as there was osmosis and interpenetration between the two; religion was omnipresent, and the intervention of society and, in particular, of public authorities in the life of the churches was not at that time perceived as the interference of an alien power. Relations between society and religion were experienced as a sort of joint possession which today would be considered confusing but which was not regarded as such at the time, the spirit of the age deeming this symbiosis quite legitimate.

The Confessional State: Unity of Faith, Political Unity

Under the *ancien régime* the state was confessional; just like individuals, it had a religion. It was inconceivable that it could *not* have one, as that would be to profess atheism. Now, even for an individual, atheism was banned and liable to result in prosecution. If the state had a religion, it could have only one; to practise several would be equally reprehensible. There was one exception, however, which underlines the singularity of the British case. Since 1707 the monarch had been the head of the church of England, but not in Scotland. That imperative expressed a principle which was then universally accepted and which allowed scarcely any relaxation in its application: the unity of faith of every state which governed relations between religion and society. The motto of the French monarchy, 'One faith, one law, one king' could well apply to all European rulers. Although at the end of the eighteenth century philosophers were beginning to question this in the name of freedom of conscience and to demand the right of individuals to have free choice in their religious belief, it still received almost general acquiescence. This unanimous religion could only be that of the sovereign; it was the old maxim *Cuius regio, eius religio*, which had settled the matter in the Holy Roman Empire and put an end to religious wars. Where one lived dictated one's religious adherence. The ruler's choice imposed the denomination of his subjects. Conversely, any infringement of this rule of oneness between the ruler's religion and that of his subjects was seen as an attack on the authority of the monarch and the unity of the kingdom. Sovereigns therefore did their utmost to reduce dissidence by forcible conversions or expulsions. The catholic kings had driven Jews and Muslims out of Spain. In France, after the expulsion of the Jews came that of the protestants. In 1685, the vast majority of European opinion had applauded Louis XIV's revocation of his grandfather's edict, which granted certain liberties to the followers of the religion known as Reformed. Curiously, France, the country which would later be the most welcoming to foreigners, was also the one which for centuries practised exclusion, persecuting any who held beliefs different from those of the sovereign.

There will be no mistaking the motives that inspired rulers with this uncompromising attachment to the principle of the unity of faith. The obligation was imposed on sovereigns and subjects alike. Henri IV had to renounce protestantism in order to reign over a France that had mostly remained catholic. Princesses were expected to embrace the religion of those they married and their new subjects; thus the little princess of Anhalt-Zerbst would convert to orthodoxy and even change her forename to become

Catherine the Great. In 1688, James II lost the crown of England through catholicism. Even today that principle of the religion of the ruler being the same as that of his subjects still exerts its consequences on the geographical divisions and distribution of denominations. If protestants are numerous in the Montbéliard region, it is because until the Revolution it was dependent on the principality of Württemberg, whose princes had embraced the Reformation in the sixteenth century. The principle had its own logic, of a time when religion had a presence in all social activities and the prevailing definition of truth was that it could not conceivably be relative in matters of religion, still less pluralist. There was only one truth; all the rest was error. Between one and the other there was no middle road. Each church, whether catholic, protestant or orthodox, was similarly imbued with the certainty of being the custodian of the one and only truth, and deemed a pernicious error any dogmatic assertion which deviated however little from its own prescribed precedent. It was therefore the state's duty to raise obstacles to the propagation of error and to contribute to disseminating the truth. All the churches sought the assistance of the ruling powers with a perfectly clear conscience. The king of England bore the title Defender of the Faith. On the day of their coronation, all sovereigns swore an oath to serve the state church.

Here, for example, is the text of the oath still taken in 1837, almost half a century after the French Revolution, by the young Queen Victoria on her accession to the throne:

> 'Will You, to the utmost of Your Power maintain the Laws of God, the true Profession of the Gospel and the Protestant Reformed Religion established by law? And will You maintain and preserve inviolably the Settlement of the United Church of *England* and *Ireland*, and the Doctrine, Worship, Discipline, and Government thereof, as by Law established within *England* and *Ireland*, and the territories thereunto belonging? And will You preserve unto the Bishops and Clergy of *England* and *Ireland*, and to the Churches there committed to their Charge, all such Rights and Privileges, as by Law do, or shall appertain to Them, or any of Them?'
> 'All this I promise to do.'

A second, more political, consideration lies at the root of the principle that a state could not admit a plurality of religions: the very widely shared conviction that loyalty towards the sovereign implies that his subjects should have the same religion, and also that a state is not united and is not likely to endure except by unanimous reference to commonly held values, which could stem only from religion. There was a perfect correspondence between religion and nation, religious loyalty and patriotism. Subjects loyal to the crown of England could be nothing else than members of the Church of England, as subjects of the Most Christian King could be none other than catholic. Everywhere religious dissidents were perceived as bad subjects, in every sense of the word; their obstinate persistence in error was a matter of distress to their sovereign and a reason to doubt their loyalty. They could not therefore be as completely national as the others and so it was logical that they should not enjoy the same rights. Thus, in the middle of the eighteenth century, those subjects of the king of France who persisted in the Calvinist heresy had no legal existence or civil status, since there was no one outside the catholic registers that recorded the sacraments. They were therefore deemed to be merely living together without benefit of clergy, their children were not legitimate, with all the negative consequences resulting from that. In England, the universities, still being church institutions, could entrust a teaching chair only to those who took the Easter sacrament in the Church of England, and Louis XV's France experienced a huge controversy on the matter of confession notes. Whatever their personal convictions, subjects were all expected to pay a tithe to the state church; so the Irish catholics had to pay it to the Church of England.

Religion governed the whole of life, both individual and collective; it presided over all social activities, nothing escaped its vigilance and control, and the state ensured that its rules of worship as well as its moral directions were respected. It occupied the entire social area, and gave a rhythm to the years; society followed its calendar for work and holidays. It solemnized all social functions. It had in its charge welfare assistance to the poor and education; universities and hospitals were institutions of religious origin and ecclesiastical status. The constraints exerted on individual consciences and liberties had their compensations: the protection of the weak, the alleviation of wrongs, assistance for the needy, homogeneity of conduct, common criteria.

In every state, ecclesiastical dignitaries were honoured and associated with government. In France the monarchy, though clinging hard to the state's preponderance over the church and taking care to protect itself from clerical meddling, often entrusted the office of chief minister to men of the church. After Richelieu and Mazarin in the seventeenth century, the cardinals Dubois and Fleury, under Louis XV, guided public affairs, and even on the eve of the Revolution Louis XVI called upon a great man of the church, the Archbishop of Toulouse, Loménie de Brienne. Bishops presided over state deliberations in the provinces which had preserved their ancient assemblies. In the early days of the Revolution, prelates often presided over the Constituent Assembly. Across the Channel, in a political system that limited the crown's prerogatives and divided power between it and Parliament, twenty-six bishops – the Lords Spiritual – sat in the upper chamber; the archbishops of Canterbury and York, as well as the bishops of Durham, London and Winchester, by right, the others in other of seniority of their accession to the episcopate.

In return, the crown drew part of its legitimacy from recognition by the church; the coronation ceremony was a religious act, the holy unction was like an eighth sacrament, the counterpart for royal office (bearing in mind the difference in the ministries) of the sacrament of ordination for clergy. Because of this, the monarch was a sacred person. In principle, the state was not only religious and confessional, it was sacral. Europe was thus wholly and entirely Christian. That by no means prejudged the inner convictions or degree of sincerity or fervour of the royal personages.

Pockets of Toleration

That was the doctrine. But the reality was somewhat different and, as the Revolution approached, practice had deviated from theory on several points. Under the constraint of certain hard facts and also the pressure of the intellectual movement that challenged the traditional system, a degree of toleration began to be accepted, more often in practice than in law. Toleration is really the apt word, provided it is allowed to retain its original sense, to designate those deviations from principles which continued to be honoured, taught and proclaimed. It was not at all a matter of formally acknowledging each person's right to profess other religions than that of the state or ruler, still less of admitting other faiths on an equal footing and granting their followers the same rights as those subjects who shared their sovereign's religion. Dissenters were merely left free not to conform to the regulations of the official church in the matter of form of worship and sacramental practice. Toleration was not the legitimation of confessional pluralism, even less the dissociation of society and state religion.

The sole experience of the legally recognized coexistence of two confessions on the same territory, among the one people and under the same crown, was that instituted in France by the Edict of Nantes, which lasted a little over three-quarters of a century. But the fact that it was terminated in 1685 by another royal edict emphasizes its precarious nature and bears witness that it was an anomaly in Europe of the *ancien régime*. The fact remains, however, that France had been the first to experience this, and that its exceptional nature was revealed as early as the end of the sixteenth century.

Toleration found its first favourable reception in protestant countries, whereas it was a point of honour with catholic kingdoms to maintain or re-establish unity in the one true faith. For some, perhaps, this was because they had had to combat intransigence, like the United Provinces which had managed to escape from the domination of catholic Spain after an interminable war. They were the first refuge of the persecuted from all over Europe, from the Jews driven out of Portugal after its annexation by Spain, to the free-thinkers who were able to work there without being harassed and publish books that were banned elsewhere. For others, because in the slow and laborious process of unification of the peoples they had not attained the same degree of cohesiveness as Spain or France, where political unity went side by side with religious unity. Thus the Germanies found religious peace only at the cost of accepting plurality. Although in each of the hundreds of units combined in the empire, oneness of faith remained the rule for relations between religion and society, and therefore the conformity of subjects to their ruler's denomination, several princes employed an intelligent policy with regard to foreigners driven from their own country for religious reasons. Sensing how much his sparsely populated state was likely to gain from an influx of protestants expelled from France by the repeal of the Edict of Nantes, many of whom were rich in ability, new ideas or scientific knowledge, the Elector of Brandenburg welcomed them with open arms. There was a time when a quarter of the inhabitants of Berlin were refugee protestants. Later, for the same motives, Catherine II took in the Jesuits who had been expelled by the catholic kings of Portugal and France, repudiated even by the papacy, and used them to help in the education of her subjects and the transformation of her empire. In these instances, it is obvious that the interest of the state had more to do with its policy of welcome than a sincere belief in the notion of toleration.

In Hungary the Lutheran and Reformed confessions had since 1686 enjoyed a status that put them on an equal footing with catholicism. In 1691, the *Diploma Leopoldinum* admitted confessional pluralism into Transylvania. In 1781, Joseph II issued an edict of toleration granting freedom of worship to Lutherans, Calvinists and members of the orthodox church. He also began to emancipate the Jews.

Great Britain was another land of toleration. In the course of his stay there, Voltaire discovered ten or fifteen denominations living on good terms with one another, and in his *Lettres anglaises ou philosophiques*, written in 1727 and published in 1732, he praised confessional plurality. Two very dissimilar churches had the same sovereign: in England and Ireland, where the Anglican church preserved the essentials of tradition prior to the split with the rest of catholicism, and in Scotland, where the presbyterian church had repudiated the hierarchical constitution and simplified dogmatic teaching. The British Isles was experiencing a regime of juxtaposed pluralism, but one that did not revise the fundamental legal inequality between the denominations and, in particular, brought about no lessening of the discrimination that affected followers of the dissenting churches, and papists even more.

The idea of toleration progressing and gradually imposing itself on minds contemplating relations between religion and society cannot be more clearly shown than by developments in France in the last years of absolute monarchy. Of all the European countries France had clung most tenaciously to the unity of faith, and from that principle had drawn the most rigorous applications against religious minorities. But in 1787 a royal edict granted protestants civil status together with freedom of conscience; they ceased to be pariahs with no legal existence. Mental attitudes had matured sufficiently not to be shocked when a Genevan protestant gained one of the highest offices in the kingdom, general control of finances. The only concession to prejudice was that the title conferred upon him was not that of his predecessors, and he was denied entry to the Council. The popularity enjoyed by Necker, which would force the king to recall him after his fall from favour, emphasizes the extent of the change in outlook and paved the way for the distinction between personal choice in the matter of faith and public responsibilities. France was ready to make the leap from simple toleration to full and complete recognition of religious freedom, implying the dissociation between faith and citizenship, and thereby opening a new chapter in the history of relations between religion and society in Europe.

3

The Breach

France was the country to make the first breach in the old order founded on the principle of state religion and one of the closest overlappings of religion and society, even if with some sovereigns political motives took precedence over religion. For the first time in a European society, belonging to a denomination would no longer be a measure of individual rights or a condition of citizenship.

The Founding Initiative:
Dissociating Denomination and Citizenship

The founding act was the drawing up of article X in the Declaration of the Rights of Man and the Citizen adopted by the Constituent Assembly on 26 August 1789. Re-reading this article two hundred years later, it is rather hard to understand its exact meaning and appreciate its scope: 'No one may be harassed because of his opinions, even religious ones.' This minor wording seems today more restrictive than liberal. It is the word 'even' that raises difficulties; we tend to see in it a limitation to freedom of conscience and to interpret it negatively as if, at the moment of proclaiming religious liberty, the members of the Constituent Assembly had faltered and conceded it only reluctantly and in a forced manner. In fact, this wording was disputed by the clergy's delegates who feared its probable consequences. To be correctly interpreted the article must be placed back in its own time, barely two years after the monarchy had granted protestants minimal recognition.

This document brought about a double break: with a centuries-old tradition in historical continuity, and in relations between religion and state. By putting religious convictions on a par with ordinary opinions, and extending to denominations the benefits of the freedom of choice enjoyed by the latter, the declaration undid the historical link between catholicism and political society. In April 1790 the Assembly confirmed its position by rejecting a motion acknowledging catholicism as the state religion. In future it would no longer be necessary to prove one's adherence to the catholic faith in order to enjoy all the rights, civil and political, attached to citizenship, as set forth in the other articles of the Declaration. In fact, several months later, the Assembly drew its own inferences when it granted full and complete citizenship, first to protestants, then to Jews in 1791. Henceforward in the eyes of the law all Frenchmen were equal, whatever their religion. Citizenship was uncoupled from denomination. For a long time France was the only country to have put this major and radical dissociation into operation. We shall see what timespans were necessary elsewhere, including the reputedly liberal countries. The Assembly members instituted a new concept, of a people composed of equal citizens, disregarding all the particular features that differentiated between them. They were laying the foundations of French political tradition dismissing all consideration of special conditions and any recognition of communities. This break had another consequence that was just as decisive; since non-catholics could be as good citizens and irreproachable patriots as catholics, so the link between catholicism and nation was also stretched. Religion was no longer the main basis of unity or the criterion of national identity. The catholic church could no longer claim to personify the whole of France or even the one true France. There could be any number of schools of thought. That would be challenged, for example, by the rebellion in the Vendée; the title 'catholic and royal army' affirmed an adherence to the old order which identified the nation with its loyalty to Rome.

Despite its low-key wording, the historical scope of the article was considerable. It contains in embryo the entire future of relations between religion and society. No regime in France would go back on this innovation. Not the Concordat of 1801; though it re-established part of the catholic church's privileges and restored

it to a more than honourable situation, this was justified by a
factual consideration: catholicism was 'the religion of the majority
of the French' and of the three consuls. It was a simple matter of
fact and not a religious truth. Even in its most reactionary phase
and under the inspiration of ultraism, the Restoration would not
question this established fact. In its article 5 the Charter of 1814
guaranteed the freedom of recognized forms of worship. From then
on there was no obstacle to non-catholics holding important
responsibilities in civil society or attaining the highest state offices.
As pronounced a protestant as Guizot was head of government for
seven years under Louis-Philippe, apparently without anyone
taking umbrage or making a public objection. Early in the Third
Republic the dismissal of catholics even gave protestants an over-
representation. In the first government constituted in 1879 after the
victory of the republican party, led by Waddington, they comprised
the majority of ministers. French history has experienced only one
tragic departure from the application of the principle laid down in
1789 – the policy of discriminatory exclusion decreed in 1940 by
the Vichy regime against the Jews. This deprivation of ordinary
rights was based, it is true, more on racial than religious criteria,
but belonging to Judaism was nevertheless one of them. With this
one grievous exception, the principle set forth at the dawn of the
Revolution definitively opened a new chapter for French society in
the history of relations between religion and society.

Not Yet Secularity

Although this initiative was destined to have such prolonged influence, the Constituent Assembly members were far from foreseeing
or desiring all its consequences. It would be an anachronism to read
into it the first assertion of our modern idea of secularity. Their
conception of the relations between religion and society was as far
as possible from our own and has little to do with today's debates.
Their entire ecclesiastical policy is a striking demonstration of this.
They shared the conviction, then generally held, that a nation
cannot do without a common religion to cement its unity. Thus
when the time came to celebrate the achievement of the great work
of remodelling all institutions – political, administrative, judiciary
and financial – and in the festival of the Federation solemnly to
make manifest the renewed unity of the nation through the freely
given consent of the citizens, for the anniversary of the taking of

the Bastille, the symbol of monarchic absolutism's defeat, it was unthinkable that the ceremony should not begin with a mass celebrated by a bishop delegate of the Constituent Assembly, accompanied by some three hundred priests. There is no better illustration of the extent to which, in that period, the idea of a separation of religion and politics was foreign to the spirit of the times, even to the nation's elected members.

They were also the heirs of the regalian or regalist tradition, intent on preserving the state's control over the ecclesiastical institution; the proof lies in the vote for a civil constitution of the clergy, two days earlier, on 12 July 1790. Contrary to the interpretation that might be inferred from a knowledge of the events that would follow from this document, it was not dictated by any animosity towards the catholic church, and still less by some antireligious design, despite counter-revolutionary theories. While not understating the hint of anticlericalism among the Jansenists, whom a long opposition to Rome had made receptive to Richerist arguments for a clerical democracy and the limitation of hierarchical power within the church, or a protestant desire for revenge, it has to be admitted that the Constituent members neither wanted nor foresaw the consequences that would emerge from this constitution. They had no real choice. They were prisoners of their earlier decisions. In November 1789, to set right the public finances whose parlous state had been the cause and the reason for the convocation of the States General, and to avert the bankruptcy whose spectre Mirabeau had evoked in such moving terms, the Assembly had decided, at the instigation of Talleyrand, former agent general of the clergy, to place at the disposal of the nation the possessions of the clergy, the kingdom's largest landowners. In return, the Assembly had undertaken to provide the clergy with a reasonable remuneration; this was the origin of the ecclesiastical budget. It was an initiative heavy with consequences: on the one hand the secularization of works of charity and education, which had for centuries been a part of the church's social function; on the other, now dispossessed of its own properties, and their income, the clergy was dependent on the state for its survival. Churchmen became *ipso facto* official agents paid out of public funds. The establishment of lists of holders of these public offices and the definition of their status was at the origin of the Civil Constitution.

Even more than from the necessity caused by the nationalization of the clergy's wealth, the Civil Constitution proceeded from a political will to harmonize the ecclesiastical organization with the new social order. The Assembly members had just reformed all the other institutions; why should the church remain outside this great movement? As well as their conviction that all the institutions in a society should necessarily be inspired by the same principles, their desire to bring the ecclesiastical organization into line with general principles was all the keener since it was their intention to entrust the church with a mission in society. If they had entertained any idea of secularity, however slight, such a thought would not have entered their heads, and they would have refrained from interfering in the church's internal functioning.

When they overturned its traditional organization they did not feel guilty of inadmissible meddling. They were doing no more than had been done before them by the kings of France. Since sovereignty had passed from the monarch to the nation, it seemed only fair that the latter's representatives should have the same right to intervene as the king's lawmakers. For centuries the Holy See had left it to the crown to appoint bishops; it seemed no more scandalous to have them elected by the citizens, as were the magistrates and local administrators. A few intellectuals who knew their history could argue that it was a return to the practice of the early church. The monarch had always assumed the right to regulate the life of the church. Parliaments had decreed the dissolution of the Society of Jesus, and on its own authority the Regular Clergy Commission had decided to do away with or merge a number of monasteries. Sovereigns abroad acted in the same way. Joseph II had undertaken a recasting of the rites and customs in his patrimonial states. The Constituent members, therefore, had not calculated the full scope of their initiative.

When they refused to negotiate with Rome over the change of status, and unilaterally substituted a bill for the Concordat of 1516, they broke with diplomatic tradition, but they also intended to establish themselves as continuing the political Gallicanism which had always made sure that the Holy See's right to supervise the church of France was kept within the limits. Had not the Parliament of Paris assumed the right to oppose the publication of papal bulls and the reception of the Councils' decrees in the kingdom?

The Constituent Assembly overturned the church's organization from top to bottom without burdening itself with its specific constitution. At one stroke of the pen, or more precisely, one ballot, it put an end to the existence of dioceses which prided themselves on having their origins in the first centuries of the Christian era, and mapped out ecclesiastical districts based on the new divisions of national territory, the *départements*, whose boundaries they adopted. Since election was now the source of all power and the way of allocating every office, parish priests and bishops were to be designated by voters, of the canton for the first, the *département* for the second. For the latter, episcopal consecration would be conferred by the bishops of neighbouring dioceses. The Holy See would simply be informed, but this was the procedure to which Rome had already consented with the Concordat of Bologna. The authors of this great upheaval could not honestly have believed that the new organization would obtain the approval of the Holy See. In any case, it hardly mattered to them. However, this reform which interfered so profoundly in the church's internal organization was in its inspiration as far removed as possible from a conception of the laicity that would be based on the distinction between the religious and the political. In this regard, despite certain circumstantial analogies, there was neither continuity nor relationship between the Civil Constitution of the Clergy in 1790 and the law of Separation of the Churches and State in 1905. The inspiration for the former was closer to that of Philip the Fair's councillors or Louis XIV's ministers engaged in disputes with the Holy See, than to the outlook of a man like Briand, spokesman for the law of 1905.

By its consequences, the 1790 initiative irreversibly altered relations in France between the political power and society on one side and religion on the other. This was due in part to the conflict engendered by the Civil Constitution; after keeping silent for too long, on 10 March 1791, Pius VI issued the papal brief *Quod aliquantum* condemning the provisions of the law and still more its inspiration, which was confused with that of the Declaration of the Rights of Man. The annexation of Avignon and the Comtat, the pope's property, which had been ratified in the interval by the Assembly, was perhaps not unconnected with the papacy's hardening attitude. It was an early example, before the complications of the Roman question in the next century, of the effects on relations between the Holy See and governments of combining two sovereignties in the person of the supreme pontiff, that of the spiritual head of the community of the faithful and that of the temporal sovereign exerting his authority over a territory and subjects.

The Split in National Conscience

Following the passing of the law and its condemnation by Rome, all the catholics in France, at that time almost the entire population, were called upon to choose between respect for the law passed by the nation's representatives and obedience to Rome; above all the clergy who had been elected curés and the bishops torn between two loyalties. The Assembly grew impatient and soon imposed on all ecclesiastics exercising public office an oath of loyalty to the Constitution, including adherence to the contentious bill. The members could not conceive that a public servant would not be devoted to the government that was paying him. Moreover, imbued with the idea that a state could not do without the co-operation of a church to assist it, the Assembly was not impartial in the schism dividing the catholics of France; it took up arms on behalf of the constitutional church and used the machinery of repression against the non-juring priests.

A First Step in Secularization

What followed belongs to general history; the rending of the national conscience and a division into two camps that were irreconcilable for a long time to come. However, the overall measures which resulted from the conflict between the two sides and punctuated its gradual radicalization stemmed directly from the history of relations between religion and society. In the wake of 10 August 1792 and royalty's downfall, the Legislative Assembly adopted measures which proved to be a great stride forward in the secularization of society. The institution of a civil registry – the expression is significant – dispossessed the clergy of a social function it had fulfilled from time immemorial, recording the highlights of individual existence, and similarly robbed religious instruments of their legal validity. The registers kept by the officers of the civil registry – again note the expression – replaced catholic records. It was no longer baptism that marked entry into life and the national community, but the declaration made at the town hall of one's birthplace. The same applied to marriage, with the institution of civil marriage and the obligation, under pain of punishment for any religious minister who contravened this regulation, to give precedence to civil over religious marriage. In any case, the institution of secular formalities would have been made necessary in order to register non-catholic affairs; but instead of maintaining several civil registries according to denomination, as in other countries, or recognizing the legal validity of religious documents, France chose the solution of a single, neutral civil registry. Society began to live a life that was distinct from the church community and denominational differences. This development reached its epilogue in 1872 with the disappearance of any mention of religion from census forms.

In the same movement, the Assembly took measures against the religious orders. The continuity is clear on this point, too. The monarchy had always mistrusted monastic orders, over which it did not enjoy the same means of control as over the secular clergy. They were suspected of being more devoted to the Holy See than loyal to the crown. In the eighteenth century that suspicion was coupled with a real aversion. Although even the least religious minds admitted the social usefulness of parish priests, if only as guardians of morality, no one any longer understood the reason for becoming a monk. The existence of the orders had become completely foreign to the spirit of the times, which regarded them as idle and useless. Above all, their existence and way of life clashed profoundly with the individualist inspiration of the first revolution, which was even more hostile to intermediate bodies than to the absolutism of monarchic government, for they represented a more direct and potentially more dangerous threat to people's individual freedom than did royal administration. In comparison with other bodies, monastic orders presented an additional disadvantage for the economy and society, and that was their immortality, which rendered their properties possessions in mortmain, thus avoiding the periodic redistribution that occurred with all other possessions on the occasion of inheritances. Most of all, the fact that an individual could take vows that committed him for life appeared to followers of the philosophical spirit as an unacceptable alienation of liberty. In February 1790, therefore, the Constituent Assembly declared that vows were invalid and banned them from being taken in the future, ordering the monastic orders to disperse. The controversy bounced back early in the twentieth century, and not for the last time. The argument that has arisen in our own era about sects accused of undermining individual freedom is somewhat comparable. For the same reasons, the Assembly abolished priests' celibacy.

This state of mind favouring the emancipation of individuals also inspired another initiative, which in this case concerned the laity: the ability to break the marriage vow. The Legislative Assembly instituted divorce; since marriage in the French legal tradition as in church law was based on the free consent of the two spouses, it seemed right that the two parties could correspondingly put an end to their union. This was a major initiative for relations between religion and society. It was the first time that behaviour contrary to the teaching of the catholic church was legalized. Until then, it had been inconceivable that civil and moral law could diverge, *a fortiori* become opposed. The vicissitudes of the status of marriage and divorce, almost to the present day, accompanied relations between religion and society in France to the rhythm of changes in regime and the overturning of majorities. Conservative governments, and even more so, reactionary regimes, would repeal divorce or make its application more difficult; liberal majorities and democratic governments would re-establish it or make its conditions more flexible. Thus the second Restoration abolished it in 1816; the republicans re-established it in 1884; the Vichy government, without going back on the principle, would extend the time requirements and increase the number of obstacles.

If France was one of the first countries to adopt a legislation that deviated from the teaching dispensed by the churches and to call into question the principle of the indissolubility of marriage, its example was followed after large lapses of time. Today divorce is accepted in all member countries of the European Union, but the achievement of this form of secularization was staggered over nearly two hundred years.

Though the revolutionary assemblies increased the initiatives that widened the split between the catholic church and new society, and set them on the path to a total break, even with the constitutional church which was decreed in 1795 by the post-Thermidorian Convention, it was not because the revolutionaries were converted to the idea of a distinction in kind between the political and the religious. On the contrary; they remained just as convinced as in the early days of the Revolution that a state needed a religion and did not exceed its powers by making a profession of faith. Robespierre instituted a festival of the Supreme Being, during which he set light to a statue of atheism, reputedly lacking in civic virtues. Since catholicism had refused to be the religion of regenerated France, the unifying function had fallen on other cults; for instance, the authorities encouraged theophilanthropy, which seemed well suited to a time when the social usefulness of religion was measured by the yardstick of what it did to ease poverty, and when benevolent acts were supplanting charity.

The religious policies of the revolutionary assemblies, which were the outcome of circumstances more than of an explicit plan but which were determined, step by step, by the results of the first measures, would have a bearing up to the present day on the way of conceiving relations between religion and society and putting them into practice. That is the key to the very special problem which is a fundamental feature of what is known as the French exception; instead of taking place as in other countries, amicably and without irremediable rifts, secularization occurred amid pain and confrontation. On both sides the process left suspicion and resentment which, as recent events show, have still not been erased.

Re-establishing Relations Does Not Mean Restoring Them

The First Consul's desire to re-establish religious peace arrested the cycle of persecutions and brought to a close a decade that had been like a final religious war. Catholicism regained a social position; for example, a decree of Messidor Year XII stipulated that military honours were to be paid at the Eucharist. It was not, however, a return to the status of the old order. The clergy did not recover its confiscated possessions. In a spirit of conciliation, Pope Pius VII agreed to give up their restitution (article 13 of the Concordat). The loss was considerable, and chiefly it kept the church in a position of dependence on the state for its subsistence. Governments up to the time of Waldeck-Rousseau would not give up the weapon with which this situation provided them; they would suspend the pay of priests or bishops who made unwelcome statements. The Concordat gave no decision on the catholic church's claim to be recognized as a perfect society, custodian of religious truth; it confined itself to noting that it was the majority religion in France. The government regained the appointment of bishops. Since every nomination involved expense, which had to be included in the finance laws, every pastoral initiative was subject to administrative authorization, using the expedient of the budget. Thus the creation of a new parish to cope with an increase in the population or the development of new districts was dependent on the administration, whose concerns did not necessarily coincide with those of the religious authorities. The resulting lapse of time between a realization of the spiritual needs of the population and the response was not without a bearing on the phenomenon known as dechristianization; the forming of a proletariat who, because of this, grew up removed from any religious instruction and any acquaintance with the sacraments. The Concordat therefore mapped out a legal framework in which the regalist tradition that kept the church in close dependence would still flourish.

Another major difference from the pre-Revolution situation was that catholicism was no longer the only recognized form of worship. Seeing that the French were not all catholic, when promulgating the text of the Concordat the consular government accompanied it with the publication of the Articles known as 'Organic'. Administrative vocabulary adopted the habit of referring to them simply as the Organics. While the Concordat was the outcome of a laborious diplomatic negotiation between the French Republic and the representatives of the Holy See, the Organics were the result of the right assumed by the state to regulate the policy of religious bodies – another expression of administrative language. It is noteworthy that administrative law knew religion only in the form of types of denominations. The authorities recognized their right to intervene in this domain only by reason of its social dimension. The Organic Articles meticulously regulated the application of the Concordat for the catholic religion and endowed the two protestant denominations with a status: the Augsburg Confession, that is, the Lutheran church, and the Reformed church of Calvinist tradition. Judaism would receive the benefit of legal recognition later, in 1805, as a religious, and obviously not as an ethnic, community. The Organic Articles bestowed on each of these denominations its own organization and representation in the public authority. The restoration of official relations between religion and society was effected on the principle of confessional plurality and equality between the recognized forms of worship.

This brief account of a disturbed decade which, in relations between religion and society, witnessed half a dozen contrasting experiences and then stabilized for a century in 1801–2, comprised a blend of elements borrowed from very ancient traditions and radical innovations. The situation instituted by the consular reorganization was no longer that of a confessional state professing catholicism, even less a sacral society. Napoleon's coronation, while celebrated at Notre Dame in Paris in the presence of the pope, was in no way a consecration; all the rites that made it a sacrament had disappeared. It was no longer the old alliance of the monarchy and the church, but neither was it secularity. Society was not secularized; religion had not been driven back into the sphere of the private individual. Nevertheless a seed had been planted in the bills which would lead by stages to an increasingly pronounced distinction between religion and social practice until their total separation in 1905. Citizenship was now irrevocably dissociated from any denominational reference; enjoyment of civil and political rights was no longer subordinate to any sort of adherence to an established religion. Freedom of worship was instituted for all recognized faiths on the basis of equality between them.

The range of this history did not stop at the borders of France. Its chief vicissitudes also influenced the course of relations between religion and society in other countries. Contrary to the saying attributed to Gambetta, according to which neither secularity nor anticlericalism were export articles, the French Revolution well and truly exported its religious policies and legislation. First, by conquest, in the wake of its armies; in all the occupied and annexed territories, such as Belgium and the left bank of the Rhine, it seized and put up for sale the church's possessions, and scattered the religious orders. With the civil registry it instituted the distinction between citizenship and faith, and equality of rights. Geography ensured that mainly catholic countries bore the full brunt of the upheaval in traditions and the disruption of customs. The coincidence of European catholic regions and the policy of brutal secularization practised by the revolutionaries had decisive importance for later relations between religion and society. It is not by chance that it was precisely in this part of Europe that the conflict between the spirit of the Revolution and attachment to catholicism experienced its greatest violence and took the turn of an ideological war dividing peoples among themselves. Only Spain, which was not invaded until later, at the time of the great Empire's hegemony, proved an exception. Instead of clearing the way for secularization, French occupation welded together Spanish patriotism and the most uncompromising catholicism, while simultaneously rejecting the invaders and French ideas.

The influence of French policies made itself felt even beyond the conquered and annexed territories; notably across the Rhine. Declaring the dissolution of the Germanic Holy Roman Empire in 1803, Bonaparte imposed a decisive change on the Germanies. He brought them out of the middle ages, of which this edifice, more mystical than political and to some extent mythical, perpetuated in the eighteenth century an archaic vision for which the Romantic movement would later preserve a nostalgia. The empire linked several hundred disparate units of territory – principalities, duchies, imperial cities, Hanseatic cities, bishoprics – and super-imposed on them the imperial dignity, theoretically elective, supposedly conferred by a college of elector princes, but which for centuries had been held uninterruptedly by the Habsburg house and was an integral part of that dynasty's patrimonial states. The Recess that put an end to the Holy Roman Empire in 1803 at the will of Bonaparte was a major date in Europe's political and re-ligious history; it signalled the end of the middle ages. The belated nature of the event perhaps explains the resurgence of medieval attitudes in Germany's public life right up to the twentieth century. Having reduced traditional institutions to a *tabula rasa*, Bonaparte set about rebuilding them. The Recess effected a redistribution from which a Germany emerged regrouped in a smaller number of states which were more compact and modern. It completed the movement begun by the Reformation and pursued by enlightened despots. After the secularizations carried out in the sixteenth century the last landowning bishoprics disappeared, together with many wealthy property-owning chapters and monasteries. It was also the end of an era of catholicism in Germany.

After some dozen troubled years, half of the continent, following the initiative of France, found that it too had lived through a real revolution in relations between religion and society. The transfor-mation was irreversible, and its effects have continued to evolve ever since.

Part II

Permanent Facts

4

The 'Religious Question': Issues at Stake

The French Revolution had opened a breach in the traditional edifice of relations between churches and society. It had shaken the system to its very foundations by dissociating creed and citizenship. Twenty-five years of unrest had ended in a compromise that had partially re-established the old order. At one time there was a belief in a return to the past and some people based their political programme on its total restoration. This hope, or illusion, was soon given the lie by reawakening controversies over the religious question. The latter occupied a central position in Europe's political history throughout the nineteenth century and, although these days it has perhaps lost some of its sharpness and seriousness, it would be premature to assert that the matter had found a definitive solution. From time to time it crops up again forcefully and upsets political positions. Like its metamorphoses, its developments and sudden revivals form yet another fundamental chapter in the continent's contemporary history.

The expression 'religious question', although classic, is not the most apposite, for what politicians of yesteryear and historians of today so describe deals with only one aspect, which is the least religious: relations between the public authorities and confessional institutions, states and churches. This is a question that concerns the law and politics, but has nothing much to do with religion, strictly speaking. Such an approach shows little interest in the specifically religious matter of faith, with all its consequences on the existence and behaviour of believers.

The religious question understood as the issue of relations between state and churches is itself only one aspect of a much vaster problem – the one that forms the subject of this book – of relations between religion in all its forms and society as a whole, not just in its political expression. Put into perspective, it is equally concerned with individuals and with governments, the private as well as the public, and leads to an examination of the boundaries of their respective areas, the fundamental issue being nothing less than religion's demand for the power to fill the whole of existence, both individual and collective, and to be omnipresent in the social domain and, in the opposite direction, the aspiration of both society and individuals to escape from religion's domination. In short, the basis of the dispute was none other than the secularization of society, civil and political alike.

This was the issue faced sooner or later by all European societies; none could elude it. All branches of thought were forced to find their own definition in relation to it. One might justly say that the question was truly universal.

However, it was not posed everywhere with the same violence as in France, where the problems it aroused would long be marked by the wounds of the religious war which had been a component of the Revolution, or as it had been in Spain. In Great Britain, for example, the matter had never divided opinion so profoundly. Nevertheless, hostility to popery would explode with great force in the nineteenth century when Pius IX re-established the catholic hierarchy, and interaction between Irish national feeling and catholicism would cause serious disturbances in the United Kingdom's internal order.

From one country to another, or rather from one Europe to another, the question was raised in very different terms according to the dominant confession: Roman catholicism, reformed Christianity, orthodoxy. It also changed according to political traditions and the memories of a tormented past. However, the religious question comprised, and still does, a body of common data that permit a general outline of its implications to be drawn up. By making a separate study, as is usually done, of the vicissitudes and episodes of particular histories, one loses sight of the consistency of positions and the way in which developments converged. The distinct elements of national histories do not invalidate a reasoned and analytical presentation of all the aspects of an argument which has widely dominated political confrontations and philosophical controversies throughout Europe for some two hundred years. We will return later to these various developments and problems.

Must the State Have a Religion?
Can the People Do Without One?

The first question is absolutely fundamental: must the state be religious? Can it exist without any religion? And, closely connected, is the question of the status of religion in the state and the nation. Under the *ancien régime* we have seen that it was the general rule which admitted no exception; even if government tolerated the expression of other beliefs on its territory, there was an official religion, a state church, whose recognition was one of the pillars of social order and, in return, was the basis for the legitimacy of the ruling power.

In monarchic regimes, that alliance took a personal turn. Traditional titles explicitly acknowledged this by qualifying the monarch as Most Christian King, His Apostolic or Catholic Majesty. The accession of a new sovereign was consecrated by a liturgical act, the rite of crowning, which was one with the ceremony of the coronation. And, unlike those that had embraced the Reformation, this took place even in states where the sovereign was not also the head of the national church. These principles and customs were maintained after the turmoil of the Revolution. In 1825 Charles X would revive the ancient pomp of the crowning rites; the marshals of the empire took their place among the peers of France. But that was to be the last royal consecration in France; in 1830 the religious act was replaced by a civil ceremony, when the Duc d'Orléans swore an oath of loyalty to the revised Charter. It was a symbolic substitution that marked a further stage in the secularization of French political society. Everywhere else the rites and ceremonies perpetuating the alliance between the ruling powers and the state church, as between the church and the nation, would survive.

As a result of this close association, the sovereign, unlike his subjects in all countries that had accepted freedom of conscience, was not free to choose his religion. As it was the rule to take a wife from or marry into a foreign royal house, often of a different faith, the spouse was obliged to abjure his or her own religion and adopt that of the new country. In 1840, on the announcement of the young Queen Victoria's engagement to Prince Albert of Saxe-Coburg, the Tory opposition to the Liberal government was disturbed by the rumour that he might be catholic, accredited by an official declaration that had omitted to mention that the fiancé was protestant, and let it be known that if this was the case the deposition of the sovereign would inevitably follow, since the 1707 Act of Settlement, which was the charter in this instance, made adherence to the Church of England a *sine qua non* for accession to the throne. To allay this fear, it was necessary to make it clear that the prince was really protestant. One and a half centuries later, this sort of demand has not entirely disappeared; when passing through Rome, the Prince of Wales, heir to the throne, was prevented from attending the private Mass of John Paul II in the name of constitutional tradition and his own obligations.

In the nineteenth century, when the movement of nationalities brought about the formation of several new nations which had to look for sovereigns among the royal houses of Germany or Scandinavia – usually protestant – the monarchs in Greece, Bulgaria and Romania had to convert to orthodoxy, as a pledge of their adherence to their new homeland and a condition that would ensure the loyalty of their subjects. The question of profession of faith was similarly put to peoples who did not live in a monarchy, for it was addressed just as much to nations, since nationality was distinct from the crown; the issue was whether the peoples could do without a religion. This seemed all the less acceptable as it was the generally received idea that nations had a truly religious vocation; God was watching them, and destined them for the accomplishment of His plans; in times of ordeal they sought His divine protection. These were all reasons that contributed to the establishment of a union between religion and nation which took over from the old alliance between religion and dynasty.

Thus being Spanish was identified with catholicism, Poland was the rampart of catholicism against orthodoxy, the empire of the tsars defined itself as Holy Russia. The German protestant states were not far behind in proclaiming that they had been chosen by providence to defend the true faith. The motto *Gott mit uns* was inscribed on the sword belt of Prussian soldiers. As for France, the seniority of its evangelization assured it of an unrivalled position: it was the Eldest Daughter of the Church, with the consequent prerogatives and duties. Christ loved the Franks and France was chosen to accomplish the *Gesta Dei* in history. In 1638 King Louis

XIII had consecrated his kingdom to the Virgin; the birth of Louis Dieudonné, future Sun King, had been heaven's reply. Every year on 15 August, on the feast of the Assumption of the Virgin, all the parishes in France renewed the vow; that was the significance of the processions which in every village honoured Our Lady Queen of France on that day.

But France was also the first nation in which a section of the citizens intended formally to dissociate national destiny from any religious reference; that was one of the implications of the dissociation between citizenship and confession. From now on the question of formal recognition of God and an explicit reference to His rights over the state and nation were the subject of discord and a factor in political struggles. Imbued with the idea that to omit such a reference was an act of impiety and equivalent to a declaration of atheism, catholics – attached to the traditional notions of the nineteenth century, along with their successors in the twentieth – fought ceaselessly for a public reaffirmation of the reign of God over society.

In the nineteenth century, their demand for a solemn attestation of faith by the authorities took the form of a public consecration to the Sacred Heart. For half-political, half-religious reasons, and partly those of circumstance, devotion to the Heart of Jesus, connected to the revelations of the blessed Marguerite-Marie Alacoque in the sixteenth century at Paray le Monial, took on a conservative political significance and gained a counter-revolutionary connotation. The Royal and Catholic Army of the Vendée had thus turned the heart surmounted by a cross into the emblem of its loyalty to the traditional order. In the aftermath of the tragic year 1870–1, after the defeat of France and the civil war, under the eyes of the enemy there developed a movement for the building of a basilica on the hill of Montmartre, where the Commune had begun with the massacre of generals Lecomte and Thomas. This would raise to the capital's sky the monumental sign of France's repentance for the crimes and failings which had brought down divine punishment upon it. *Gallia poenitens et devota* would be the watchword inscribed on the pediment of the building. In 1873 a majority of the National Assembly adopted the vow of a national consecration to the Sacré Coeur, to the irritation of republicans and all secularly inclined thinkers. The monument would remain a subject of division up to the present day. A century later, the year of the Commune's centenary, in the aftermath of May 1968, a handful of left-wing catholics occupied the basilica as a sign of revenge on the Versaillais and clerical reaction.

Early in the Third Republic, the hymn 'Save Rome and France in the Name of the Sacred Heart' linked in the same sentiment of dolorist piety the cause of the pope, robbed of his states and captive of the Piedmontese, and that of the bruised homeland which had fallen into the hands of the impious. From time to time the demand arose for the inscription on the white part of the tricolour of the sign of the Sacred Heart which, baptizing the Republic, would make it acceptable to catholics. In 1900, at the congress which on the initiative of Abbé Lemire, a republican deputy, assembled some four hundred clergy to greet the new century, a priest from the Gers, Abbé Castarède, who had already persuaded thirty-two municipal councils in his *département* to consecrate their commune to the Sacred Heart, proposed extending its recognition to the whole of France to combat official atheism. The organizer of the congress in person, Abbé Lemire, gave him his answer and stood out against the motion; it confused two absolutely distinct things, religious order and political order. In a desire to serve the one, it misjudged the other. A flag was not a banner.

The idea would recur periodically, however; during the Great War more than one catholic believed that such a consecration would ensure France's victory by drawing divine protection upon its weapons. Even today the concept has not disappeared. Certain supporters of French Algeria not so long ago, and today the movement inspired by Abbé Georges of Nantes, which calls itself Counter-Revolution, adopted the cross surmounted by the Sacred Heart as a sign of rejection of modernity, laicity and democracy. It was learnt that on Sunday 4 August 1996 in a Toulon church in the presence of the curé, the National Front elected mayor and his majority recited a prayer of consecration to the Sacred Heart as they emerged from mass. The next day the local press, as well as publications close to this extreme right-wing group announced that the town of Toulon had been dedicated by its councillors to the Sacred Heart, provoking a clarifying restatement by the bishop in terms approaching those of Abbé Lemire's assertion: 'This prayer must be considered as a private act, and cannot commit either the diocesan authorities or the Toulonnais as a whole. It is merely a religious gesture involving those who asked for it.'

Although this matter of an official consecration of the nation assumed such importance in France, it was also raised elsewhere and in several countries received a positive response. In 1889 Leo

XIII had issued an encyclical which dedicated humankind to the Sacred Heart. At the time the church extolled the example of the president of Ecuador, Garcia Moreno, who had consecrated his country to it. Spain and Belgium officially celebrated the cult of the Sacred Heart. The introduction by Pius XI of the feast of Christ the King into the liturgical calendar meant that everything must be subject to His monarchy and, indirectly, that of His church.

Independently of these acts of consecration, political life arranged other forms of homage to religion, such as the public prayers at the opening of parliamentary sessions to call for God's blessing on the work of the Assemblies. Similarly, honours were rendered during religious ceremonies. In catholic nations, sounding the *General salute* at the elevation of the Host, or the command given to soldiers to *Present arms*, in other words, the honours usually reserved for heads of state and civil authorities implied official recognition of the catholic dogma of the real presence.

From the same spirit proceeded all legislation making provision for specific punishments for misdemeanours or crimes related to the faith of a church. Thus there were especially severe penalties for blasphemy, or laws, like the one adopted in France in 1825, which imposed the same punishments on sacrilege as on parricide. In England, a twelfth-century law punished anyone who reviled Christianity or used improper and offensive language about God, Christ or the Bible. It would still be invoked in the twentieth century, the last time being in 1977.

For the churches, these honours, considerations and distinctions flowed logically from a simple recognition of the truth. Without falling into impiety the state could not avoid recognizing the true religion and granting it a privileged status. As soon as they came into power, the laics would find nothing more urgent than to rescind measures that they held to be contrary to the distinction between the political and the religious, and offensive to those who did not share the beliefs of official religion. These differing practices clearly revealed the diametrical opposition of the two ways of thinking about the confessionalism of both state and society.

From the state the argument indeed extended to all institutions in civil life, especially over religious emblems; the crucifixes whose presence or absence are for religious minds the symbol of a people's loyalty to their faith or, on the contrary, of their apostasy. Keeping or removing the crucifix in courtrooms, hospitals, classrooms and public buildings, as well as taking the oath on the Bible became the issues in impassioned battles; all the more so when they applied to institutions whose origins were often religious, such as hospitals. Then indignation over what was regarded as despoilment was added to the scandal of impiety. Two contradictory views clashed: for one, there could be neither a state without religion nor a society which did not profess a belief; for the other, the church's grip on society was an assault on liberty of conscience and contrary to the independence of civil and political society. On one side were the laws of God and the church; on the other, the liberty of individuals and the state.

One Religion or Several?

Nothing being more contrary to the idea of plurality than religious truth, the assertion that the state should be confessional generally involved the proscription of any religion other than the one that had its allegiance. Nevertheless, as we have seen, well before France legalized the pluralism of religious beliefs by dissociating confession and citizenship, in several countries a certain toleration admitted that inhabitants could belong to other faiths. Freedom of conscience, which is an individual's right and ability to hold convictions different from the official religion, was an established fact, but not freedom of worship, which acknowledged the right and ability of religious minorities to celebrate their faith communally. Controversies on this subject, battles to introduce a certain freedom of worship, the search for a compatibility between the existence of a state religion and confessional plurality went into the composition of another chapter in the history of relations between religion and society almost up to the present day. The Waldensian church had to wait until the Piedmontese entered Rome before it could have a church at its disposal in the capital of Christendom. Up to the last years of Franco's regime Spain obstinately refused protestant churches equality in the matter of freedom of worship. Since the fall of communism in Russia, part of the orthodox hierarchy has disputed the Roman catholic church's right to carry out missionary work, on the grounds that it would be interfering in an area that belongs exclusively to orthodoxy. Depending on the country, liberty and equality between the cults were ensured either by extending to other confessions the conditions and benefits previously reserved for the only recognized religion, or through the state's neutrality, or by the withdrawal of all recognition and the severing of all connections between state and religion.

The Rights and Liberties of Ecclesiastical Institutions

The confessionalism of the state and, secondarily, of society was not only adherence in principle to a truth of faith; it carried with it consequences for the status of the state church. The proclamation of what the churches sometimes called God's laws was extended by a demand for church freedoms which the latter made legitimate. In the same way that state confessionalism turned dogma into a legal truth, it implied that civil law should conform to the law governing the organization of the ecclesiastical institution, that is to say, for catholicism, canon law. As a result a special status was created that removed from clerics part of the obligations imposed on others, and exonerated the church from certain constraints that burdened the rest of society. Thus clerics were privileged and answerable only to ecclesiastical jurisdictions, even for violations of common law. But this did not mean impunity; the cleric found guilty of a crime would perhaps be as severely punished as by a civil court, but the ecclesiastical institution did not allow a cleric, who by his adherence to a faith had a sacred nature, to be judged by laypeople. Another example of which the preservation or repeal aroused lively controversy in the nineteenth century was exemption from military service. This was an issue which hardly arose in *ancien régime* societies, where soldiering was conducted by volunteers or professionals, but following the example of revolutionary France the majority of states having gradually adopted the principle of universal armed service inspired by conscription, the exemption of the clergy assumed the significance of a privilege and thus a violation of democracy. In the name of canon law, which forbade the clergy to shed blood, the religious authorities claimed a dispensation for priests and those destined for the priesthood. They had other motives for claiming this exemption; the bishops feared that some seminarists would abandon their vocation. A third privilege, which concerned institutions rather than individuals, was fiscal immunity. This claim went back a very long way; in all *ancien régime* societies the clergy were exempt from taxation. In France the amount of their contribution to the royal treasury was left to their own judgement, and the term used to describe it was significant: the free gift. But in the democratic societies of the nineteenth and twentieth centuries which aimed at an equitable division of taxes in accordance with each person's ability to pay, exemption took on a very different significance, quite at odds with the attitudes that had dictated the abolition of privileges. Claims which, in traditional societies, had not jarred with their tenets and rules were perceived as deviations after the disappearance of the *ancien régime*. The principle of equality carried the seed of the repeal of all special status, while the churches, in the name of the specific nature of their mission, declared that they should not be reduced to the precepts of civil society and intended to remain special societies preserving their own status. The contradiction became increasingly pronounced with the development towards democracy.

The regular clergy, subject to monastic rule, posed particular problems. They almost exclusively concerned catholicism, as the churches of the Reformation had not generally kept the tradition of monastic orders. But it has always been like this; all regimes, even the best disposed, have had difficulties with religious orders and have adopted special legislation relating to them. The regulating of congregations was a subject of dispute between catholic states and the Holy See. Two reasons, among others, explain this.

First, is the fact that as a general rule religious orders were answerable directly to the Holy See, and had the benefit of an immunity that removed them from the authority of the ordinary, or diocesan bishop; because of this, governments too had no hold over them. For the same reason, they did not necessarily get much sympathy from the secular clergy or bishops, who were not always in a hurry to take up their cause. Directly dependent on the pope, they were naturally suspected of being the instruments of foreign-inspired politics, unlike the secular clergy whose patriotism and devotion to the public good were popularly praised. Their superiors often lived outside the country. This suspicion nurtured, for example, the disconcerting hostility that fell on the Society of Jesus, which crystallized every suspicion of internationalism. Another, more material, reason also worked against the congregations: mortmain. When a monk or friar died the state received no death duties; the possessions of religious orders never re-entered the chain of property transfers. The wealth of congregations was thus destined to grow indefinitely. Economists worried about this sterilization of resources which they regarded as badly managed. Thus governments had been forced to take measures to control the development of congregations, limit their communications with Rome, monitor their exchanges and impose taxation upon them. Such initiatives naturally encountered resistance and protests from the interested parties, and these differences gave rise to endlessly revived arguments which affected relations between society and religion.

Although they were specific and sharper, the financial problems posed by the congregations were not the only ones to interfere with these relations. The churches' activity was essentially spiritual, but they nevertheless experienced material difficulties in providing for their upkeep and ensuring that they could function. The livings of clergy, the studies of future priests, the maintenance of buildings and the costs connected with teaching and charitable institutions represented considerable expenditure. In economies that were still close to rural societies the church budget was of prime importance. To meet their expenses the churches had available two main kinds of resource, the tithe and the income from their patrimony, both based fundamentally on the produce of the land, the first taking a portion of the crops, and the second being revenues from property.

Society acknowledged the eminent role played by religion, and the tithe was the price to be paid; it was incumbent on the community to bear the cost of maintaining serving priests as a return for the worship and prayer which were their functions in the allocation of activities. Like any levy, the tithe, which came on top of seigniorial dues and state taxes, was unpopular, and its removal much desired. Its abolition was accepted by the clergy's representatives in the generous enthusiasm of 4 August 1789, which swept away all privileges. The example was followed in all the countries reached in their turn by the revolutionary fervour, to the great satisfaction of the peasants. Later, rumours that the tithe was to be reintroduced was enough to set the country areas in an uproar. In Great Britain, where even the followers of other denominations, notably the Irish catholics, were obliged to pay a tithe to the Church of England, it was the object of conflict between the crown and its subjects.

Moreover, the churches obtained income from their possessions. Their wealth was derived essentially from property, their heritage composed of buildings usually put to various uses: housing clergy, presbyteries, bishops' palaces, seminaries, monasteries, universities, charitable institutions and hospitals. This patrimony had been gradually built up from gifts made by the faithful out of generosity, for the salvation of their soul or the redemption of their sins. It was a considerable fortune; in many countries the clergy were the leading landowners and owned a large proportion of urban buildings. The income from these possessions supplied their needs, ensured the financing of worship and other activities; above all, it guaranteed the independence of the church.

Such wealth aroused the envy of a society for whom the possession of land was the sign of great affluence, the criticism of economists who took a harsh view of the church's poor use of its resources, and the covetousness of ever-impecunious governments. From time to time rulers with few scruples, or driven by necessity, had confiscated part of the church's wealth. Philip the Fair had set the example when he seized the riches of the Temple. In the sixteenth century the desire to pillage the possessions of an opulent abbey or appropriate the revenue of a diocese was not always unconnected with the decision of this or that ruler to embrace the Reformation. The term secularization was then used for the first time to designate these expropriations, well before it was applied to the process of dissociating religion and society.

When the French Revolution took place, the operation was repeated on a much larger scale in all the countries occupied by French armies, with the connivance of populations who were only too happy to lay hands on monastery lands or clergy buildings. In France it took more than a century for the church to rebuild its patrimony, as Pope Pius VII agreed in 1801 not to reclaim the restitution of national possessions, in order to keep the public peace. It underwent another total expropriation following the passing of the Law of Separation, another pontiff, Pius X, having forbidden the church of France to form the religious associations to which the legislator had planned to transfer the whole of the ecclesiastical patrimony. Its possessions were seized by the state, and bishops' palaces, large seminaries and monasteries were allocated to public administration, to be used as revenue offices, assembly halls and so on.

In the east of the continent, in countries that had fallen under soviet domination in the wake of the Second World War, communist regimes confiscated all the churches' possessions, including places of worship, some of which were destroyed or transformed, as the French revolutionaries had done, for other uses, such as warehouses, garages or cinemas. Since the fall of communism, their restitution has been on the agenda. The Russian government of its own accord returned to the orthodox church some of the churches that had not been destroyed; it even took the initiative of rebuilding the basilica of the Holy Saviour in Moscow, on the site of which a swimming pool had been built in the 1930s. Nothing was too good for this reconstruction, and the Federation government and city of

Moscow vied with each other for the honour of working towards its completion. In most of the satellite countries the situation proceeded less happily. The churches demanded reparation; the fate of the possessions confiscated in the Czech Republic where the catholic church owned vast forests, as in Hungary, was a subject of dispute between governments and the catholic hierarchy.

At all events, everywhere the removal of ordinary resources by the abolition of the tithe and the confiscation of the churches' own possessions left unsolved the problem of financing confessional activities and religious institutions. In November 1789 the Constituent Assembly had undertaken to step in and had instituted a budget for religions that did not survive the altered relations between the catholic church and revolutionary Assemblies. The Concordat had honoured the Constituent Assembly's undertaking and had extended its benefits to the other denominations recognized by the Organic Articles. For 104 years in France the public budget ensured their upkeep. The Law of Separation put an end to it, and since then religions in France have existed only through the generosity of their followers.

In several European countries which accepted the principle of a certain participation by society in the functioning of a religion, the method known as the ecclesiastical tax took over from the budget for religions – with two special features. On the one hand, without being a completely spontaneous gift because it was levied with the overall sum of public taxes by the fiscal administration, the taxpayer could freely choose to which of the churches his contribution should be allocated, and usually also had the opportunity to refuse its donation to an ecclesiastical institution. Thus non-believers were not forced to take part in financing a religion to which they did not belong. Collection of money by administrative means was no more than a convenience similar to the arrangements used for a number of parafiscal taxes. On the other hand, and here lies a great difference from the confessional state – these measures concerned a plurality of religions. The tax guaranteed the churches substantial resources and revenue; thus the catholic church of Germany was the richest of the European churches, and ensured that all the poor churches in other continents greatly benefited from it. Moreover, its generosity established the influence of catholicism across the Rhine; it supplanted the church of France which, in the last century, accounted for half the number of European missionaries in the whole world. The institution of the ecclesiastical tax is challenged today, especially in Germany where every year several thousand taxpayers ask to have their names removed from the lists. First posed in 1789, the question of whether society should finance religion still remains controversial.

The Independence of the Churches: Free Self-administration

If discussions over the methods of financing religions and the churches' resources occupied such a large amount of time, it was because their independence was at stake. No sooner had the ecclesiastical officials been forced to cease exercising their authority over the state than their most constant and pressing preoccupation was to find ways of preserving that independence. Governments too, whether pledged to religion or distancing themselves from it, had no more enduring concern than to keep the churches under their thumb. The most favourable and sincerely religious firmly intended to keep them in check, even if it meant breaking off all links. And even in that instance governments rarely gave up exerting some control, for no one could totally ignore an institution with such an influence over a proportion of subjects or citizens.

What was chiefly at stake in this ever-open competition between churches and civil authority was the appointment of people at all levels, from the humblest serving priest in a rural parish, to the curé in the big town, as high as bishops and even the supreme pontiff. The churches demanded free choice in their officers, while the governments determined to reserve the right to inspect nominations. Under the *ancien régime* nearly all states had won their case; in catholic countries the Holy See had usually conceded the appointment of bishops to the sovereigns. In France, the king held the list of benefices and saw to all episcopal appointments; in Spain, he had enjoyed the right of presentation of clergy since the sixteenth century. In protestant countries, the ruler was generally the head of the national church and had the same prerogatives; in constitutional monarchies, it was the government that dealt with nominations. In the Russian Empire, since the reforms of Peter the Great, the church had also been answerable to the tsar. But after the French Revolution, the catholic church, now having to deal with governments that were less assured in their religious convictions and more dependent on a public opinion which no longer accepted the interference of the clergy in political life, sought to regain the right to choose its leaders. A movement developed within it to break free of a state supervision that was increasingly un-acceptable. In parallel with the gradual secularization of the state and society, winning independence was like the corollary and counterpart of the slackening of relations between civil society and religion. This desire for freedom in the matter of appointments lies in the texts of the Concordats between the Holy See and the states. Formerly they had nearly all included measures by which Rome yielded part of its rights to governments; the later concor-dats restored to the Holy See the sole initiative for episcopal appointments. A similar tendency took shape in protestant countries to emancipate the churches, even in England; the queen herself raised the question.

The clash between the ecclesiastical wish for independence and the state's firm intention to limit it did not spare the head of the catholic church and his relations with national churches. From time immemorial governments had assumed the right to control communications between the Roman Curia and the national clergy, and to oppose the circulation of papal bulls or the appli-cation of council decrees. Under the Second Empire, the imperial government barred the publication of the syllabus. Again in 1904 the prime minister, Émile Combes, quoted the Concordat as his reason for banning the bishops of Dijon and Laval from comply-ing with a summons to the court of Rome. In the talks that would result in the signing of the Lateran Agreements, the Vatican attached great importance to the Italian state's commitment never to raise obstacles, even in time of war, to bishops coming to Rome to visit the supreme pontiff, or to impede the holding of a conclave.

The same movement inspired the Holy See's policy of abolishing practices or repealing laws which limited its own freedom of action. Thus when convening a Council in 1868 Pius IX refrained from following the usual custom of inviting state representatives; several heads of government were upset by this departure from tradition and took counsel together to find a way of thwarting it, but then gave up. In 1959, when the second Vatican Council was convened the question would no longer be raised. Similarly, for the election of the pope; Austria, Spain and France had historically held the right to debar whichever cardinal they feared, rightly or wrongly, might not be favourable to their interests. In 1903, for the successor of Leo XIII, Austria still made use of this right against Cardinal Rampolla, secretary of state to the dead pope, whom Vienna judged to be too much won over to the views of France. The College of Cardinals bowed before this ban and instead gave its votes to Cardinal Sarto but, after his elevation, he hastened to repeal this right. Since then no state has dreamed of reinstating it. The freedom of the churches thus went side by side with secularization.

Although the clash of opposing ambitions between churches demanding their freedoms and governments jealous of their authority took priority in the attention of contemporaries and gets preferential treatment from historians, the competition between them was not confined to relations between those at the summit; it was also to be seen daily at the grassroots and fed all kinds of disputes at village level. Among other topics, two gave rise to innumerable squabbles which were widely talked about and fuelled the deliberations of administrative tribunals until they became the symbol, on the one hand of religious freedoms which in the eyes of the faithful had been jeopardized by the intolerance of the impious, and on the other of clericalism threatening freedom of conscience and public order; these were the ringing of church bells, and processions along the public highways.

For centuries the bells had provided the rhythm for the passing hours, dividing time, in the absence of other means of measuring and announcing it. Morning, noon and evening, the Angelus punctuated the working day. The bells still announced all the events in village communities, glad tidings or sad, baptisms or deaths, and also accidents such as fires. Before radio, and later television, brought immediate, on-the-spot news of great historic events, it was the tocsin that kept villagers informed. Around 5 in the afternoon of 1 August 1914, throughout the whole of France peasants busy gathering in the harvest learned of the mobilization; four years later, it was still the bells that announced the end of fighting. On the evening of 24 August 1944, they told the Parisians of the arrival at the Hôtel de Ville of the advance detachment of Leclerc's division and the end of the black night of occupation. Hence the strength of feelings attached to the ringing of bells; if catholics were pleased that these auxiliaries of religious worship were associated in this way with all the events of civil life, this occupation of air space by the bells jarred the sensibilities of those who were militating for the secularization of society. Anticlerical mayors used the pretext of the annoyance caused and the need for rest in order to ban or limit the bell-ringing.

Bells invaded the air space, processions encroached on public places. The clergy were free to organize processions within the churches as they pleased, but to emerge from the edifice and impose the spectacle of banners and statues on all inhabitants and make them listen to hymn-singing, was to assert a right over the thoroughfare that recalled the time when those who lived along the route were obliged to decorate their house when processions passed and to hang out white sheets on the facades to honour the Holy Sacrament. Therefore, using their policing rights, many mayors issued by-laws strictly regulating processions, or simply banning them. Even more than in parliamentary debates or press campaigns, it was locally, in these petty wranglings and interminable proceedings before administrative courts, that the battles for secularization were fought.

Not one of the numerous subjects in dispute just referred to was entirely unprecedented in the nineteenth century; nearly all, under the regimes prior to the Revolution, had provoked and sustained differences between society and religion. Only the context had been altered by the slackening of the ties between them and the fact that dissociation had begun. Other issues then arose to join the earlier ones and these, paradoxically, emerged from the beginnings of secularization. In fact, as soon as the churches had lost the monopoly of certain functions or had been removed from their dominance over civil institutions, they had to redirect their efforts to the new framework they had created, over which they intended to keep exclusive control. A varied network of confessional institutions was thus gradually built up, outlining the shape of a complete society within an overall one. Ousted little by little from running civil society, the churches turned their hopes to the organization of a confessional system. For instance in teaching: keeping pace with the state which, filled with consciousness of its responsibility for organizing schools, created a public service removed from the control of the ecclesiastical authorities, and with even greater justification when the government, in the name of a certain concept of secularity, believed that any religious reference should be excluded, the catholic church set up a network of school establishments of a firmly declared religious nature, which began to compete with the public service. It was the same for hospital and charitable bodies which for centuries had been created and run by religious congregations; driven from the public hospitals, they re-formed confessional establishments.

In both instances, the activities concerned were almost as old as the societies and churches. Social transformations and technical progress gave rise to opportunities to create new confessional institutions. Thus in the nineteenth century the rapid development of the press, encouraged by the spread of education and made easier by lower costs and increases in circulation, brought about the appearance of a religious fourth estate. For a generation of young priests at the end of the nineteenth century it was proof that if Saint Paul were to come back he would be a journalist. This very varied output, ranging from parochial newsletters to high-quality dailies, demanded the benefits of the freedom granted to the press. Christians, too, intended to profit from the opportunity grabbed by the working-class movement to form organizations to defend workers' rights; so religious trades unions were created which referred to the Vatican's teachings on social questions. To remove children and adolescents from the perils of the streets and prolong the religious instruction of the catechism, in the last few decades of the nineteenth century the various churches formed all sorts of organizations: young people's clubs, study circles, educational movements, of which they fully intended to keep control.

So, by what only appears to be a contradiction, the more society became liberated from the supervision of the churches and restricted their intervention in communal institutions, the more the churches were led to invent new forms of presence which widened their sphere of influence. These new institutions then became a fresh battleground with governments, one more pawn in their rivalry; for governments were not at all eager for these new sectors to escape their control. The nucleus of confrontations shifted; in the twentieth century it would be less the traditional subjects of contention – ways of appointing bishops, allocation of ecclesiastical benefices – and increasingly the status of religious schools or the freedom of youth organizations. In more than one country the education issue set the confessional school against the state one; both sides imagined, not without some self-deception, that the future would belong to whoever could become master of scholastic institutions, which were deemed to train generations to come. With the regimes inspired by totalitarian ideologies, disputes revolved around the religious press and youth organizations; a crisis over these matters erupted in 1931 between the papacy and the fascist regime as it did a little later with the Third Reich. The independence of religious youth movements would be a cause of discord between the French episcopate and the Vichy regime, which wanted to train and supervise young people.

Preaching Morality: Moral Law and Civil Law

By nature and tradition, religion and morality are intimately linked. No church, even the most respectful of people's individual liberty, consents to confine its role and teaching solely to preaching the faith. Every ecclesiastical institution, therefore, considered itself duty bound to preach morality and give timely, or even untimely, utterance to those commandments it deemed necessary for the salvation of souls and the well-being of the people. For their part, societies expected churches to co-operate in the moral education of individuals. In return, the churches expected the public authorities to give them their support; it was up to the state to set forth what was permitted and what was forbidden, since it alone possessed the power to compel and to punish offences. Consequently the law must write the essentials of God's commandments into both civil and penal codes. The churches could not conceive that civil law could differ from moral law, still less contradict it. They considered themselves guardians of moral law; it was up to legislators to build it into the rule of law which was imposed on everyone. In the nineteenth century, the vast majority of public opinion was not far from this way of thinking, even those who thought it unnecessary to base moral obligation on the affirmation of a transcendence and who upheld the idea that moral law was justified in itself without having to refer to the existence of God. It was not difficult to see the similarity between Christian morality and natural morality, and this remained a traditional position of catholic doctrine.

For God's commandments, that was all well and good, but by no means for those of the church; it was over the latter that disputes arose, especially in catholicism, but the protestant churches were also concerned about private morality. The churches expected the law to impose respect for the obligations which they had set. For example, the churches fought for a ruling to ban all activities on the Sunday rest day. The public authorities were therefore required to impose the hallowing of Sundays, ensure that it was respected and to punish those who worked. Nowhere was regulation in this area pushed as far as in protestant countries, especially Victorian England, where Sunday was sacred. All chance of amusement was removed by the obligatory closing of museums and the banning of shows.

Society, too, obliged everyone to conform to the morality defined by religion; by way of legislation the churches intervened in private life and governed individual conduct. Having regard to the ties between religion and personal morality, every religion considered that the definition of ethical standards came within its competence. As for relations with the political authorities, there was but one choice: either the churches challenged their right to make decisions on it or they expected them to see that their own regulations were observed; in any case it was a source of disputes.

Marriage was often a subject of contention between church and state, especially the catholic church; the latter made marriage a sacrament and always claimed the right to define the conditions that validated conjugal union. Consequently it demanded for its own jurisdictions, diocesan tribunals and the Roman court of the Rota, exclusive authority on matrimonial cases. It also asked the civil authorities to recognize the legal validity of religious marriage, which would make the secular deed superfluous, except for non-catholics for whom it would admit, if absolutely necessary, a special ceremony. Above all, it intended that civil law, being based on traditional doctrine, should guarantee the indissolubility of marriage and exclude any possibility, other than the death of one of the spouses, of breaking the commitment and dissolving a union contracted for life. It was up to the legislator, therefore, to impose the model proposed by the Gospel, interpreted by the church, of a union founded on the mutual consent of a man and a woman, with the intention of welcoming in their home all the children God would send them. It was up to the law to suppress any deviation from this conduct; adultery must be severely punished, children born out of wedlock branded as shameful at birth and throughout their life; and with even greater reason, children born of adultery, the fruit of a guilty union. As for relations between people of the same sex, they were regarded as infamous; those that practised them were outcasts of society and their actions subject to punishment. Thus the civil code and the penal code were the translation into law of the moral code decreed by the churches. The public powers were therefore required to ensure that individual behaviour conformed to the commandments of God and His church.

In countries with confessional pluralism, where the catholic church in particular could not claim to impose its own laws, marriages were no less a source of tension; especially mixed marriages between catholics and protestants, which the catholic church accepted only reluctantly. It tolerated them on condition that the couple promised to raise their children in the catholic faith. After the French Revolution, in Germany, the catholic clergy became more obdurate about this principle and repudiated measures in the opposite direction taken by governments anxious to keep the peace and maintain an equal balance between religions. Its hardening attitude led to open conflict, notably in Prussia. In 1837, the archbishop, who had not long occupied the see of Cologne and was a member of the aristocracy, Mgr von Droste-Vischering, denounced the agreement reached by his predecessors with the authorities on the subject of mixed marriages, and brought back into force the old ecclesiastical canons which strictly limited the practice. The Prussian government, vexed by this initiative, had him imprisoned. What was called 'the Cologne incident' had wide repercussions throughout Germany, and even in Europe. Historians are agreed in dating the reawakening of German catholicism from this affair.

The churches naturally took an interest in everything connected with sexuality. As long as it stayed contained within the private sphere, the churches' attitude concerned only the particular dialogue of individuals with their conscience and the religion to which they belonged. But the moment society was involved in the definition of what was permitted or forbidden, *a fortiori* if it adopted a position which deviated from the teaching of the churches, sexuality and the transmission of life became a subject of discord and conflict. This was so for laws authorizing contraception and, still more, abortion. On these issues the catholic church took the most intransigent stance. It had always reproved the 'dire secrets' that prevented sexual relations from producing their natural results. Even though the theology of marriage has moved forward and nowadays admits that the union of a man and woman may have other ends than the propagation of the species and increasing life, it continues to condemn any means of birth control other than natural. After a period of hesitation over the new possibility of avoiding conception which the discovery of the pill offered women, in July 1968 in the encyclical *Humanae vitae*, Pope Paul VI spoke out against reputedly artificial methods; the church allowed no other form of contraception than keeping to the natural rhythms of fertility. This position put the Vatican at odds with all governments practising or encouraging the sterilization of men and family planning campaigns, as well as with international organizations trying to stem the population growth in the earth's poorest countries.

The condemnation of abortion was even stronger, since the catholic church – and it was not alone – regarded it as murder.

Consequently, its officials disapproved of parliaments and governments which legalized this act of death. In many countries the episcopate campaigned to prevent or, if it had already been passed, to repeal legal abortion. Nowadays there is no topic on which the opposition between the catholic church and a certain section of thinking and legislation is more manifest.

If life is a matter for dispute between religions and society nowadays, death also was, and sometimes still is, a subject of discord. As their mission is to prepare the way from earthly life to the next world, the churches considered that everything connected with death pertained exclusively to their sphere of authority. They were the ones to judge whether the deceased deserved a religious funeral – refusal of which could be a means of coercion and punishment – and burial in Christian soil. The expression is significant: cemeteries, generally situated around religious buildings, were blessed sites which had a sacred nature. Consequently, only baptized Christians who would there await the resurrection of the body, could be interred in these places. But society was less and less willing to accept this discretionary power of the clergy; often the populace insisted that the coffin should pass through the church. A movement grew to extract all religious character from cemeteries and to secularize them. If the churches had taken an unfavourable view of civil marriage, they were even less inclined to accept civil burials, the ultimate challenge of free-thinkers. So they put pressure on civil authorities to deprive such funerals of any publicity; if they could not be banned, let them at least be carried out as discreetly as possible, furtively, at nightfall, without a cortege. Regulation of the trappings of death, burials and cemeteries, thus formed another chapter – and by no means the least – in the equable or conflicting relations between religion and society.

If the most personal and even the most intimate acts of private life, relative to the forming of the couple and procreation, already gave rise to differences between churches and governments, despite the recognition by most regimes of the eminent distinction between the private and public spheres, relations would naturally become a greater source of conflict if churches meddled in society's problems, and still more if they interfered in political debates. Governments of whatever kind had little liking for religious authorities pronouncing judgement on their actions. In the nineteenth century this type of intervention was generally viewed as an unlawful interference and denounced as typical clerical behaviour. Of all denominations, it was most often the catholic religion that entered into dispute with states over such subjects. The reformed churches ordinarily observed greater discretion and refrained from adopting a stance; the orthodox religions were too dependent upon the ruling power to raise an independent voice.

In the wake of Pius VI's condemnation in March 1791 of the Declaration of the Rights of Man and the inspiration of the Revolution, all the Roman pontiffs fulminated against modern society. Gregory XVI denounced the freedom of the press as deplorable; Pius IX anathematized all contemporary misdemeanours. For a hundred years interventions by the Vatican all took the form of uncompromising condemnation, without any positive proposal other than the restoration of a fairly idealized traditional order in which society had to conform on all counts to the church's teachings, and people were left with no alternative between estrangement from religion and a return to the *ancien régime*.

The last decade of the nineteenth century saw the dawning of a more positive tendency. Without overtly breaking away from the denunciation of modern transgressions or revoking the condemnation of liberal theories, in a series of small touches the popes defined a more forward-looking conception of society. The turning point was reached in 1891 with the encyclical *Rerum novarum*, which opened a new chapter in relations with society. Its scope was far wider than the theme of the text, the social question viewed as the condition of workers in industrial society; its implication was that the catholic church considered that everything concerning the organization of life in society fell within its sphere of authority. It was a challenge to the liberal premise according to which the functioning of collective life should be outside moral judgements. At the same time, it was an affirmation that nothing – politics, the economy, international relations – was exempt from moral judgement, that ethics prevailed over any consideration of efficacy, expediency or reasons of state. This set of assumptions contained the seed of conflict with governments and everyone responsible for social organization.

In the twentieth century the extent of papal intervention has been gradually enlarging to embrace every aspect of social relations. With Pius XI the catholic church took an interest in interstate relations, condemned nationalism and adopted a position in favour of a juridical order. After the Second World War, attention shifted towards the organization of peace, development, and the reduction of inequalities between rich and poor countries, to the point of embracing the whole of society's problems. National episcopal conferences would take a stand over the sales of arms and the strategy of dissuasion.

It was a far cry from the problems that had once made up the fundamental points at issue between churches and governments – the status of congregations or the appointment of bishops – although those questions had not entirely disappeared from the agenda. But others had arisen: some born of the results of advances in knowledge and science or emerging from the development in relations between peoples; because churches no longer accepted being confined solely to the defence of confessional interests, but increasingly claimed that their followers could not be uninterested in the behaviour of society. In other words, the boundary between the religious and the social shifted; it was no longer conceivable to reduce religion to the sphere of individual privacy, and this at a time when societies were becoming more and more secularized. The apparent contradiction between these two major trends is the outcome of a history whose vicissitudes must be retraced; they account for that paradox.

5
Opposing Forces and Traditions

If the history of the religious question contained many important issues, it also set at loggerheads a large number of interested parties. Consequently it permits several parallel readings. The most obvious aspect is the competition for power between the two rivals – churches and state – which each sought to exercise over society a control that neither side was prepared to yield or share. But their opposition was not confined to this commonplace dimension; it also contained a significance of a spiritual nature which transformed their disagreements into battles of principles. In all contemporary history there is perhaps no debate in which the ideological aspect has played such a determining role. The churches' ambition for power proceeded from the certainty that they possessed the truth, and found its justification in the desire to communicate that truth, a zeal to win souls and the determination to bring salvation to others, even if they did not want it. Far from being dulled by time, these motives, as old as religious faith itself, found a redoubled intensity in the struggle against the advance of impiety, even after the revolutionary break. In the opposing camp, philosophical considerations came from a more recent past. In the age of the monarchies, sovereigns generally shared the religious convictions of their peoples, and intellectual motives were less crucial than a concern to have the sovereignty of the state respected and not to tolerate an independent power, or the avarice that often drove rulers to appropriate the wealth accumulated by the churches. But with the coming of regimes that relied on the support of public opinion, and the advance of philosophical concepts, the traditional conflicts between powers became battles of ideas.

When these arguments overflowed into the political arena they unfailingly brought with them a simplification of the explicit issues and forced the adversaries to enter willy-nilly into a dualist system which no longer admitted nuances of thinking or middle positions. Everyone was called upon to take sides, and there were only two. Thus in the nineteenth century the religious question divided opinion between clergy and laics: between these two opposing blocs were the voters, who made their decision and gave to one or other side for a time the power to regulate relations between religion and society according to its own ideas. Belgium presented the spectacle of successive reversals which brought liberal majorities adopting legislation of secular inspiration, especially over the matter of education, and catholic majorities which hastened to restore a more favourable status to the religious schools. Similarly, in Spain the alternation of liberal and conservative regimes punctuated the variations in the status of religious orders, the fate of ecclesiastical possessions and the settlement of all the issues contributing to the litigation between state and church.

This outline of the two opposing forces rather tends to water down a far more complex reality. The complexity lies in the philosophical and spiritual dimension of the argument. If, in fact, the bitterness of the combat brought about its simplification, in return the ideological aspect gave rise to a variety of points of view. This diversity of standpoints explains the ambiguity of certain bills which attempted a synthesis of differing positions, or sought a compromise.

Although there can be hardly any argument about the general trend of development over the past two hundred years – towards an increasingly marked distinction between religion and society – the unfolding of the events that gradually dispersed the confusion inherited from the *ancien régime* was far from moving in a perfectly straight line, and secularization was even farther from coming about as the result of a single ideal. It was the outcome of the evolution of power struggles between trends and traditions. There were at least half a dozen of these components.

Some extended the oldest traditions that had not yet breathed their last, such as regalist thinking, which conferred on the state the right to intervene in the life of the churches and control the regulation of cults. It re-emerged strongly after the revolutionary turmoil. Opposed to it was a tradition of unconditional loyalty to the church, which claimed for religion the right to dictate private and public conduct, as well as the church's total independence in relation to the secular authority. In the nineteenth century this idea found a systematic expression in catholic intransigentism and achieved an incomparable dynamism in ultramontanism.

More than these traditional or archaic views, it was liberal thinking that fashioned nineteenth-century history and inspired government policies. Its intention was to base freedom of conscience on the distinction between the private sphere, to which religious beliefs belonged, and the public area in which religion would have no place. Under its inspiration the transition would be made from the confessional to the liberal state. Often a rationalist conception interfered with it, fighting against any religious expression as a vestige of the past, a challenge to reason and a threat to liberty and democracy. In short, religion maintained contact, sometimes of alliance sometimes of opposition, with the thinking, the feeling, the reality of the nation which, after the French Revolution, had become one of the mainsprings of history.

Amid these currents, forces and values, relations continually altered from one country to another, depending on the period, and according to the issues at stake. The following chapters intend to retrace the main vicissitudes of this complex history and distinguish between the trends which resemble various threads in its plot. We shall start with the oldest elements.

The Regalist Tradition

If the guiding principle for setting out these various components is to be chronological, priority undeniably goes to the tradition known as regalian or regalist, from the name it had under the *ancien régime*. It asserted the superiority of the secular power over the churches and therefore intended to keep them subject to its sovereignty. This is the oldest stratum. The tradition, which was common to all state powers, came from time immemorial. It did not necessarily proceed from animosity towards the church, and still less from any disagreement over dogma; the same power that closely controlled the clergy held them in honour and showed consideration and respect for religion. *Ancien régime* governments shared the conviction, then generally held, that society was unable to do without religion and that the state had authority and responsibilities in the matter. When they intervened in its operations sovereigns believed they were rendering the church a service; it was incumbent upon them to arbitrate over internal disagreements. By obliging the church to reform itself, carrying out the changes which it was incapable of effecting on its own, even if that meant imposing their will, they were helping it in its mission and bringing it into harmony with the spirit of the times. So thought Joseph II when he reorganized the church in Austria, or Louis XV's ministers, proceeding unhesitatingly with the Regular Clergy Commission to close numerous monasteries and regroup religious orders.

In the eighteenth century it had been a long time since the churches had dreamt of opposing these interventions by the secular power. The question obviously did not arise for the protestant churches, which were national and state institutions. They acknowledged the ruler's right to take a hand in their life, and since they had separated from Rome they could no longer turn to an external body. But the situation was hardly different for the catholic church. The papacy had conceded to those sovereigns who had remained obedient to it the power to administer the church and, in particular, the right to appoint bishops; the kings of France, Spain and Portugal freely disposed of ecclesiastical benefices and allocated bishoprics and abbeys. They even meddled in doctrinal arguments. Since 1682 the monarchy in France had imposed the teaching in seminaries and theology faculties of what was known as the declaration of the four articles, which formulated a Gallican ecclesiology. Louis XIV, and later the parliaments, did not refrain from intervening in the Jansenist dispute and the crown had imposed on all clerics recognition of the bull *Unigenitus* as a state truth.

Although it substantially altered the nature of relations between religion and society, the Revolution neither abolished nor even suspended the regalist tradition. Quite the reverse; the Civil Constitution of the Clergy was in some way the ultimate outcome of its logic. Nothing was farther from the modern idea of secularity than such interference in the religious domain, whose autonomy and special nature were totally ignored by this venture of reorganizing the catholic church. The restoration of religious bodies in 1801–2 by the Concordat and the Organic Articles stemmed from the same spirit and represented the triumph of regalist inspiration; it was the model of administrative catholicism. A telling example, of that mindset was the First Consul's choice of religious festivals that would now be obligatory. Even today, if all activity in France comes to a halt on 1 November and 15 August it is the result of Bonaparte's personal decision, decreeing that these should be the feast days on which the faithful would be indirectly obliged to hear mass on pain of mortal sin. It illustrates the ambiguity of the association between religion and society. Religion's control over civil society was ensured since it regulated the use of the calendar, but the political authority was also involved, dictating to the church and its followers alike what they must do.

Following the upheaval of the Revolution, this tradition remained the rule for relations between political powers and church institutions. All the governments in Europe at that time considered that the regulation of cults, to use the administrative language term, fell within their competence; today we would say that there was a public policy for religion. Although regalist thinking, imbued with the idea of the state's natural supremacy over any other institution, continued to inspire legislators and governments, two new factors, or ones that had gained greater importance, affected its application. The first was the result of the upheavals wrought by the Revolution. When they eliminated an age-old heritage, annulling the special statutes which in many countries had ensured the autonomy of the state church, and through confiscation of its possessions removing the regular resources that had guaranteed its financial independence, the revolutionaries caused the churches to fall into a close dependence on the ruling powers, from which the state emerged remarkably strengthened.

The second factor relates to the development of attitudes that were now less willing to accept the church's authority, backed by the state, over individual conduct. Even those states most attached to the principles of a state religion had to come to terms with public demand for freedom of conscience and even freedom of forms of worship. The era of the sacral state was over; the last attempt to restore it in France was probably the ceremony of Charles X's coronation in 1825 which aroused more derision than fervour, its failure emphasizing the irremediably archaic nature of pretensions to revive it. The regalist tradition therefore had to compromise with liberalism.

The conjunction of these two changes led the majority of European societies to pass by stages from a confessional to a liberal state, showing consideration for choices of conscience and working out a regime of confessional plurality. The churches, hitherto dominant, saw their hold over society challenged at the very moment when that of the state was tightening upon them; so they were the losers on both counts. Hence their reaction, and we shall see its preambles and developments, linking an uncompromising recall of the principles which the catholic church considered inviolable and the demand for independence. That was the thrust of the ultramontane movement, a major component in the nineteenth century of the history of the interaction between religion and society.

In the nineteenth century the regalist principle had asserted itself in all states, without exception. In France it could take advantage of a very long tradition and make reference to a doctrinal corpus worked out by jurists and theologians, which was taught in seminaries and universities. A Directorate of Public Worship, attached sometimes to the Ministry of Justice and at others to the Ministry of Public Education, consistently applied a policy that was careful to maintain state control. The administrative department which had the task of appointing bishops generally chose good priests of irreproachable background, who would make sound administrators and offered guarantees of discretion and loyalty; close surveillance was kept on their communications with Rome. Against those who might show signs of too much independence, the administration did not hesitate to call for sanctions, in which it had the backing of administrative jurisdictions. Thus in 1828 the archbishop of Toulouse, Mgr de Clermont-Tonnerre, was brought before the Council of State, according to the old procedure, accused of misusing his position of authority, and deprived of his salary for having publicly protested against the decrees issued by the Martignac government, one of which reactivated former measures targeting the Society of Jesus and the other restricted the number of students admitted into minor seminaries to 20,000. This incident had a decisive effect on La Mennais' way of thinking, persuading him that it was urgent for the church to dissociate its destiny from a monarchy that had become disloyal to its vocation.

Even when tempered by a certain liberalism, the regimes following the Restoration insisted just as strictly that the state's authority must be respected. For a time the Second Empire heaped honours and benefits upon the catholic church, but then made it feel the weight of its authority as soon as the Roman question had altered the church's relations with the regime. On 16 October 1861, the Minister of the Interior, Persigny, decreed the dissolution of the St Vincent de Paul central organization of assemblies. This association had only charitable aims but, in the absence of any other body, it acted as a means of expression for catholics in France; federating some thirteen hundred local assemblies, grouping more than thirty thousand affiliated members, it disturbed the authorities, who applied the severity of the law which in that period did not tolerate gatherings of more than twenty people.

After 1879 it was the republicans' turn to act as faithful disciples of the king's lawmakers. In 1880 Jules Ferry dispersed the Society of Jesus and all unauthorized religious orders by the application of a cabinet decree. In 1901 Waldeck-Rousseau had a law passed which instituted an extremely liberal regime for associations, excepting religious congregations to which a discriminatory statute was applied, its constraints reflecting the *ancien régime* monarchy's and parliaments' traditional mistrust of religious orders. In 1904 Émile Combes forbade the bishops of Dijon and Laval to comply with a summons to go to Rome. In reality, the regalist tradition continued to inspire the actions of all French governments. The break with it came neither in 1791 nor 1801, nor even with the republicans' coming to power in the 1880s. The real rupture was brought about by the Law of Separation in 1905; severing the last links connecting churches and state, it deprived the latter of all chance of maintaining its control over the former. It was that prospect which held back many politicians, who had no real motives for wanting to keep the presence of religion in society, from repealing a concordat which subjected the churches to the control of the public authority.

Most of the other states were very careful not to go so far and deprive themselves of the advantages of which they were particularly assured by agreements made with the Holy See. In Spain the crown jealously preserved the right of patronage which it had been granted by the Concordat of 1753. Even the Cortes, meeting in Cadiz during the war of independence against France, who in 1812 had drawn up one of the most liberal constitutions, had retained recognition of catholicism as the state religion. Portugal had not forgotten the tradition made famous in the preceding century by the Marquis of Pombal. The abolition of tithes in 1832, taking away from the clergy one of its main regular resources, made it dependent on the state. Two years later, all religious orders were suppressed and their possessions confiscated. In its article 75 the constitutional Charter of 1835 laid down that the king was to make all the appointments to episcopal sees and provide for all ecclesiastical benefices; furthermore, he had the power to authorize or refuse consent to council decrees and apostolic letters. He thus exercised an unopposed right over communications between the church of Portugal and the Holy See. This was a strict application of the regalist tradition.

In the Italian peninsula, which at that time was no more than a geographical expression, after the Congress of Vienna which restored the *ancien régime* dynasties, the majority of states signed concordats with the Holy See re-establishing relations on the former principles; they restored to the catholic church part of the privileges it had lost under the French occupation, like that of the ecclesiastical tribunal in the kingdom of Sardinia; in exchange governments recovered their prerogatives in the matter of keeping a control over religious bodies.

It was the same in the catholic German states, where Josephism remained the inspiration. The various Concordats negotiated after the Congress of Vienna confirmed the rights of the secular power to regulate religious life. In catholic Bavaria, Montgelas attended to the strict application of the Concordat of 1817, which placed the church in tight subordination to the state. Bishops' pastoral letters were subject to the administration's authorization and their correspondence with Rome was monitored.

In the protestant German states the practice was similar, the only difference being that governments did not have to reckon with an external partner. The protestant churches were territorial and the principle of *Landeskirche* placed them under the authority of the ruler, who held extensive powers in religious affairs. Prussia was the most unusual case; the state had a tradition of tolerance, and since it had been enlarged protestants of various traditions coexisted with catholics. The interests of the Prussian state made tolerance a political necessity. The Minister for Religions, Altenstein, clearly defined the state's official position on the subject: 'The Prussian state is a protestant state that has taken over one-third of catholic subjects. It is a difficult situation. The best solution is for the state to take care of the protestant church for pleasure and the catholic church out of duty.'

Whether from pleasure or conviction, all the kings of Prussia paid close attention to the protestant church, intervening in its internal organization and even in its religious life. In 1817 King Frederick-William made all the protestant churches, Lutheran and Reformed, regroup into a united evangelical body which would survive the fall of the empire even up to the Third Reich. He gave this church an internal set of rules and even dictated its liturgy. The measures taken by Bismarck in Prussia at the time of the *Kulturkampf* against the catholic church, such as the obligation of every future priest to follow the teachings of the public universities, belonged to this tradition of state interference in the organization of the various forms of religion.

In the Netherlands, the king also imposed a set of regulations for the reformed church, in 1816. In Switzerland the Confederation authorities assumed the right to allow or forbid religious expression; the creation of new catholic dioceses was subject to the consent of the authorities in Berne. After the Vatican Council, the Federal Council decided to create an old-catholic diocese, bringing together those priests and faithful who had not recognized the new dogma of papal infallibility; by doing so it interfered in an internal debate of the catholic church.

In the Scandinavian kingdoms the Lutheran church, which had been the state church since the Reformation, was subject to the sovereign. In Sweden relations were defined by a law of 1686 which applied equally to the Grand Duchy of Finland, whose transition to Russian domination had not changed the status of the Lutheran church.

As for Holy Russia, in the nineteenth century it was the perfect example of the closest fusion of the political and the religious, and of the most extreme subordination of the orthodox church to government since the reforms of Peter the Great. Through the intermediary of the Procurator of the Holy Synod the tsar exercised sole control over the life of the church.

A liberal state if ever there was one, nevertheless England did not accord much liberty to the official church. Government intervention was not confined to discipline and the liturgy; it even ventured into doctrinal territory. In 1850 the Queen's Privy Council gave its judgement in a dispute between the bishop of Exeter and one of his priests on the subject of baptism. The prelate considered the priest's position to be contrary to orthodoxy; by saying he was in the wrong, the Privy Council assumed the right to define the sound doctrine in a sacramental matter.

Throughout the length and breadth of the continent, in the aftermath of the revolutionary upheaval that had shaken the old order and destroyed the foundations of the ancient alliance between religion and society, the regalist tradition of intervention by the public powers in the organization of forms of religion and the subjection of the churches to political authority thus remained the rule. Although the churches received consideration and certain advantages, they paid for them with the loss of their liberty. The abolition of special status, the confiscation of their wealth, increased their dependence. Nowhere were churches completely free in their words or deeds. So the phrase usually employed to define their relations in that period, the alliance of the throne and the altar, seems hardly suitable, unless it is to make clear that it was an unequal alliance between the states, which emerged strengthened from the revolutionary crisis, and the churches weakened by the ordeals they had undergone.

The Utopia of Restoration

Although the regalist tradition thus formed a kind of hyphen between the *ancien régime* and post-1789, at the same time adjusting to some of the changes brought about by the Revolution, in 1815 there were many minds which rejected the latter's achievements wholesale, and advocated a simple return to the old order of things. It was even the official argument of most regimes: the principle which prevailed over the reorganization of Europe was one of legitimacy, and the crime of which the Revolution was accused was of forming a new order based on different principles from those which had been hallowed by time, the revolutionaries' unpardonable sin being to have wanted to break with tradition. If there was one domain where tradition reigned alone and was revered more than elsewhere, it was religion; after all, the teaching of Christian churches rested on handing down a revealed tradition. In return, religion conferred legitimacy on the political power, and assured it of the obedience of its subjects.

The Revolution's religious policy had thrown the catholic church into the camp of the Counter-Revolution. Pius VI had condemned the Declaration of the Rights of Man. Under Bonaparte, with the re-establishment of freedom of worship and the restoration of religious peace, the signing of the Concordat, and the young emperor's invitation to the supreme pontiff to come and consecrate his new dignity, it had been possible for a time to believe in a reconciliation between the heritage of the Revolution and traditional religion. What followed had swiftly proved that hope false. The abduction of Pius VII and his imprisonment, the excommunication fulminated against the emperor, who was identified with the Anti-

Christ, the tension between the Episcopate and the imperial regime, had managed to convince catholics of the impossibility of an entente between religion and the principles of 1789. There could be no future for catholicism except in the uncompromising affirmation of the truth. That was also the condition for society's salvation. Only one conclusion could be drawn from this succession of unhappy experiences: the restoration of social order would come by way of recognition of the principles which in the past had ensured the greatness of states and the peace of their peoples, without the slightest concession to the spirit of the times. That restoration would naturally begin by re-establishing the true religion in all its rights and prerogatives.

In more than one country, the defeat of the French armies and the restoration of peace effectively signified the return of religion in force. In both Spain and Portugal catholicism emerged strengthened because during the war against the occupation and French ideas it had identified with the mother country. In these two lands uncompromising catholicism and its claim to rule society would hold firm for over a century, from the Carlist wars to Francoism, with the most conservative tendency closely linking religion and reaction. In Italy, the restoration of the princely dynasties was accompanied by the re-establishment of the catholic church in its secular privileges. This happened in the kingdom of Naples, Piedmont-Sardinia, and with even stronger reason in the Papal States, where Napoleon's fall had been followed by the restoration of the pope's temporal power. As there was a total merging of his spiritual authority and his temporal sovereignty, there was nothing to oppose a full return to the old order, unless it was the nostalgic memory left by France's presence to the patriots and liberals who dreamed of a united and independent Italy. In the Habsburgs' patrimonial states, since the Counter-Reformation catholicism had been a federating element for the associated peoples, and at the root of legitimacy for the emperor.

Reference to the religious foundations of the political order was no less explicit in protestant or orthodox states. In England the Anglican church was a pillar of the establishment which had not been shaken by the revolutionary upheaval. In the Russian Empire, Orthodoxy was an integral part of autocracy. Throughout Europe the principle of legitimacy that proceeded from submission to a divine providence was triumphant. The pact of the Holy Alliance concluded by the sovereigns at the end of the Congress of Vienna makes explicit reference to it. It is true that historians hesitate to take this document seriously and usually view it merely as a fantastic idea inspired in Alexander I by Madame de Krudener, to which the other signatories would have subscribed only to please the tsar. Probably the other monarchs did not attach the same importance to it that he did, but it is nonetheless obvious that the text did not run counter to their own convictions. It was even in harmony with the conclusions reached by some sections of public opinion after a quarter of a century of wars with the Revolution. The idea that religion must be the foundation of restored order and the cornerstone of the European edifice inspired the actions of governments.

Even in France, which had had the audacity to challenge tradition, the old order returned; the regime prided itself that it was closing the parentheses opened in 1789 and relinking the 'chain of time'. It was called the Restoration – both political and religious. Catholicism was re-established in its position as state religion. The Ultra party had on its agenda the restitution to the clergy of civil registration and the confiscated possessions. A few even advocated bringing back the tithe and recognition of catholicism to the exclusion of all other faiths. Since the restored monarchy was unable to allow its relations with the church to be governed by a concordat signed by the usurper, the ministry engaged in negotiations with Rome to replace the Convention of 1801 with an agreement more in keeping with an orthodox definition of relations between church and state. In 1817 the outcome of these talks was the drawing up of a document which, however, remained a dead letter. The unsuccessful fate of this still-born Concordat is perfectly symbolic of the twist imparted by the Revolution to relations between religion and society; it illustrates the failure of plans for an integral restoration of the traditional order. Although in 1817 the liberal government of the Restoration gave up the idea of submitting the plan for the concordat to the Chambers, it was because its contents seemed incompatible with the commitments made by Louis XVIII and the promises in the constitutional charter. True, the latter mentioned catholicism as a *state* religion, but it was not *the* state religion and liberty was guaranteed to other forms of worship. It was impossible to go back on the changes brought to relations between religion and society; they were irreversible. In other countries too governments similarly realized the impossibility of closing the parentheses opened by the Revolution; the break was well and truly irremediable. In any case, the ruling powers were not really that keen to re-establish the privileges of the church. They all found some advantage from pairing regalist tradition with the heritage of the liberal revolution. None seriously envisaged returning civil administration to the clergy. Almost all were satisfied for education and social aid to remain within the competence of the state.

6

Rome and the Papacy

The Ultramontane System

The failure of plans for a total restoration, partly because of governments, profoundly disappointed the most intransigent elements, and their resentment had no small consequences for their attitude on relations between religion and society. They were generally people with an absolutely rigid outlook for whom truth must never compromise with any considerations of circumstance or opportuneness; if contradictions arose between them and reality it was up to the latter to adapt, and not the other way round. They had an abiding horror of 'deals' and concessions. A man like La Mennais is typical of that outlook in his fervour in claiming for the catholic church an absolute right to direct the conduct of states, and his vehemence in denouncing the weakness of the country's rulers. He was far from being alone in this thinking. In other countries, too, authors, theologians and political writers came forward, sharing the same vision of history, and called on the political powers to make themselves the instrument of restoring a Christian order; Görres in Germany, Donoso Cortes in Spain and in France, in the next generation, Louis Veuillot. If the state shirked its religious duties, it deserved neither trust nor obedience; the state that did not proclaim its religion loud and long was an atheist one. At that time no distinction was made between religious neutrality and declared impiety; any measure allowing a certain freedom of impartiality was held to be apostasy. That was the view inspired in John Keble, one of the future leaders of the Oxford Movement, by the Whig government's decision in 1833 to abolish eight of the Church of England dioceses in Ireland, acceding to the demand of the island's catholics.

For people with this outlook, the return to the past which they advocated was not a return to just any past. It was certainly not the restoration of the declining *ancien régime*, which was held responsible for all its own misfortunes and downfall; already sullied by impiety, the French monarchy had paved the way for the Revolution. By setting absolute power above laws and rules it had cleared the way for Jacobinism and Napoleonic despotism. There was therefore a need to go further back in time, before Louis XIV and Richelieu, who was similarly not forgiven for having subordinated the interest of religion to those of state, and rallying to heretical Sweden and the German protestant princes against catholic Austria. How could Christian France, the daughter of St Louis, the France of the Crusades, protectress of the Holy See, have concerns other than those of religion? In a way, the intransigent catholics of France belonged to the tradition of the League and the catholic party. This orientation would reach its full dimension in the second half of the century over the Roman question.

The rejection of part of the past included the repudiation of Gallicanism and Josephism. Political Gallicanism – which banned the Vatican from all interference in the kingdom's politics – but also religious Gallicanism which, in the tradition of the Councils of Basle and Constance and in keeping with the teaching of the Sorbonne, contrary to the pretension of the Roman pontiffs to hold sovereign rule, declared that the pope should exercise his spiritual power in harmony with the universal church. Traditional teaching advocated a government combined with the church, associating the monarchic principle with papal primacy and the aristocratic principle expressed by the Episcopate. It also affirmed the autonomy of national churches. This was the position of the church of France, proud of its ancient lineage, tenacious of its freedoms, opposed to ultramontane aspirations. Only a few religious orders, with the Society of Jesus in the forefront, did not adhere to this body of doctrine on which the crown, parliaments and the university were all in accord. Josephism was its Austrian version that inspired most of the princely courts of Germany.

After the Revolution, however, positions were overturned. Some

of the wisest minds, the most respected thinkers, founders of religious institutions, now adhered to an ecclesiology based on the
authority of the pope and obedience to Rome: ultramontanism.
This was a major event for the history of relations between religion
and society, and perhaps historians have not given it enough attention; probably because of its name, which restricts its scope,
whereas ultramontanism was, in fact, a complete and coherent
system around which the catholic faith reassembled itself in the
nineteenth century. This system put forward an overall view of
the world and offered the answer to all the problems of human
destiny and the life of societies, in the same way as liberalism or
Marxism, to quote but two of the ideologies which have had most
influence on opinions and the course of events. Since this system
lost its coherence and its grip on the faithful, after the second
Vatican Council had withdrawn the support conferred on it by
the first, ninety years earlier, it is easier to recognize that ultramontanism characterized an era in the history of catholicism. Just
as it had already redefined itself in the sixteenth century in reaction
to the Reformation, in the aftermath of the French Revolution
catholicism reconstructed itself in contrast with the modern society
that had emerged from 1789.

The system was formed in concentric circles from the starting
point of the papal institution. Reference to Rome pervaded everything: thinking, piety, discipline, liturgy, culture, politics, society.
The pope was the symbol and the personification of the principle
of authority, the antithesis of the spirit of free enquiry, which was
the destroyer of faith. The pope set forth and expressed the truth;
he was incapable of error and defined the faith of believers. Adherence to the utterances of the Vatican was the certainty of
following sound doctrine, and unconditional obedience to the pope
was the criterion of belonging to the church. The response, whether
true or apocryphal, attributed to a catholic journalist who is said
to have answered someone questioning him on the content of his
faith. 'Go and ask in Rome', although it may not actually have been
spoken, is nevertheless a good illustration of that attitude of mind
which excluded all doubt and all question. There was no need to
convene new councils; the dogma had received its definitive formu-
lation. Ultramontanism was linked to a literal interpretation of
tradition that left no room for innovation. Ultramontanism and
dogmatic intransigentism merged. The theologian therefore had
nothing to learn from modern philosophies, which were the expression of the pride of the human intellect. Liberalism was the enemy,

and all modern philosophical systems were merely its embodiment.
It put truth and error on the same level, led to relativism and in-
differentism. It was the heresy of modern times, the offspring of the
Reformation which had ruined the unity of Christendom. The
Roman pontiffs vied with one another to fulminate anathema
against liberalism, and denounced the pernicious effects of the
practice of freedom, whether of conscience or the press.

The papacy was not only an institution; it was also a person –
the pope. Ultramontanism was not only a way of thinking; it was
also a cult – of the sovereign pontiff. This feeling of fervour for
the Vicar of Christ was a relatively new phenomenon; formerly, the
faithful barely knew the name of the reigning pope. In the nineteenth century, not only was he well known, but he also inspired
piety and devotion. Certain events contributed to the creation of
this feeling, especially the misfortunes of the holders of the supreme
office: Pius VI snatched from his palaces and dying in exile at
Valence, and the imprisoned Pius VII inspired respect for the
dignity with which they had endured snubs and captivity. Later,
there would be sympathy for the woes of Pius IX, driven out of
Rome by riots, then robbed by the Piedmontese and, in the imagination of the faithful, turned into a prisoner in the Vatican. The
exceptional length of two of the reigns contributed in no small way
to familiarizing European public opinion with the popes. Pius IX
was the first in history to outstrip Peter's number of years, in-
validating the very old idea that no pope would reign longer than
the Prince of Apostles; and by an extraordinary coincidence, his
immediate successor, Leo XIII, repeated the feat. Between the two
of them, they guided the destinies of catholics for fifty-seven years,
from 1846 to 1903.

With their impetus, the Roman component of catholicism was
considerably strengthened, to the point of becoming identified with
it. Pius IX and Leo XIII systematically practised a policy of tightening links between the centre and the churches of the whole
world, attracting to the Eternal City the mother-houses of religious
orders, procuracies, or general Curias, opening seminaries for different nations, or welcoming the most gifted candidates destined
for the episcopacy. The Curia was internationalized and the practice of regular visits *ad limina* of bishops to Rome became an
institution. This centralization of the church was helped by the
technical advances which reduced distances and shortened waiting
periods, facilitated by the building of railways, the telegraph and
also the development of the press which circulated the pontiffs'

pronouncements. Rome attracted ever-increasing numbers of the faithful who came on pilgrimages from all over Europe and returned to their provinces with the lifelong memory of having seen the Vicar of Christ with their own eyes. 'The characteristic feature of this era,' wrote Mgr de Salinis, a former disciple of La Mennais, 'is the movement towards Rome. Rome is the centre of catholicism, and therefore it is from Rome that the movement for the regeneration of human societies must start.'

Priests and their faithful flocks made it a pious duty and a point of honour to imitate the customs and practices of the Eternal City in their parishes; everything was done as it was in Rome. The old local liturgies were dropped in favour of the Roman rite; even the Roman pronunciation of Latin was adopted. In everything, reference to Rome became the rule, inspiring artists and authors. Religious architecture reproduced the model of the Roman basilica, and artists' brushes brought back to life the first Christian meetings in the secrecy of the catacombs, which the excavations of the archaeologist Gian-Battista de Rossi had made familiar to the French public through the works of Gabriel Boissier. Louis Veuillot wrote 'Parfums de Rome', a hymn of love for the city. Two novels enjoyed immense success throughout Europe and endeared the church of the early centuries to young people: *Fabiola ou l'église des catacombes (1854)*, whose author was no less than Cardinal Wiseman, and *Quo Vadis (1896)*, by the great Polish writer, future Nobel prizewinner, Henryk Sienkiewicz.

Although ultramontanism numbered great thinkers in its ranks, and found well-reasoned and argued justifications, it also reached the masses and contained a popular dimension. Ultramontanism spoke as much to the heart as to the intellect. A vast number of people had access to a press with a wide circulation, took part in pilgrimages and went to pray at the great sanctuaries. To some extent, ultramontanism was the counterpart of what the protestant churches experienced with pietism, with the one difference that the ecclesiastical authority always kept a close control on its expressions. If one looked today for what might be the extension or equivalent of this great momentum of popular piety, it would probably be the charismatic movement which has enjoyed a certain success in catholicism since the 1970s.

Ultramontanism was not only an ecclesiology, it was more than a theology; it was also a vision of history and a social and political philosophy or, to be more precise, its ecclesiology shaped catholic thinking about society. The same principles, in fact, applied to the organization of civil society as to the ecclesiastical institution, starting with that of authority without which there is nothing but disorder. The principles of '89, the expression of liberalism and rationalism, brought in their wake the destruction of the natural order willed by God, and unleashed individualism, the triumph of egoism and anarchy, the source of injustice and generator of domination by the strong over the weak, the rich over the poor. From the social situation created by the political and industrial revolution, ultramontane thinkers drew a picture whose blackness did not yield before the criticism of socialist schools of thought, and they gradually erected a system advocating a return to the institutions that structured medieval society and were deemed to have ensured the happiness of the peoples. Any separation of society and religion was naturally rejected as contrary to the design of providence and the salvation of society. Religion must inspire the conduct of individuals and governments alike. Here and there, this programme of restoration of an order transferred from the church started to take place and could boast of symbolic figures. For instance, Garcia Moreno, president of the Republic of Ecuador, in 1862 had signed a concordat which completely satisfied Rome's demands and based public law on canon law. The ultramontane press praised his work of restoration of a Christian society in the face of impious liberalism. His tragic death – he died at the hands of an anarchist – made him a martyr and a model for the veneration of the faithful and imitation by catholic politicians. In today's terms, one would say that ultramontanism was a form of integralism.

It was a doubly reactionary integralism. The society for which ultramontanism drew up the ideal plan ran counter to democracy; there could be no legitimate power other than that delegated by God, and ultramontanes could not conceive that it could proceed from appointment by the rank and file. Inequality among men was a fact of nature according to the will of providence; although they were all equal in the sight of God for their spiritual destiny, and all called to the salvation of their soul, on this earth they were necessarily different from one another and unequal, because they were destined to fulfil distinct functions of disparate importance. Ultramontanism was inseparable from an organicist view of the social body as a living organism in which the limbs had various functions and the organs were specialized. Inequality was accompanied by hierarchy; some had to obey, others to give orders and be in charge. To work for the equality of individuals would thus be to go against divine will.

Ultramontane integralism was also reactionary through its nostalgia for a largely mythical past: a Christianity supposed to have known a 'golden era' in the middle ages. The imagination of the Christian populace was fed on the memory of a time when the popes laid down the law to princes and imposed a respect for morality on them. From the catholic people a cry went up to the Holy See. Parish priests, sometimes the butt of their bishop's pedantic authority, turned their eyes towards the supreme head of the church; clerics and faithful exposed to administrative harassment addressed themselves to the supreme pastor and, for support in the face of political oppression, counted on the backing of the power of the pope. Peoples of catholic tradition whom the vicissitudes of history had subjected to the foreign domination of schismatic or heretical beliefs saw loyalty to Peter's See as a means of preserving their national identity: the Irish oppressed by protestant England, the Polish annexed by Russian orthodoxy. Italian patriots dreaming of their homeland's unity and independence expected the pope to head the liberation movement in the peninsula; it was a reawakening of the old Guelph dream against domination by the *tedeschi*. Following Joseph de Maistre and La Mennais, some people hoped to rebuild the unity of Christian Europe around the papacy.

By an unforeseen twist of history, in the nineteenth century the pontifical institution took on a political significance. First, it was a denial of modern society, the rejection of the principles of the Revolution and a plan to restore the traditional order of things. It was also the demand by and for the catholic church, a society reputedly perfect and superior to anything of human construction, for its independence in regard to any political power. Lastly, it represented the entry of a new player into the system of international relations.

Antipopery

Offsetting the new fervour for Rome and the person of the pope there came a growing animosity. Hostility to the papacy certainly went back a long way and had played no small part in the secession of the northern European countries. But though it is true that in the countries which had remained obedient to Rome the majority of governments had never consented to its involvement in their internal affairs, anticlericalism had only rarely attacked the pope, who was too distant a figure to arouse the wrath of pamphleteers and who normally did not interfere in the daily life of the national churches. The authority of the supreme pontiff was called into question only indirectly and in a roundabout way. For example, the Jansenists held a grudge against him for his condemnation of the five Propositions; it was one reason among others for their affinity with the Richerist doctrine, which took its name from a Paris curé, Richer, who claimed the right for his colleagues to have a hand in the running of the church, harking back to the succession of the seventy-two disciples of Christ, as the bishops boasted of the succession of the twelve Apostles. The Jansenists, too, advocated a more democratic organization within the church. Nevertheless, because the pope's power was reduced it did not provoke great opposition.

On the contrary, in the nineteenth century neither the pontifical institution nor the pope personally left people indifferent, and public opinion was divided between unconditional loyalty and bitter loathing. It was partly the consequence of the Revolution, which the Holy See had condemned in circumstances that have already been mentioned. Revolutionary propaganda enveloped the papacy in its denunciation of thrones and despots. It is true that the sovereign of the Papal States was being targeted rather than the supreme pastor, but how could the two be dissociated when the pope himself maintained that the two offices were indissolubly linked and that his spiritual ministry required his dominion over a territory, which made him a head of state like the rest? The feelings of hostility aroused by the papacy were also the product of his increasing intervention in the life of the universal church and world affairs. The catholic states, who willingly tolerated a feeble and docile papacy, and even looked for its approval of their own policies, resented its interference. They were loath to let the Holy See escape their control; in 1868 the governments of catholic nations were indignant when Pius IX convened a council without giving them prior warning of his intention, and even more because he had not invited them to be represented as usual, so accustomed were they to nothing being decided without their consent, even in religious matters.

Not only catholic countries were upset by Rome's initiatives in the nineteenth century; they were given no better reception in nations won over to the Reformation, especially when some of them clashed with the national feeling that for three hundred years had fed on mistrust of the papacy. In 1850, taking note of the

conversion movement that for some time had been bringing back
university men and ecclesiastics to the church of Rome – the most
shining example being Newman in 1845 – Pius IX re-established
the catholic hierarchy in England which, since the sixteenth
century, had been little more than a mission land under the aegis
of the Roman Propaganda Congregation. He revived the titles of
the ancient episcopal sees and placed at the head of the reconstituted Episcopate an Archbishop of Westminster. Now, these titles
had been borne by prelates of the Church of England, who regarded
themselves as the legitimate heirs of the apostolic succession; in
their eyes, the catholic bishops were usurpers. The papal decision
rudely reawoke in public opinion the spectre of a papist return. The
politicians' reaction was one of extreme violence. Twenty years
later, the Vatican Council's proclamation of papal infallibility as a
dogmatic truth provoked fresh controversy. Even someone as
open-minded as Gladstone then wrote a book denouncing catholicism. Parliament retaliated in 1851 with a law declaring the
illegality of ecclesiastical titles borne by clergy of denominations
other than the established church and reserving to the crown the
creation and allocation of titles. If the reaction was so sharp, it was
also because in the United Kingdom the question of catholicism
became entangled with the Irish problem; the conjunction of the
two was not favourable to the extinction of prejudices that dated
back to the religious wars.

There was the same reaction in the Netherlands to a similar
initiative; in 1853 Pius IX re-established the hierarchy there with
an archbishop in Utrecht, in the heart of Calvinist Holland. A vast
movement of petitions demanded an answer and reanimated the
anti-Roman feeling inherited from the long struggle waged in
the sixteenth and seventeenth centuries by the United Provinces
against catholic Spain. A quarter of a century later, when the
catholic hierarchy was re-established in its turn in Scotland,
emotions ran less high; opinion had grown accustomed to the idea
and experience had disproved certain anxieties.

In German protestant countries, mistrust of the papacy was no
less strident; the German *Los Von Rom* echoed the British *No
Popery*. Catholicism was regarded as an adverse force by patriots
anxious to unite Germany, especially those who hoped it would be
achieved around Prussia, partly because of Austria's identification
with catholicism. The Prussian state had joined battle with the episcopal hierarchy in 1837, at the time of the Cologne Incident. Later,
catholics would long remain suspected of being less loyal nationals

than the rest because of their allegiance to Rome. This suspicion was one of the motives for the policy carried out in Prussia by Bismarck against the catholic church, under the watchword of *Kulturkampf*, fight for culture.

This name throws light on some of the reasons why, in the nineteenth century, so many intellectuals, writers, learned men and philosophers in Europe were determined opponents of the papacy and ceaselessly fought against its positions and interventions. In their eyes it was an obscurantist power hindering freedom of thought and the progress of reason. They did not necessarily set all religion in opposition to science; within protestant denominations attempts were made to reconcile the Christian revealed religion and the experiences of scientific knowledge, some of these conciliations, in the case of so-called liberal protestantism, going as far as the eclipsing of Christian dogma. It was with catholicism that there appeared to be a total contradiction, to the point where many considered that the triumph of reason and the advance of science required the catholic church to lose all influence over the training of intellects and the conduct of societies. At the time, the popes did nothing to dispel these prejudices, systematically condemning all the aspirations of modern society and putting forward the most intransigent version possible of catholicism. Between the spirit of free enquiry and teaching by authority, between the primacy of critical reasoning and unconditional submission to the Vatican, reconciliation was inconceivable. Therefore, bearing in mind the increasingly frequent intervention of the papal institution in intellectual and political debate, opposing feelings crystallized on that and the person of the pope.

The Papal States

The fact that the head of this church was also the sovereign of an earthly state did little to improve the papacy's image. To understand the vehemence of passions aroused, it would be impossible to pay too much attention to this particular aspect and its consequences, especially to the problematics of what was then called the Roman question, which in the nineteenth century occupied an important place in international relations.

Until the French Revolution the dual sovereignty of the pope, spiritual and temporal, was beyond question; it was a relatively commonplace situation in a Europe where ecclesiastical office was often accompanied by territorial possessions, which were originally justified because they were supposed to ensure the material security and legal independence of their holders. In the Germanic Holy Roman Empire, for instance, which in Enlightenment Europe remained the most precise example of the medieval spirit, several bishops were landowning princes who exercised a dual authority over their subjects and flocks. When all was said and done, if the pope, the supreme head of the church, also reigned as absolute master over a vast territory that stretched across the Italian peninsula and extended from one sea to the other and from the banks of the Po to Campania, he was merely at the summit of a legal edifice which, throughout Europe, combined religion, possession of land and political power.

On this point as on many others, it was the French Revolution which shook traditional order and changed outlooks. The secularization of the clergy's possessions in all countries occupied by the revolutionary armies and, with the Recess of 1803, the disappearance of ecclesiastical principalities in Germany, left the church states in a more exposed position. People questioned the legitimacy of a joint possession which began to be perceived as a sign of confusion between functions that would gain by being differentiated and dissociated; it was the start of the first controversies over the Roman question.

There had actually been a precedent which is often omitted from comparisons although it played a far from negligible part in the change in relations between the papacy and the Revolution: the fate of Avignon and the Comtat Venaissin which had been in the pope's possession for centuries. In 1790 a section of the people of Avignon, from sympathy with the ideas of the Revolution, and also perhaps to escape the authority of the pope and his legates, expressed the desire to become French and asked to be part of the kingdom. After some hesitation, to be quite sure of the population's feelings, the following year the Constituent Assembly arranged a consultation that was known as a plebiscite. This was the very first application of the principle of the rights of peoples to decide their own future, in open opposition to the principles of division among sovereigns for which the unfortunate Poland had paid the price. The result was perfectly clear; the inhabitants of Avignon and the Comtat, including the enclave of Valréas in the *département* of the Drôme, declared themselves by a strong majority to be in favour of joining. Today, a stele in the town centre of Avignon perpetuates the memory of this event (1791). The papacy, considering itself robbed, protested against this brigandry, which was not likely to make Pius VI favourably disposed to the Revolution.

The domination of the pope over his states was again called into question in 1797, once more on the initiative of revolutionary France, when Bonaparte invaded Italy and by the Treaty of Tolentino imposed on the pope an amputation of his states. Napoleon reoffended in 1809, when he quite simply incorporated Rome into the French Empire, reducing the Eternal City to the role of capital of the French *département* of the Tiber. The pope had refused to close his states to British trade and support the continental system. Thus the eldest daughter of the church, who had so often been the protectress of the Holy See, had three times in twenty years aimed a blow at both the theory and the reality of the pope's temporal power.

The Congress of Vienna re-established the pope's authority over all his states, with the exception of Avignon. But no restitution could erase the memory of what had happened. Papal domination over Latium or Romagna was henceforward at odds with the aspirations of Italian patriots for the unity of the peninsula, and in contradiction with the principle of peoples' right to self-determination. It was an odious concept in the view of the Vatican, which did not refrain from denouncing it. Gregory XVI had condemned Poland's insurrection against the tsar. It was therefore out of the question that the papacy should recognize the justice of the patriotic claim, or make the slightest concession to liberal thinking; the power of the pope-king was absolute.

If only his states had been a model of paternal administration! But they had the not ill-founded reputation of being the worst governed of all the states in the peninsula. Corruption was endemic, and there was nothing to encourage initiative or stimulate the economy. In contrast to a Europe which was gradually seeing the results of an increasingly clearly perceived distinction between religion and society, confusion was the rule in the Papal States, whose title emphasizes the very essence of this particular territory. It had properties which appeared unacceptable to public opinion: the commandments of the church were the state laws, canon law replaced the civil code.

One incident made the archaism of the situation very obvious, and had considerable repercussions throughout Europe: The Mortara affair. The facts can be told in a few lines; on a June night in 1858, in Bologna, there was a knock at the door of a Jewish family who had long been settled in the Papal States. A man accompanied by two police officers asked to see one of the children, aged six, young Edgar Mortara, and took him away. The motive behind this abduction was soon revealed. Some years earlier, when the child had fallen ill, a young girl who was a servant in the family had become worried about his salvation and had had him baptized without his parents' knowledge. The secret had been kept until the death of another Mortara child, who died unbaptized. Stricken with remorse, the servant had confessed the matter to a priest who immediately informed the archbishop of Bologna. The latter, considering that by his baptism the child belonged to the catholic church, which was therefore under an obligation to see that he was instructed in the true religion, took the decision to remove him from his family and place him in a house in Rome where he would be raised as a catholic. Nothing could show more clearly the catholic church's intent to ensure that God's laws, and its own, prevailed over the rights of the natural family. Contemporaries saw it as a proof that the church respected no other laws than its own, in contempt of individual rights and liberties. The episode caused an immense outcry; emotions ran high and there was widespread indignation. Even governments could not keep silent; Napoleon III instructed his Minister of Foreign Affairs to make representations to the Holy See to have the young Edgar returned to his family. He received a negative reply.

Far from distancing themselves from the position of the Roman authorities, the intransigent catholics did their utmost to explain that the religious authorities could not have acted otherwise. Any alternative on their part would have been a failure in their duties to the truth of which the church was custodian. Anticlericals of all shades and liberals took note of the incompatibility between church law and civil law; yet another reason for working to free society from the clerical grip. The Mortara affair thus contributed to hastening the secularization of society. It also helped greatly to spread the conviction that temporal power was an archaic institution.

The Roman Question

A prey to liberal agitation, at loggerheads with demands for unity, in order to maintain its authority over his subjects the pope's government was compelled to resort to harsh measures that did not exclude capital punishment. There was indignation in Europe that an ecclesiastical government which drew its inspiration from the Gospel could execute men whose only crime was too much love for their native land. After 1850 Victor Hugo, in his *Châtiments*, would become the eloquent spokesman for moral awareness against the barbarism of the priests' government.

After the revolutions of 1830, and still more of 1848, it became evident that the maintenance of temporal authority would henceforward depend on the backing of other powers. From then on the Roman question not only set the pope against part of his subjects; it also assumed an international dimension, similar to the so-called eastern question posed by the decline of the Ottoman Empire. The link between the two issues was the impotence of an archaic government. Although the protestant states did not disapprove of the weakening of a government whose very existence seemed illegitimate to them, the catholic states for their part could not remain passive or simply indifferent. In any case, the papacy, which was incapable of resisting by itself and therefore reduced to seeking help from abroad, would increasingly rely on diplomacy through the intermediary of national churches invited to put pressure on their respective governments. But catholic powers did not share the same views or interests; they were more anxious to prevent their rivals from gaining an advantage than in providing the Holy See with unselfish assistance. In 1831 Austria's intervention to help the pope against his rebellious subjects in Romagna had provoked France into occupying the port of Ancona.

Of all the peoples interested in the Roman question because of their catholicism – Austria, Belgium, Spain and France – the latter was most closely associated with the vicissitudes of the matter. Its involvement began with the Second Republic; the revolutions of 1848 had had repercussions in the Papal States. This time it was not only in the northern provinces that the disturbances erupted, but in the very heart of Rome itself, following the refusal of Pius IX to take part in the patriotic war against Austria for reasons similar to those which had formerly motivated Pius VII's refusal to close his states to England at the time of the continental system. A triumvirate had seized power in Rome and proclaimed the Republic. Pius IX had fled his capital and found refuge in the kingdom of Naples, at Gaeta. The faithful in every country were shattered by the thought that the pope was no longer in Rome, especially the French, who put pressure on the prince-president to whose election they had largely contributed. Louis Napoleon therefore sent an expeditionary corps whose official mission was to reconcile the pope and his subjects. The expedition quickly became a trial of strength. The grandsons of the gendarmes who forty years earlier had led away Pius VII besieged the city in order to hand it back to his successor. From the heights of the Janiculum the French artillery bombarded Rome. A month later they overcame the resistance and the pope was able to return home.

For the next twenty years France was linked with the destiny of the Roman question, the survival of the pope's temporal power and the existence of the church states dependent on its support. The Italian policy of the Second Empire, espousing Piedmont's ambitions and declaring war on Austria, unleashed a process that it was unable to control. Napoleon III would have wished to confine the territorial reorganization to the north of the peninsula, thus avoiding touching the totality of the Papal States but, clandestinely encouraged by Cavour, the movement for unity inspired by Garibaldi swiftly overflowed the frontiers assigned to it by cautious governments. One after another, Romagna and Emilia, Umbria and the Marches joined the nascent kingdom of Italy. After the incorporation of the kingdom of Naples, which managed to encircle the pontifical domain, the fate of what remained of it was extremely precarious. It was the final obstacle to the achievement of unification, and abroad many tended to view this last residue as no more than the survival of an age that was over everywhere else and thus destined for a swift demise.

But at the same time, throughout catholic Europe a movement of sympathy and solidarity with the pope was taking shape; some ten thousand volunteers of twenty-two nationalities, including three thousand Frenchmen under the command of General Lamoricière, flocked to assist in the defence of the Holy See, in the same state of mind as their ancestors who in times gone by had donned the cross to liberate the tomb of Christ. Despite the difference in their ideological outlook, this noble impulse had some analogy with the movement of the International Brigades, a century later, to defend Madrid and bar the way to fascism. The papal combatants, however, had less luck; they had no Malraux among them to hymn their epic, no Hemingway to say for whom the bell had tolled at Castelfidardo. Their cause, it is true, also had less future; the defenders of the pope were fighting a rearguard action which international opinion considered they had lost in advance.

From 1860 there was no longer anything between the pope and Italy but the French garrison in Rome, whose presence cost France the moral advantage of its intervention on the side of Piedmont.

Through the Convention of September 1864, French diplomacy, trying to extricate itself from the trap, obtained the commitment of the king of Italy not to invade what remained of the Papal States; the French division could therefore leave Rome. But a surprise attack by Garibaldi obliged the French to make a hasty return, although the Piedmontese kept their word and halted the Redshirts' march on Rome. France's defeat at Sedan and the deposition of the Emperor, to whom Victor Emmanuel had felt personally committed, allowed him to take back his promise. On 20 September 1870 the Piedmontese mounted an attack on the Eternal City, and opened a breach in the wall level with the Porta Pia. After a symbolic resistance, Pius IX gave the order to cease combat. The last vestiges of the Papal States disappeared, together with the temporal sovereignty of the pope.

Although it was resolved by force of arms, the Roman question was by no means settled. The pope, and with him the catholics of the whole world, refused to recognize the fait accompli. Pius IX denounced the despoilment and demanded compensation. He rejected both the damages proposed to him by the Italian government and the assurances of the law known as the Law of Guarantees passed by the parliament in 1871. He and his successors now regarded themselves as prisoners; since their domain had been taken from them by violence and the town of which they remained the legitimate sovereigns was occupied by usurpers, they would not emerge from the Vatican. Upon his election a new pope would solemnly reiterate his predecessors' protest and enclose himself in the apostolic palaces, a voluntary recluse. The catholic world was moved by the plight of the august captive; in all the churches in Christendom prayers were said for the restoration of his power. In France the hymn 'Save Rome and France' associated vanquished France and the imprisoned pope in the same dolorist piety. Pilgrims flocked annually to Rome in ever-growing numbers to receive his blessing and acclaim the pope-king, in defiance of the Piedmontese.

From the opposite point of view, this demonstrative solidarity of the clergy and faithful rendered them suspect to their fellow-citizens. In 1877 the campaign of French bishops in favour of re-establishing temporal power provoked Gambetta to denounce clericalism as the main enemy. Their patriotism was doubted, as the loyalty of communists would be later. This comparison is not fortuitous; in 1924 when the French radical party chose as the watchword of its electoral campaign *Ni Rome ni Moscou*, the

Rome thus rejected was not that of fascism but of the Vatican. At that time the radicals put loyalty to the pope and alignment with the Comintern on the same level.

The Roman question continued to weigh on international relations well beyond 1870. It seemed absolutely insoluble, like all those in which two entities covet the same territory and fight over its possession. It is the same problem as that of Jerusalem claimed by two peoples and three religions. In both cases a religious factor is added to the strictly political claim, making an amicable solution even more improbable. The desire of Pius IX's immediate successor, Leo XIII, to ensure France's help in its settlement perhaps played a part in the origins of the invitation addressed to French catholics to rally to the regime. In the opposite direction, in 1915, as the price of its intervention, the Italian government demanded from France and Great Britain a pledge to exclude from the future peace conference any representation of the Holy See. This it obtained without difficulty from protestant England and a French government that had had no connection with the Holy See since 1904. The question was finally settled by direct negotiation between the Italian government and the Vatican in 1929. But for almost a century it had weighed on international relations and, in every country in which catholics were in the majority, on relations between them and their government, thereby adding an international issue to all the many others that were the subject of dispute in relations between religion and politics.

7

Religion and Nation: Two Universal Realities

Since European societies were defined as much by reference to actual nations as by their formation into political entities, relations between religion and society usually included the latter's attitude towards the idea of nationhood and the feeling of belonging to a national community. This notion was not compatible with the interaction between religion and political power, if only because nation and state did not always coincide in the history of European societies; they were sometimes opposed and frequently involved in combat. Even today instances of discord between them are not rare and are at the root of some of the disputes tearing the continent apart and disturbing the peace.

Religion and nationhood are connected by more than one feature; they are the two most universal social factors. In all countries human beings have for centuries adhered to one or other of these two types of community. It is true that they had hardly any chance of escaping them, but why should they have wanted to? There was no greater calamity for anyone than to lose his native land or be exiled from it; bewailing the misfortune of the exile or refugee is a constant theme in every country's literature. In the present time, the fate of the expatriate still arouses compassion. As for belonging to a religion, it was imposed on everyone from birth; one could no more choose one's religion than one's family or country. The nation chose on behalf of its nationals. Even today, that is the situation in Scandinavian countries, where one is enrolled at birth into the state church. Although a free-thinker was always at liberty not to belong to the faith professed by the nation, society would not tolerate open withdrawal; it was more willing to accept hypocrisy than apostasy.

Another feature of kinship was that neither religion nor nation was prepared to share; people belonged to one nation alone, and the same applied to religion. Both demanded an allegiance that excluded any other attachment, and in both cases it was for life. Changes of homeland remained the exception and were generally looked on as a betrayal. One was baptized for all eternity; it was not only the cleric who was ordained *in aeternum*, so was every baptized person. Adherence to either could go as far as sacrificing one's life; the idea was inculcated that to die for one's homeland was the finest and most enviable lot. Many true believers have aspired to becoming martyrs, with a burning desire to testify to their faith even under torture.

Religion and nation similarly transcended the span of individual existence; homelands did not die, they outlived the citizens who made them, and their immortality was built on individual sacrifice. As for religions, they lay outside and beyond time and history since they announced a truth which foretold a world where time would be abolished.

Recent history, moreover, has proved the ability of these two realities to endure. Notably, it has invalidated the predictions of Marxism, which forecast the ineluctable decline of both when the day came for the disappearance of those socio-economic conditions on which, according to the system, their existence depended: bourgeois domination and the class struggle. Half a century of pitiless application of Marxism-Leninism has made short work of the premise that saw both national feeling and religious belief as no more than the sublimation of a transitory phase in the relations of social forces. This premise can be seen today for what it is: an ideological *a priori* closer to an act of faith than a scientific finding. In all countries that have been subjected to communist rule since the Second World War, religious feeling has resisted attacks and, far from disappearing, has triumphed over ideology. As for national feeling, not only has it failed to disappear, it has been revitalized, with a strength redoubled by having been long repressed or forfeited. Religion and nation found themselves in the same camp, waging a common battle against the same adversary.

Meeting in the hearts and minds of people, nation and religion had to recognize each other; they needed to continue to interact, and over the centuries relations have been close and very varied. Their history alone would fill an entire book; it would not be out of place, if only to describe the diversity of these relations and retrace the way they followed on from one another. There is every kind of example. Relations between religion and nation did not have to be of competition and rivalry; the most usual and long-lasting kind was an interdependence between religious and national adherence. Without going into an abstract outline, basically three successive eras can be distinguished, their forms intertwining, transition from one era to the next not immediately obliterating any trace of the one before. At the end of the twentieth century, Europe still juxtaposes situations inherited from each of these three eras.

The Era of Symbiosis: The Holy Nations

The first, and most common, era is also the one that lasted longest, and is characterized by a close interdependence which reached a stage of symbiosis between religion and nation. If it contained such involvement between the two realities, it was because to a certain extent their origins were intermingled. Peoples simultaneously attained a consciousness of both. In Europe, the birth of a nation often coincided with the transition from paganism to Christianity; conversion also meant access to a superior civilization. That was particularly true of those who entered a second circle of European Christendom, at the time of a second phase in the evangelization of the continent, around the year 1000: the countries of northern Europe and those of central and eastern Europe. For Norway or Denmark, Poland and Hungary, it was the conversion of their sovereign along with that of the people, and his baptism that is still celebrated today as the nation's birth certificate. Popular piety mingling with love for the homeland became canonized. The case of Gaul is not at all similar, although a certain tradition dates the birth of Christian France to the baptism of Clovis, and for an obvious reason: when the chief of the Franks decided to embrace the religion of his wife Clotilde, Gaul was already christianized. St Martin, to whom tradition attributes rural evangelization, had already been dead for a century. Unlike other sovereigns, whose personal choice committed their people, Clovis rallied to the religion of his subjects. Whether they belonged to the first wave of evangelization, like the countries that had been part of the Roman Empire, or had not joined them until five or six hundred years later, like all the peoples who had remained outside its boundaries, all European peoples, whether inhabitants of their territory from time immemorial, or recent invaders like the Hungarians, subsequently combined nation and the Christian religion in a common piety. The conflicts that frequently erupted between royal powers and churches, the disputes setting sovereigns against primates and arch-bishops, pope versus emperor, in no way affected the symbiosis between religion and nation. The whole of society was steeped in a sacral ambience, which enabled Marc Bloch, when speaking of the French monarchy, to talk of the Reims religion.

At the roots of this intertwining lay a conviction that was not always explicitly expressed but was unanimously accepted, and concerned a certain theological view; the nation was a living entity, a spiritual reality, which existed in God's eyes and possessed a soul. Providence had plans for it; it was summoned to a holy mission. Thus for a subject to serve his king and fight for his country was to obey God. Each nation believed itself called upon to play a part in the accomplishment of God's plans. Spain's mission was to repulse the infidel and free the peninsula. When the *reconquista* was achieved under the catholic kings with the fall of Granada in 1492, Spain's mission was transferred overseas; it was to preach the Gospel in the new world and win over the recently discovered lands to Christianity. At the other end of Europe, Poland's geographical position dictated its mission: to be the rampart of the Latin west against schismatic Russia. As for Russia itself, Byzantium's heir since the fall of Constantinople and invested with the dignity of the third Rome, its destiny was also expressed in re-ligious terms. It was holy Russia, guardian of orthodoxy and charged with responsibility for all those people who shared its faith.

It was perhaps in France that the identification of religion with national destiny was oldest, because it was one of the oldest nations. At a very early date, a tradition accredited by the abbey of St Denis presented the kingdom of France as the chosen nation, called upon, after Christ's coming, to be the one to carry on the Israel of the Old Testament; hence the adage *Gesta Dei per Francos*. God had a special fondness for the French. Two historical figures illustrated and helped to found this religious interpretation of national history. One was the pious king St Louis, the model of a Christian sovereign, causing justice to reign in his kingdom, a knight going off to the Crusades and dying in a distant land. The other was Joan of Arc, whose story is more mysterious. In the fifteenth century, in fact, the nations of the west still regarded themselves as parts of a relatively united Christendom. That did not rule out conflict between them, but apparently without religious significance since all sides shared the same faith and were in communion with the Holy See. The war of succession which set the two monarchies of the west at loggerheads could not therefore be thought of as a war of religion, since French and English professed the same faith. Moreover, it was a church tribunal, constituted by English catholics, that condemned the catholic Joan to the stake, to be burnt by soldiers who shared her faith. Nevertheless, her suffering and death assumed a religious significance; she was acknowledged to be holy as much because of her mission as for the sanctity of her brief existence. One cannot therefore speak of her as a martyr, since she was not put to death out of hatred for her faith; the opposite was the case, since the indictments against her were for heresy and witchcraft. She was, however, canonized, and even the French laics acknowledged her as a national saint. This indissoluble mixture of religious elements and what may already be termed patriotic feeling in the cult of Joan of Arc is an essential ingredient of her mystery and historic role. In the play that the shepherdess from Domremy inspired in such a nonconformist intellectual as Bernard Shaw, he clearly showed that when Joan of Arc burst upon the history of Europe she presaged the end of medieval Christendom's undividedness, and the birth of modern nations.

The Era of Modernity: Religion and Nationality

The second era in the history of relations between religion and nation is clearly distinguishable from the preceding one by the splitting up of European territory into national entities. Of course, the first era was not unaware of territorial divisions and it would be an illusion to picture medieval Europe as a united and homogeneous world. But with the notable exception of the severance from the Christian east, dramatically illustrated by the sack of Constantinople by the Crusaders from the west in 1204, its divisions belonged to a universe that recognized the religious authority of the Roman pontiff, even if sovereigns did not refrain from flouting his orders and challenged his right to intervene in their kingdom's affairs. With the protestant Reformation in the sixteenth century, the ties linking Christianity with the real life of nations were not done away with but substantially transformed by the shattering of religious unity and the parcelling out of Christendom. The union of the religious and the political would henceforward operate within the more confined framework of the nation. It was the principle of national churches coinciding with the state, on the model of the German *Landeskirche*. Although it is not possible to determine with any certainty what was cause and what was effect, the concomitant emergence in the sixteenth century of modern nations and national churches was a great historic happening, which constituted modernity. The religious reference was a people's means of affirming its national singularity, and a component of its particular identity in the European ensemble. Northern Europe's choice of the Reformation, though fundamentally inspired by religious motives, was also an opportunity for that part of the continent to escape the control of Rome and win its cultural as well as its political independence. At the end of the middle ages, Bohemia had undergone a similar experience with the cult to the memory of Jan Hus, which signified a rejection of Roman authority and the affirmation of the Czech nation. The same movement then aroused the recognition of the vernacular as the language of religion, administration and culture; from then on it was permissible to pray to God and listen to His word in ordinary language. Luther's translation of the Bible, and England's adoption of the book of common prayer were contemporary with Villers-Cotteret's edict imposing the use of French in administration and the law. The bond between religion and nation was tightened, and for nations which had broken with Rome antipopery became an ingredient in the national persona.

Although the transition to this second era in the history of relations between religion and national awareness chiefly concerned the nations that had embraced the Reformation, those who had made the opposite choice and remained obedient to the Holy See also accomplished a similar movement. The Counter-Reformation had comparable results; remaining loyal to the traditional faith helped to accentuate the identity of catholic nations. For Bavaria or Austria, the struggle against the protestant heresy took over from Christendom's fight against the pagans or the infidel. The war that for thirty years, from 1618 to 1648, tore central Europe apart, was in some aspects a religious one, setting catholic Austria and Spain against the rebel Czechs, the German protestant princes and the Lutheran Sweden of Gustavus Adolphus, whose soldiers fought for their faith and sang hymns after battle. It was also the choice of different denominations which caused the dismemberment of the seventeen provinces composing the old Netherlands and brought about the separation of the Calvinist United Provinces from Belgium which had stayed catholic.

The key feature of this second era, in the wake of the dividing up of Christian Europe, is the coincidence between the parcelling of territory and confessional division. Splitting the continent into separate entities from then on had its counterpart in the religious domain. Far from the bonds being strained between the two realities and the feelings they inspired respectively, their almost perfect simultaneity, hallowed by the principle *cuius regio, eius religio*, increased national feeling and turned religious adherence into the criterion and foundation of political society. We have seen its effects on the earlier regime of relations between religion and society.

The period of European revolutions initiated a third era which was characterized by a growing dissociation between religion and nation. It is the intention of the following section to retrace the process by which these two great realities diverged, sometimes to the point of opposing each other. But entering a new era does not mean an end to those that have gone before. As the religious era lasted a long time, they survived well after the causes of their appearance had vanished; the long gone circumstances of their formation continued to live on in people's memory, imagination and conscience. It was that coexistence which provoked disputes and fed arguments over the religious question. In France, vestiges of eras prior to the Revolution partly explain the bitterness of the battles aroused by entry into the third of the periods described here.

Not everything of the first and second eras disappeared immediately when France dissociated national and confessional adherence. That dissociation was perhaps the most fundamental reason for the conflict between catholicism and the Revolution. It is customary to lay more blame on the contradiction of political and social philosophies, the incompatibility of an individualist society based on the primacy of liberty with a traditional order which promoted the higher interest of groups over personal aspirations. This contrast was certainly a determining factor, and its impact even grew as, during the nineteenth century, the Vatican increased its anathemas against liberalism, to which it imputed responsibility for all the ills afflicting society, from atheism to social injustice. And yet, for the catholics of France who for centuries had identified patriotism with their faith, who knows whether the feeling of being suddenly deprived of the nationhood that belonged to them in their own right may have been just as decisive a factor in their rejection of the Revolution. It was henceforward possible to be a full French citizen with the same rights as other compatriots, without being a Roman catholic. Catholics could hardly have failed to interpret this upheaval as disloyalty on France's part to its origins and its vocation. They had even greater justification when the Revolution's heirs challenged their mystical vision with a different and contradictory Messianism, making France the missionary of the principles of 1789, the propagandist of the revolutionary gospel. From then on, two equally idealistic views, adding a religious or ideological dimension to patriotism, fought to win the hearts of the French.

The religious concept of France as the eldest daughter of the church lasted beyond the events of the Revolution and continued to inspire all sorts of initiatives, such as the repeated proposals for the consecration of France to the Sacred Heart and suggestions that the image of the suffering Christ be superimposed on the tricolour. How many fervent catholics fell on the field of honour convinced that they were dying for both their well-beloved homeland and their religious convictions! During the ordeal of the Great War, the two concepts drew closer. On 11 November 1918, announcing the signing of the armistice to the Chamber of Deputies, Clemenceau was able to reconcile them in the same burst of oratory, celebrating France as 'yesterday the soldier of God, today the soldier of Right'. In July 1937, Cardinal Pacelli, Secretary of State to Pius XI, returning from the eucharistic Congress of Lisieux, where he represented the pope, gave a memorable speech from the pulpit of Notre Dame de Paris on France's Christian vocation. There were scarcely any anticlericals then to take offence at what in other times would not have failed to be interpreted as clerical meddling and an attempt by catholics to monopolize the nation. Opinion was more interested to see it as an expression of the Vatican's sympathy for France and for democracies engaged in a trial of strength with totalitarian regimes. Three years later, in May 1940, in a dramatic situation – the front had collapsed, the Germans were a day's march from the capital – the public authorities rediscovered the ancestral instincts of the ancient alliance between religion and homeland. The government in a body attended a ceremony of prayers for France in the capital's basilica.

This behaviour in times of trial, the heritage of previous eras, was not peculiar to France alone; it belonged to all peoples, whatever their politics, even those most hostile to every religious belief. Thus the soviet regime, although holding religion to be a superstition and persecuting the churches, found no more pressing need, when faced with the invasion of the German army in June 1941, than to call for the moral support of the orthodox church, and to mobilize religious feeling for the salvation of the homeland.

Religion Saves the Nation

Identification with religion, whether catholic, protestant or orthodox, was not and is still not as developed anywhere else as in nations deprived of political existence, those which have never had a state to defend and represent them, or have lost it. For a people who have been conquered, oppressed, subjected to foreign domination, especially if their faith is different from that of their oppressor, religion ensures the preservation of their personality and encourages awareness of their identity. The church becomes the Ark of the Covenant of their homeland, the repository of the nation's soul. Events help to make the church and its ministers guardians of the national memory. The church or temple are the only places where the population can assemble, where the inhabitants have the right to meet and can publicly practise a collective sociability. It is also the only place where relatively free speech can be heard, of the celebrant, priest or pastor, preaching from the pulpit. In the absence of political leaders, or for want of educated worthies who might be the spokespeople for their citizens, the clergy, the only cultivated elite, take on a role of leadership, especially in rural societies mostly composed of peasants enslaved by foreign landowners. Like the Polish or Slovakian peasants, the Irish peasants, reduced to the condition of farm labourers for Anglican landlords, naturally placed themselves behind their parish priest. Thus catholicism ensured the survival of an Ireland subjected by force to protestant England, as it did of Poland, dismembered and divided between schismatic Russia and heretic Prussia. On the other hand, relations with the occupying power were the least strained in those territories annexed to catholic Austria. The difference in religion had also played an important role in 1830 in catholic Belgium's rising against the Calvinist kingdom of the Netherlands. Yet the rebellious movements of catholic populations against foreign sovereigns of a different religion rarely met with encouragement from the Holy See, the prisoner of its tradition of respect for established power and haunted by fear of revolutionary agitation; in June 1831, more concerned about preserving good relations with the monarchs than pandering to public opinion, Gregory XVI rebuked the Poles for rebelling against the authority of the tsar.

The religious factor was also important in the break-up of the Ottoman Empire, which was hastened by the movement for emancipation by the Christian peoples of the Balkans. The sultans had not, however, tried to convert the conquered nations to Islam; they had allowed them to practise their own religion and the Porte honoured their religious leaders, whose loyalty guaranteed the docility of the populations. In the early nineteenth century the situation started to unfold; the Christian peoples roused themselves and looked for independence, and religious feeling played a large part in this movement. It also explains the sympathy developing throughout Christian Europe for the Greeks rebelling against the Turks. Forgetting the differences between Roman catholic and orthodox, the French felt a solidarity with the rebels. Victor Hugo hymned 'The Greek Child', demanding gunpowder and bullets, and Delacroix painted the Chios massacres. The philhellenic movement that would force governments to intervene combined love of liberty, memories of ancient Greece and the solidarity of Christian Europe: the battle of Navarino was like a replay of Lepanto. All the other Christian peoples in the Balkans – Serbs, Bulgarians, Romanians – rose in their turn, fighting for both their independence and for orthodoxy. Even today religion plays a part in the animosity which continues to set Greece and Turkey, though secularized, against each other.

Religious involvement in the struggle for national independence, the close association of the patriotic cause and traditional religion, turned the great nationalistic movement that disturbed the whole of Europe in the nineteenth century into the extension and outcome of the second era in relations between religion and nation.

Even today the traces of that symbiosis are not all erased, if only because not all peoples are freed from dependence on a foreign domination of a different faith. So with northern Ireland: even if the strictly religious dimension of the conflict has faded and almost evaporated, in Ulster people continue to speak of catholics and protestants. And in former Yugoslavia religious differences are one explanation of opposite choices, and the violence that sets them at odds is the expression of the refusal of populations of different religions to live together in one political entity. The separation is made on the criterion of religion, orthodox Serbs on one side, catholic Croatians on the other, and Bosnian Muslims caught in the cross-fire: the result of the historical link between religion and nationality.

In the states that were constituted after the disintegration of the Ottoman Empire as the peoples were emancipated, the orthodox churches, on the initiative of the Serbian, Bulgarian and Romanian governments, made themselves independent by a movement similar to that of the Reformed churches. Thus over some three hundred years the great tide that tended to make ecclesiastical structures keep in step with the emergence of nations continued across Europe. By bringing the eastern churches closer to those of the protestant west, it deepened the gap with the catholic church which, at the same time but in the opposite direction, tightened the hold of the Holy See over national churches.

The historical circumstances which, in several countries, had made the catholic church the custodian of the nation and the guardian of the national soul, left traces which have continued to the present day in ways of thinking and institutions. In the old Republic of Poland where royalty was elective, if the crown was vacant the primate, the bishop of Poznan, was the *interrex*, ensuring the continuity of government in the interim period. This custom, which made him a source of historical continuity, explains why under the communist regime the Poles naturally turned to Cardinal Wyszynski to defend their country's loyalty to its traditions. This was also the origin of the disagreement which, after the fall of the regime, set the ambitions of part of the catholic hierarchy and clergy against those of the Poles who were demanding the state's complete autonomy with regard to the church. In the name of a certain vision of Poland and with reference to the major role played by the church in the fall of communism, the first group considered catholicism to be the constitutive and distinctive element of Polish nationality. That is why Cardinal Wyszynski's successor, Cardinal Glemp, thought it his duty to encourage candidacies in competition with some of the personalities who had played a great part in the liberation of their country but had the irremediable drawback, in his eyes, of being Jewish. In neighbouring Hungary, the catholic church occupied a somewhat comparable conventional position; fortified by this tradition, Cardinal Mindszenty stood up to the communist government, and it was for the same reason that the regime took action to discredit him. In orthodox Greece, during the troubles that followed the liberation of the country in 1945 and divided public opinion, the regency was entrusted to the primate of the orthodox church, Archbishop Damaskinos. In Cyprus, the Greeks who were fighting for the liberation of the island and its union with Greece, made Archbishop Makarios their leader, rather as Mgr Tiso had formerly in troubled circumstances personified the aspiration of Slovakians to escape the grip of Prague. Over the whole of Europe, therefore, religion played an incomparable role in the defence of particular identities and the movement to set up independent nations.

On the other hand, in states that had long been established and were heavily centralized, religion often protected regional cultures and ensured the survival of small individual areas. Without necessarily calling into question adherence to a much larger ensemble, for small regions it played a role fairly comparable to the one it filled elsewhere against foreign administrations. In France, a nation that had been established longest and was probably the most united, the catholic church had preserved local traditions and regional tongues against the Jacobinism that followed on the heels of the absolute monarchy. Counter to Abbé Grégoire's declared intent to substitute French, the language of the nation and democracy, for local dialects, which were the remnants of feudalism and supposed obstacles to consciousness of belonging to a common native land, and unlike state education, which banned the use of dialects, the clergy, using Breton, Provençal, Alsatian or Flemish in both catechism and preaching, ensured the survival of those languages before governments recently decided to authorize their use when it no longer seemed to threaten either democracy or national cohesion. For the clergy, the use of these dialects, like adherence to regional traditions, was a means of saving the faithful from the harmful influence of the capital and halting the spread of evil doctrines. To proclaim oneself catholic and a Breton, to sing in Provençal, was less a show of opposition to the French homeland than a display of loyalty to ancient France.

The role of catholicism was even more important in Spain for the Basque and Catalan peoples. Although in 1936 the Basque country chose to stay loyal to the government of the Republic, it was less from sympathy for the parties that formed it than from attachment to its liberties which it feared the nationalists would do away with, and which it held to be inseparable from its religious convictions. Similarly, it was the abbey of Monserrat, capital of the Catalan nation, which raised obstacles to the wish of Franco's regime to eradicate memories of Catalonia from the Generality.

Religion thus found itself sometimes the cement of national unity and sometimes the protectress of regional cultures. In both cases its historical role was of major importance.

Nation against Religion

The period of revolutions inaugurated a new era in the history of relations between religion and nationality; it began a separation between the two that would not be completed until much later, and in some instances is not complete even today. It is uncertain whether it ever will be.

Formerly, relations were of the closest kind: the rule of coincidence between ecclesiastical community and national identity had hardly any exceptions. The French Revolution announced the end of that symbiosis, at least for France. Dissociation belonged to the logic of the movement that had begun to separate denomination and citizenship; henceforward one could be a full citizen just like the followers of the state religion, even if one belonged to a different denomination, and religion could no longer be the criterion for being a part of the nation or the principle of political unity. Simple recognition of the plurality of religious expressions turned belief into a factor of differentiation and even an element of division among citizens. Sharing religious convictions was no longer anything more than one feature among others in the diversity of a people, neither more nor less than having different jobs or coming from this or that region. From being the basis of unity which it had been in earlier times, religion was reduced to no more than one of the numerous variables that distinguished between subjects or citizens. There were now more in the nation than in the faith: it alone held together the totality of individuals who were separated by their religious convictions. The nation replaced the church as overall society and no longer needed to refer to a higher authority. Emancipated from all dependence with regard to religion, it became a secular reality.

To assert itself and form an autonomous entity, the nation had to reduce the pretensions of religion. Hitherto associated in the hearts of individuals, often merging their causes, nation and religion became rivals: they fought to win over minds and the fervour of feelings. The nation became a religion in its turn, a secular religion; it changed into an absolute and the feeling of sacredness which was deserting religion was transferred to the nation. People devoted their lives to it, died for it, dedicated all their thoughts to it, fought for its liberty or its greatness. The competition between these two absolutes imposed heart-rending choices that divided the national conscience, and this great split affected all countries as each was touched by the revolutionary contagion; it dominated the intellectual and political history of Europe for some two hundred years.

The conflict between the two principles, the rivalry of the two realities, were fuelled in the nineteenth century by the great movement which worked on all European societies to merge national bodies into a more homogeneous entity. The second era of this history already contained that aspiration towards unity; it then passed through the break-up of Christendom and the constitution of national churches. In the nineteenth century the movement continued and finished in the break with religion, essentially catholicism, because it was the least confined in the framework of nation-states.

In all the multi-confessional countries seeking to unite, catholicism was suspected of being a hindrance to its achievement. The antagonism was especially evident in Germany, where the unitarian movement materialized on the initiative of and centred around protestant Prussia, by the exclusion of catholic Austria and the absorption of the catholic states in the south and west into a Reich dominated by the Reformation. The partisans of unity mistrusted the German catholics, whom they suspected of being less in favour of it. Although protestants did not have to prove the sincerity of their patriotism, catholics had to give pledges of their loyalty.

The dispute between patriotism and catholicism was even more marked in Italy. The reason did not lie, as in Germany, in the plurality of denominations and the minority status of catholicism. On the contrary, the whole of Italy's population was catholic. The real reason we already know: the existence of the Papal States, the pope's unconditional attachment to the integrity of this temporal domain, which he regarded as the means of his independence, and the sacred character which catholics throughout the world ascribed to it. In short, the Roman question, whose apparently insoluble nature hampered the realization of the peninsula's unity and presented Italian catholics with only one painful alternative. For a time catholic patriots had believed it possible to serve both causes with the same enthusiasm; the Risorgimento had numbered in its ranks, and even among those who inspired it, some of the most devoted to the pope and the church: Manzoni, Gioberti, Silvio Pellico, who all dreamed of a free and united Italy under the aegis of the sovereign pontiff. It was the old Guelph plan. The 1848 revolution had left their hopes in ruins, and afterwards the divorce was finalized between traditional religion and the desire for unity which ran counter to the church. The new Italy was built without the catholics and against them, as the pope had forbidden them by the *Non expedit* to take part in any way in the political life of the state that had been built on his despoilment: '*Ne eletti ne elettori*'. The intransigence of the papacy perpetuated the conflict between patriotic feeling and loyalty to the church at least until Italy's entry into the war in 1915. Only after the victory did the birth of the Italian Popular Party in 1919 begin the reintegration of catholics into the nation and political society.

In the states whose unity went further back in time, to a moment when religion had made a contribution to its achievement or affirmation, the problem appeared in a very different guise. In protestant states where protestant churches had been immediately included in the national framework, there was not usually any conflict between nation and religion. Things were not the same in the predominantly catholic nations, where religion was often perceived as a threat or obstacle. And this was due to two distinct reasons that combined their consequences.

The first has already been mentioned; it resulted from the political plan and its inspiration. 'The people' was constituted from the whole body of citizens, themselves defined by what they had in common, disregarding anything that might introduce differences, including those of religion. This was the principle formulated by Clermont-Tonnerre at the time of the debate over the incorporation of Jews into French society, recommending that they should be granted everything as individuals and refused everything as a nation. For the meticulous guardians of revolutionary tradition the principle was equally valid for or against catholicism. The Republic was one and indivisible. Denominations, introducing diversity, were the source of discord. The monarchic *ancien régime* had maintained a multiplicity of special statutes, but henceforward there was only one law, the same for all: democracy was synonymous with unity. The old watchword of the French monarchy, 'One faith, one king, one law', was replaced by the unity of the sovereign nation, the sole source of law, which ruled out reference to a religious transcendence and arrogantly paid no heed to the various denominations. This was the basis of the secularity of the church, the schools, society. The nation appropriated the church's concept of unity and secularized it.

Accustomed to enjoying a privileged status, and having for centuries ordered social life, the catholic church could not interpret this development as anything other than a drive to uproot religion from the soul of the nation. So catholics fought every inch of the way against the secularization of society. When they were forced to the conclusion that it was irreversible, they behaved like their fellow-catholics in the countries where they were a minority, Germany or the Netherlands. They organized themselves into a special society with its own confessional bodies, aiming to include all ages and all sectors of activity in a tight network of institutions controlled by the church: schools, trades unions, associations of every kind. This system of counter- or parallel culture no longer endangered society's independence, but it did pose a potential danger to unity. That was the fear of those who denounced the division of two groups of young people who were brought up separately, and opposed a unitarian logic to the demand for recognition of the pluralism of denominational communities.

As noted, there was a second reason for the opposition between religion and nation in the case of catholicism: its universalism aroused mistrust and anxiety. As the nation had become an absolute, it was jealous of its sovereignty and would not agree to sharing with others the allegiance of its citizens and the adherence of their hearts and minds. The fact that catholics expressed their loyalty to a foreign sovereign, the pope, led to doubts about their patriotism; the dual allegiance was perceived as duplicity. If they were compelled to choose between the two, where would their loyalty lie? They challenged not only those laws that undermined the rights which the church considered its own, but also those that contravened the Vatican's moral teaching; and in addition, they declared themselves in solidarity with the pope's temporal interests, at the risk of harming their homeland's and running counter to its diplomacy. Thus in the disputes setting France against Weimar Germany over the execution of the Treaty of Versailles, notably on the occasion of the occupation of the Ruhr, the disapproval shown by the Vatican would lend substance to the argument that the pope was giving allegiance to the ex-enemy. In the eyes of others, catholics could not be completely patriotic like anyone else; catholicism was the foreign party. This accusation would be taken up systematically under the communist regimes in eastern Europe in order to destabilize the church. Defenders of the colonial system after 1945 who strove to maintain the mother countries' domination over their empires would take up the same theme when the Holy See supported the legitimacy of coloured peoples' desire to gain independence.

The suspicion cast on their patriotism often had the unexpected effect of leading catholics to go one better. From the time of the Dreyfus Affair in France catholics sided massively with nationalism. It could be said of the *Action française* school of thought, which defined itself as one of integral nationalism and exerted great intellectual influence on catholics, that it was itself catholic in so far as it saw in this the opposite of universalism. This interpretation had something to do with its condemnation in 1926 by Pius XI. In the recently unified countries, the split between nation and catholicism diminished. The two world wars contributed to this; even if Italian catholics in general were not in favour of their country's entry into the war in 1915, they did their duty like their compatriots. In 1914 German catholics were already well integrated into the Reich. In France the Sacred Union laid aside the religious quarrel and opened the way to reconciliation.

However, the last word has not yet been uttered on relations between religion and nation. Since the end of the Second World War there have been further developments, partly owing to the increasingly frequent Vatican interventions in international questions. Successive pontiffs and Fathers of the Council have insisted more and more on states' duties to solidarity, and condemned the deviations of nationalism, at the risk of going against governments' interests and disputing their strategies.

Part III

The Liberal Era of Secularization

8

From the Confessional
to the Neutral State

The process of secularization which at first brought about the dissociation of church and state, then separated religion from society, spanned a period that varied from one country to another; in any case never less than some hundred years, often more. Even today it is not complete everywhere. From one country to another, long timelags in applying the measures reflected the diversity of situations and heritages. One must be careful not to speak of 'delays', as if all the countries, by a sort of unwritten law of historical development, should have followed one and the same path that would of necessity lead to the same ending; such a view would have more to do with an ideological *a priori* than an objective observation of the comparative history of European peoples. With regard to relations between religion and society there is not one formula that takes precedence over the others. No one nation is entitled to advocate the solution which it adopted as the universal model to be followed by the rest: not the confessionalization established in the Netherlands as a basis for the organization of society, and which inspired the policy known as 'pillarization', extending to all sectors, including radio and television networks; any more than the method of the ecclesiastical tax instituted in Germany during the second half of the nineteenth century, based on the taxpayer's declaration of his religious denomination and allowing the fiscal administration to pay back a proportion of tax revenues to the various recognized churches; nor yet French-style secularity which, since the passing of the Law of Separation in 1905, is supposed to rule out any recognition of forms of worship by the Republic.

In any case there is not one of these countries today where the current regime does not voice criticisms calling the matter into question. In the Netherlands there are doubts about the relevance of the 'pillarization' system; in Germany the very principle of the ecclesiastical tax is questioned, if for no other reason than the annually increasing number of citizens asking to be crossed off their church registers; in addition, the reunification of the two Germanies has upset the situation because of the vast number of taxpayers of the former Democratic Republic who belong to no recognized religion. In France, as we shall see, practice has diverged considerably from the concept that directed the passing of the law.

Yet despite the differences in timespans, the disparity of routes and the great variety of regimes, it is not impossible to discern a general direction in which nearly all European societies in their turn were headed. They all took their inspiration from a few ideas and referred to a few principles that formed a kind of common denominator and were gradually brought in as state law. During the nineteenth century they almost all distanced themselves from the idea of confessional state to adopt, fairly quickly and resolutely, the path of a certain secularization comprising at the least the recognition of the distinction between civil society and confessional community, and at the most a complete separation balanced by regained independence on the part of the churches who escaped the control of the public authorities.

For all countries the starting point was more or less the same: the confessional state which had a privileged relationship with the established church. Already it was no longer a sacral state. What continued out of habit to be called the 'sacre' (coronation rite) of sovereigns no longer had much to do with the conferring of a sacrament; it was simply a crowning. In this respect, Napoleon's gesture of taking the crown from the hands of the pope to place it on his own head was symbolic, as would be the failure in public opinion of Charles X's coronation ritual, a misjudged attempt to revive an obsolete tradition. Five years later, the oath taken before the Chambers by Louis Philippe, when he swore to respect the revised Charter, a contract established with the nation, signified the secularization of power.

The transition from confessional state to state neutrality in religious affairs comprised four or five successive stages. States did not all make the complete journey; some stopped half-way, without indicating whether they would go on to the very end. As for the others who reached the provisional end of the development, some went through all the stages, one after the other, with varying intervals in between; some, on the contrary, reduced the timespans, leapfrogging intermediate stages or going directly to their final condition, for example passing almost without any transitional period from the *ancien régime* to the secular state. Some, indeed, even took a step backward. Bearing in mind the variety of permutations between the rhythm followed and the ultimate regime, it is possible to distinguish several types of process in the secularization of European societies. Across the diversity of national instances large geographical blocs can be found which approximately match the various religious Europes we have seen. A Europe of the west and south, catholic; a Europe of the north influenced by the Reformation, from the British Isles to Scandinavia and including part of the Germanies; a Europe of the east, for the most part orthodox.

Great Britain is an example of a country where the evolution was gradual, the various stages following one another but not quite coming to term. In contrast, Portugal and Spain went directly from the status of *ancien régime* to a brutal secularization of deliberately antireligious inspiration; Portugal with the creation of the Republic in 1910, Spain in 1931. But in both countries this enforced secularization was followed by a restoration which re-established traditional practices; Portugal with the Salazar regime of the Estado Novo, Spain with Francoism at the end of a civil war in which the religious question had been a major issue.

France's case, too, was distinctive. It had been the first to put into effect the initial and fundamental dissociation between citizenship and confession, and we have seen that almost immediately it reaped the chief legal and administrative consequences: institution of a secular civil registry, introduction of a similarly entitled civil marriage and, even in 1795, radical separation of the state and churches, constitutional as well as traditional. Without going back on those reforms, which were enshrined in the Concordat and the Napoleonic Code, France later re-established legal relations with the catholic church in direct line with regalist tradition. For just over a century, the Concordat, accompanied by the Organic Articles for other recognized denominations, was the institutional framework for relations between the state and religion. Scrupulous observance of this set of rules by the administration did not prevent it, in the 1880s, from adopting and putting into force a legislation which aimed at an integral secularization of all political and civil institutions and forcing religious matters into a closely confined area. Then, in a different context and another state of mind, re-iterating the initiative of the First Republic, the Third finally adopted drastic measures and effected a more radical separation than in any other nation. Since then, in empirical fashion, a prac-tice of separation was instituted which was apparently far from the legislator's intentions and involved a new and original interpret-ation of relations between religion and society. Thus in two hundred years in France, at least three or four experiences suc-ceeded one another, and one may well think that this series is not far from having explored all the imaginable scenarios.

The First Stage: the Abrogation of Confessional Discrimination

The very first stage consisted in the achievement of conditions of an effective freedom of conscience; though its principle was no longer generally challenged, its practice was fettered by all sorts of measures. Its application was therefore accomplished by the suppression in statute books and legislation of what we would today call discrimination, which on numerous counts disqualified anyone who did not profess the state religion, the only one that was recognized and also the only one that assured its faithful of full civil and political rights. In most countries, under the *ancien régime* dissenters had no rights at all; usually the practice of another re-ligion was even banned and punishable by strict penalties. In France, after the revocation of the Edict of Nantes in 1685, protes-tant pastors caught in the act of celebrating clandestine forms of worship were sent to prison. In some countries, admired by the philosophers and held up as an example – England, the United Provinces or Prussia – denominations other than the official church were tolerated. The word is a good indication of the rules that were applied to them, which granted them no rights at all. Burdened by all kinds of restrictions or totally withheld, freedom of conscience was at best a precarious liberty, and one subject to conditions.

Throughout Christian Europe one category underwent an even harsher regime: the Jews were weighed down by all kinds of restrictions concerning where they lived – compelled to huddle in a ghetto or to live together in the shtetl, prohibited from following certain trades, subject to specific taxes. Unlike twentieth-century sanctions instituted by totalitarian regimes against Jews, those measures inherited from the middle ages were dictated less by an anti-semitism of racist origin than by a religious anti-Judaism. It was the Jewish people's refusal to recognize the Messiah in the person of Jesus and, above all, the responsibility for deicide imputed to them that exposed the Jews to the vindictiveness of Christians. Those of them who converted were *ipso facto* relieved of their dis-qualifications and escaped the measures imposed on their former co-religionists. Disraeli, whose name clearly reveals his origin, was able to pursue a great political career and become Prime Minister to Her Britannic Majesty in an England that until 1858 had banned an unconverted Jew from sitting in the Commons. The chiefly re-ligious nature of the animosity against the Jews did not exclude the admixture of a good dose of xenophobia in popular antisemitism, mistrust of those who were different because of their customs, dress and way of life as much as their belief, not to mention a gut re-action against those who, in the absence of credit, practised moneylending at reputedly usurious rates of interest.

The abrogation of all measures contrary to an effective equality between people in order to allow freedom of conscience, the first stage in secularization, was carried out under the inspiration of liberal thinking. As the choice of a religion was an essentially personal affair, it concerned only the individual conscience and must be free of both society's control and state interference. In England especially, the influence of liberal ideas had a decisive effect on reforms. It was strengthened by the action of religious minorities which campaigned for the repeal of discriminatory statutes; they were given consideration by governments that were henceforward at the mercy of movements of public opinion. Similarly, the action of catholic parties in countries where Rome's faithful were in the minority was a determining factor.

The British case is a textbook example. At the time when Voltaire was praising its tolerance, England was practising a graduated discrimination according to denomination. At the summit was the church known as the Church of England, that of the crown, the keystone of the social edifice. The term 'establishment' widely used today to apply to other than religious matters, in particular the social class that has power, wealth and influence, at that time desig-nated essentially the established church. Only its followers were eligible and only they could have a political career; they alone could obtain a commission in the army and navy. Only they, too, had access to the universities of Oxford and Cambridge, which still remained close to their ecclesiastical origins, and could seek the degrees which they conferred and thus teach there. Furthermore, they alone had the right to be buried in Christian soil, in the cemetery surrounding the parish church.

The other protestant denominations, nonconformist, dissenters, baptists or methodists, had a lower status. Their followers were not equal, but were considered British. It was not the same for catholics, who were at the foot of the ladder, scarcely higher than the Jews, and collected disqualifications for reasons linked with history: antipopery and the Irish question. We know how much the break with Rome and the adoption of the Reformation had been connected with the assertion of British identity. Every year popular animosity to the papacy was reactivated by the commemoration of the failure of the conspiracy known as the 'gunpowder plot'. Loyalty to the Holy See was held to be incompatible with loyalty to the crown, although a few great aristocratic families had remained true to the old faith. The rivalry between the Tudors and Stuarts, the 'glorious revolution' of 1688 mainly unleashed by James II's catholic faith, the memories of the Jacobite rebellion in the eighteenth century, kept mistrust of catholicism alive. The fact that the Irish were catholic really put papists at the bottom of society. However, on two occasions, in 1778 and 1792, Catholic Relief Acts had quashed certain civil disqualifications that affected them.

The first initiatives to dismantle the system of inegalitarian discrimination were taken on behalf of dissenters; in 1828 Parliament annulled the Test and Corporation Acts which banned them from applying for and holding municipal office, an important function in a country where, in the absence of a centralized state, the fundamentals of administrative power were exercised by local authorities. A more decisive step was taken the following year with the passing of an Act emancipating catholics. The term was judicious; until then, in fact, both English and Irish catholics were regarded as legally incapable minors. As they could not be eligible, only protestants could represent them in the Commons. Even after their emancipation something of this would remain; at the end of the century, their principal leader, Parnell, was still a protestant. In the Commons they were represented by protestants. The measure was prompted essentially for political ends, in a concern for appeasement, rather than by reasons of principle.

In the wake of the electoral reform of 1832, the arrival of a Whig majority, of liberal conviction, resulted in the adoption of a whole series of measures to do away with discrimination. The Dissenting Marriages Act in 1836 allowed nonconformists to celebrate their union outside the established church; henceforward all the events of personal life, individual and family, birth, marriage and death, for non-Anglicans were recorded by a civil registry office. A little later, dissenters were granted the right to be buried in the parish cemetery. In 1830, Jews were authorized to do business in the City, and in 1833 allowed to be called to the bar. Without affecting the privileges of the traditional universities, the government granted a constitutive charter to the new University of London, which was open to non-Anglicans. Only in 1871 came the abolition of the Test of Anglicanism hitherto required of all degree-holders, lifting the ban on teaching at Oxford or Cambridge for anyone who had not signed a declaration of adherence to the thirty-nine articles which since the seventeenth century had defined the Church of England's profession of faith. In 1858 the text of an oath taken by members of Parliament, which included a reference to the Christian faith, was altered to allow a Rothschild to sit in the Commons, and this liberalization was soon extended to higher civil servants. The last episode in this progress from confessional to neutral state occurred following the incident caused in 1880 by the election of a radical named Bradlaugh, who had not been allowed to take his seat because he had refused to swear an oath on the Bible, that formality was annulled in 1886 and replaced by an 'affirmation' of loyalty to the constitution.

It had thus taken nearly a century for liberal England, which had however preceded France in the practice of tolerance under the *ancien régime*, to reach the point at which France had immediately established itself, as early as 1790, and to achieve the conditions of an effective freedom of conscience. If it had taken so long to purge British legislation of its discriminatory measures on religious criteria, it was because their repeal did not go through without arousing tough opposition. The House of Lords, in which twenty-six Anglican bishops sat, showed stubborn resistance to all bills that would open public office to nonconformists, as they did those which admitted them to university degrees or allowed them to take their place in the offices of local councils and administration. The bill seeking to institute denominational equality for funerals aroused no less opposition. Many could not accept the fact that the established church was no longer the only one to enjoy official recognition; even in 1867 a court reaffirmed that Christianity was part of the law of the land.

For the same philosophical reasons – especially respect for freedom of conscience – most European countries in the nineteenth century committed themselves fairly quickly to the same movement of quashing discrimination based on religious adherence. As in England, the operation was balanced by a modification in the standing of the dominant religion; the state generally remained religious, but now within the framework of a confessional plurality which liberty of conscience brought as an inevitable corollary, the recognition of a certain freedom in the choice of forms of worship enabling them to be placed on an equal footing.

In France the development happened in one leap. The matter had been settled by Bonaparte when he granted the two protestant denominations, Reformed and Lutheran, and then Judaism, the status of recognized form of worship; four recognized denominations now enjoyed freedom. The Constitutional Charter's re-establishment of catholicism's position of state religion, in 1814, changed nothing despite the pleas and hopes of intransigent catholics and the Ultra party. The revision of the Charter in 1830, withdrawing the qualification of state religion from catholicism, finally cut short any attempt to revive the question. François Guizot's well-known adherence to the Reformed church did not stop him from being Louis Philippe's chief minister for seven years, and no one seriously contemplated citing his Calvinism to challenge his right to lead the French government.

Upon its liberation from Netherlands domination Belgium wrote freedom of worship into its constitution in 1831, and immediately granted recognition to protestant denominations and Judaism. This recognition was extended in 1835 to the Anglican church and in 1858 to the liberal protestant church. The Belgian action set an example; Belgian catholics had already joined cause with liberals in the fight for independence, and the example of Belgium like that of the United States was invoked throughout Europe by those who believed it was possible to reconcile Christianity with liberty. It is said that Belgium's efforts may have had some influence on Leo XIII's thinking about relations between church and state, as he had been nuncio in Brussels. At Malines in 1863 Montalembert, the symbolic figure of catholic liberalism, gave a still-renowned speech on a free church in a free state, courageously taking a liberal stance that was at odds with the papacy's intransigent tendencies. In the

Netherlands, a review of the constitution undertaken in a liberal spirit loosened the ties between the Calvinist church and the state, and achieved the equality of Netherlands citizens regardless of their denomination.

The farther one goes in Europe from west to east, the longer this liberal evolution has taken. In Germany the 1848 Revolution brought about the first changes; the Frankfurt Parliament debated on religious freedom and had an inclination to put an end to the regime of state churches. In Prussia the constitution of 1850, though not undoing the ties joining the Evangelical church with the state, granted it the right to regulate its own affairs. In 1865 the philologist Jacob Bernays was the first practising Jew to teach in a university, as 'extraordinary' professor; he would never be an ordinary professor. In Austria, the liberals had the principle of denominational equality adopted after 1866, thanks to the re-organization of institutions of the Double Monarchy. In northern Europe also the freedom and equality of forms of worship gradually prevailed: in Norway between 1842 and 1845; in Denmark in 1849, later in Sweden, between 1862 and 1866, but as early as 1858 the right of citizens not to belong to the Lutheran church was recognized.

It was a very different story in the Iberian peninsula, where brutal surges of anticlericalism alternated with periods of retrogression. The former showed themselves in the confiscation of ecclesiastical possessions and measures against monastic orders which had more to do with the regalist tradition of controlling the church than with a truly liberal inspiration aiming to establish freedom of conscience by dissociating church and state. The periods of restoration, on the contrary, reaffirmed catholicism in the status of state religion. Thus in its article 6, the Constitutional Charter of 1835 asserted that 'the Roman catholic religion will continue to be the religion of the kingdom', and from that inferred that there would be no freedom for other cults, 'other religions will be permitted only to foreigners, with their domestic cult, in particular in houses with no external appearance of a temple'. This was precisely the set of rules authorized by the French monarchy after the Edict of Fontainebleau for the ambassadors of protestant governments, allowing them to have a private chapel. Up to the last years of Franco's regime official Spain continued to refuse Christian faiths other than catholicism an effective freedom of worship.

Liberty experienced no lesser difficulties in the Christian principalities freed from the Ottoman yoke, whose national religion was

orthodoxy. Thus in the kingdom of Romania the constitution of
1866, adopted after the joining of the two provinces of Moldavia
and Valachia, lays down in its article 7 that 'only foreigners of
Christian faith can become Romanians' and affirms the oneness
of orthodoxy and nationality.

The Second Stage: Disestablishment

These concessions to the principle of liberty and the recognition of
equality opened the way to other changes which were necessarily
the result, even if they had not always been foreseen initially.
Moreover, the prospect of these developments motivated intransi-
gents' resistance to the first modifications in the administration of
forms of worship. By putting an end to the identification of the state
and, through it, of society with one religion to the exclusion of all
others, the annulment of the constraints affecting dissenters started
a movement which led ineluctably to an increasingly marked
distinction between religion and society. Religious freedom
contained a dynamic which imposed the withdrawal of the legally
obligatory nature from certain provisions. For example, the
Restoration in France in 1814 re-established the ban on Sunday
working at the same time as the obligation on all those who lived
in houses on the routes of the Corpus Christi festival processions
to decorate the facades with white sheets; but from the moment the
Charter recognized the plurality of confessions, how could it be
justifiable to force protestants who did not believe in Christ's actual
presence in the Host to acknowledge a dogma they rejected? That
would be to turn the dogmatic assertion of a church into a legal
truth.

The British example, too, shows that the emancipation of religious minorities contained in embryo the retraction of part of
the established church's prerogatives, starting with those that
comprised authority over dissenters. Here again, the Irish question
lay at the root of the change of status. The passing of the Act of
Emancipation in 1829 had certainly granted Irish catholics equal
rights in civil and political society, but it had in no way released
them from the obligations imposed on them by the church of
England, and in particular they were not given dispensation from
paying the Anglican clergy the tithe which all British subjects
owed to the established church. Forty years after the first Act
of Emancipation, in 1869, the British government passed the

disestablishment of the Irish Church, which in Ireland was the expression of the Church of England. It lost its status and the right to levy a tithe. A similar measure was taken for Wales in 1914, but was not necessary for Scotland, where the established church was Presbyterian. From then on the Church of England was linked to the state only in England, where it maintained most of its traditional prerogatives, together with its prestige.

The dissociation between religious acts, on the occasion of receiving the sacraments, and administrative acts recording life's important moments – birth, marriage, death – opened a new chapter in secularization. To ensure that dissenters had a legal existence, there was no option but to set up a civil administration distinct from the keeping of the registers that recorded the conferment of sacraments. There was therefore no middle course; either a special civil registry must be created for them, or one set up for all citizens, its universal nature offset by the removal of any religious reference. The same problem arose for marriage; institution of a civil marriage only for those who ruled out religious marriage, or a civil ceremony for all citizens without exception. Again there was the same problem for cemeteries, over whether there should be special graveyards with separate sections for the different denominations or a communal area for all. It was not a neutral alternative. The first solution would have the consequence, albeit limited, of the acceptance of confessional plurality and involved no other position on principle; the second meant a decisive step in deconfessionalizing the state and secularizing society. For a long time most countries clung to the first.

France opted at once for the more radical solution of a single status, the same for all. It was the logic of the principle set out as early as 1789 of the dissociation between citizenship and religion; it was also in tune with the definition of the people as a union of like citizens, disregarding anything that might differentiate between them. In August 1792, the Legislative Assembly instituted a civil administration, the word 'civil' at that time contrasting with confessional or religious. In 1872, the same logic dictated the disappearance of any mention of religious adherence from administrative documents. From that date onwards no question relating to religious matters appeared on census forms, and that is why today there is no accurate official information available to make a statistical evaluation of the number of followers in the various denominations. One is reduced to problematical estimates or extrapolations inferred from opinion polls. Assessments of the number of Muslims living in France today thus vary by several million. The majority of European societies followed the movement started by France, but not all went as far in its application; most continued to take a census of the followers of the various churches, but took every precaution to see that no discrimination could result. Of the current fifteen members of the European Union, Greece is the only one that still mentions religion on its citizens' identity card. This practice has already earned it reprimands and formal notices from Brussels; a proof that nowadays in western Europe there is complete dissociation between religion and people's individual status, and it is acknowledged as a modern imperative of democracy.

The same principles gradually led to the institution of civil marriage. On this point again the alternative arises: either institute civil marriage only for those who do not want a religious ceremony, and in this case recognize the legal validity of the sacraments, which remain the most common practice, or institute civil marriage for all citizens without exception. The French Revolution chose the latter in 1792. England set up civil marriage in 1837, Italy in 1866, Spain and Germany after 1870.

The churches, which were already loath to let the state recognize a union they had not blessed, were generally opposed to the institution of obligatory civil marriage for all. In any case, everything to do with marriage had always been a subject of dispute between churches and state, the former claiming exclusive competence in matrimonial matters and governments rejecting their claims in the name of personal liberty. In the nineteenth century, liberal inspiration and a concern to guarantee citizens a real freedom of choice helped to strengthen the regalist tradition and contribute to the dissociation of the civil act and the sacrament. In France the civil code made it obligatory for the wedding couple to go to the town hall before the church, and prohibited religious ministers from celebrating a marriage that had not been preceded by the civil marriage. If they infringed these measures, which still figure in the penal code, priests or pastors could face imprisonment. The enforcement of the precedence of the civil over the religious marriage was especially criticized by catholic clergy. In 1875, when Pius IX received pilgrims from Belgium, where the regulations were the same as in France, he passed censure on such compulsory precedence. In Austria, although the Concordat of 1855 satisfied the catholic church by recognizing the legal validity of religious marriage, in 1866 Chancellor Beust restricted the competence of ecclesiastic officialdom in matrimonial matters, and recognized the authority of civil courts on the subject.

Funerals raised problems of the same kind and provoked similar arguments. Was it possible to authorize civil burials about which the anticlericals made such a fuss? Most governments subjected these funerals to all kinds of restrictions that tended to make them furtive or clandestine, but were gradually compelled to lift these measures. Free-thinkers demanded the presence of state representatives at the civil funerals of the deceased who had been awarded the Legion d'honneur. In France, the national funeral decreed in 1885 for Victor Hugo, who in his will had explicitly refused any religious ceremony and whose coffin, after being on view under the Arc de Triomphe, was solemnly transferred to the Pantheon without going by way of Notre Dame or receiving the prayers of any church, marked a decisive moment in making civil funerals an ordinary event and in the secularization of French society. Two years later, a law granted this type of burial a status that made it easier.

The problem was what to do with the corpse and where to bury those who had refused to let their remains pass through a church, at a time when cemeteries were an integral part of the religious grounds surrounding the churches. Again, the alternative was the same. In early days the solution adopted was generally to have separate cemeteries for minority confessions, protestants or Jews in catholic countries, catholics in protestant countries; so in Rome, the special cemetery for English people who died during their stay in the Eternal City. Or there was the method of providing particular sections within municipal cemeteries; this was the solution decreed in France in Year XII, dividing cemeteries into various sectors for each of the recognized religious bodies. It was only a Third Republic law, adopted in 1881, that banned separate cemeteries and did away with the religious nature of these sites. In Great Britain Lloyd George campaigned for the disestablishment of cemeteries in Wales; in 1914 Parliament adopted a law to that effect, but its application was postponed until the end of the war.

Thus for each of these important events in individual existence, which also concerned the social body, the principle of religious freedom gradually wrote into the legislation the practical consequences of dissociation between belonging to a religious community and the obligations of citizenship, and caused civil society to take a second major step on the road to secularization.

9

From the Liberal State to Separation

In the majority of European societies recognition of religious freedom had the fairly swift consequence that the state, while remaining religious, had to admit the rightful plurality of denominations and the ability of all its nationals to choose their religion freely and even, if pushed, to choose between belief and non-belief, although for a long time most governments were loath to admit the permissibility of atheism, for it was still felt that an atheist could not be trusted, a legacy of the old prejudice according to which there could be no moral conduct in the absence of religious reference. Locke excluded them from full citizenship on the grounds that, unable to base themselves on a firm belief, they were incapable of loyalty. As a result, the recognized churches, even if preserving a status that earned them honours and privileges, had lost those that gave rise to confessional discrimination.

Pluralism Becomes Institutionalized

The secularization movement, already well under way, did not generally halt at this stage. There were several paths available for its continuation. One, which was mainly explored in protestant societies, consisted of recognizing the religious factor and institutionalizing it on the basis of pluralism. That was the choice made in the Netherlands; in the nineteenth century Netherlands society rearranged its organization on the principle of the coexistence of various cults of spiritual belief, extended to agnostics, who were constituted into a distinct family known as humanist. As a prelude to this reorganization, in 1879 the law had introduced into the population census forms a new heading for those who belonged to no church, the *onkerkeliken*. This was the system of 'pillarization' which has since influenced the entire functioning of its society. Today, this system is beginning to be called into question because of the need to adapt legislation, which hitherto was nothing more than a translation into civil law of the morality taught by the churches, to meet new aspirations, especially in the field of sexual morality.

Less systematic, and less far-reaching, Germany's post-war legislation was inspired by the same principles: recognizing the diversity of churches and combining them officially with the life of the nation. They had the status of public corporations; the ecclesiastical tax (*Kirchensteuer*) was merely an expression of this principle in the funding of the churches. In England, the established church had had to agree to giving up part of its prerogatives but retained, together with its prestige, the majority of its powers and even privileges. Its partial disestablishment did not mean the slightest diminution in its prerogatives or the slackening of its links with the crown, the corollary being an aloofness and reserve on the latter's part with regard to other religions and, above all, catholicism. Other protestant denominations, for instance, had to wait until 1947 before they were given access to the BBC's religious broadcasts. Prince Charles, as has been said, was still prohibited from attending John-Paul II's private mass. Only in 1995, nearly a century and a half after the restoration of the catholic hierarchy in England, did the Queen attend a catholic service for the first time – and then it was only Vespers – on the occasion of the festivals organized for the centenary of the catholic Westminster cathedral. So one is far removed from the idea of a secularity which established absolute separation between religious beliefs and political institutions.

The Third Stage: Separation and Secularization

Another type of development, following a stricter logic in every sense of the word, went farther in the dissociation between religion and society, and led the liberal state, which had however remained confessional, to a total neutrality regarding beliefs and a complete withdrawal of the state from this area. This second route was adopted chiefly in predominantly catholic societies, France being the country which took the process of secularization to its extreme, to the point of breaking off all relations between the religious factor and the social order.

Two Concurrent Inspirations

This movement took place under the influence of several inspirations which worked together and combined their results. The first is well known to us: none other than liberal thinking, whose initial applications I have already mentioned, and which continued to infer more far-reaching consequences from its assumptions. It was no longer only a matter of cutting out of the statute books those measures that offended freedom of conscience, or erasing those that perpetuated the superiority of one denomination over others. It was no longer enough to remove individual lives and personal conduct from the supervision of a church. It was now necessary to reap all the consequences of the distinction between public and private, a distinction that applied to every activity, economic as well as intangible. In the division effected by liberal philosophy between these two areas, religion was the exclusive concern of private life. From a liberal view, it was the means of guaranteeing freedom of conscience, thus no constraint could be exerted on free choice, whether by society or the political power. This was also a precaution against the ever-possible intolerance of the churches. The state must therefore be absolutely neutral in religious matters; it must not take sides among the denominations or designate which one was teaching the truth. In return, religion must not intervene in the public domain; every expression of the religious factor in the social sphere was regarded as illegitimate interference, the sign of a confusion to which the law must put an end. That was one of the motives which prevailed in the vote for the secularity laws passed in France between 1880 and 1905, in the quarter-century following the Republican party's coming into power.

To describe this legislation, the term 'laicization' is more apposite than secularization; it characterizes more exactly the other inspiration which went hand in hand with liberal thinking towards the gradual removal of every religious reference from social organization. The liberals nurtured no hostility towards religion; they were simply anxious to preserve liberty of conscience and the independence of the state. The second inspiration was very different; far from respecting religion it saw it as an adversary to be combated with every available means. This state of mind resulted from a major change which took place in intellectual movements after the revolutions of 1848, about which Roger Aubert quite rightly spoke of a profound renewal of the sources of non-belief. It was a capital event in intellectual and cultural history before it ever became political. At that time, new philosophical systems, especially positivism, took over from the philosophy of the Enlightenment, reactivating its most irreligious ferments. The motives for their opposition to the churches were no longer due only to circumstance, or borrowed from differences of opinion over morality. It was a logical, well thought out opposition, based on the assertion of a natural incompatibility between modern society and catholicism. This repudiation was in fact aimed at the catholic church; compromises seemed conceivable between reason and protestantism, some of whose expressions diverged from the traditional formulations of dogma and came to terms with liberalism. Therefore more than one intellectual or politician who believed in the social usefulness of religion and who supported free-thinking, looked to protestantism for the hope of reconciling them. In the case of protestant churches, relations between modern society and religion were very different from those with the church of Rome. The possibility of an understanding with the latter was all the less imaginable because the pope had adopted a position of total intransigence. Since the events of 1848, Pius IX had condemned any form of innovation; in 1864, in the very midst of those years when the intellectual panorama was being transformed, he drew up a reasoned catalogue of all contemporary errors, including the one containing the desire that the Roman pontiff should reach a reconciliation with modern society. The direction that the papacy thus imprinted upon catholicism played into the hands of its most determined adversaries by providing the proof they were waiting for in support of their argument. Two systems arose therefore, in direct opposition, challenging each other item by item: education through authority versus a questioning approach; unconditional obedience versus liberty; submission to the law of the group versus individual will; dogma versus reason; hierarchy versus equality, tradition versus progress and conservatism or reactionarism versus democracy.

In this pattern of themes secularization took an entirely new direction; it was no longer only a matter of instituting a regime which would guarantee equality between the denominations, and in which the state would respect religions. Now the aim was quite different; since religion posed a permanent threat to the principles and values of modern society, it was the state's duty to set up a legislation that would combat its influence. No longer could the state remain neutral; it had to take sides, work for the decline of religion and diminish its role in preparation for its disappearance. The inspiration was deeply antireligious; ideology versus religion or even new religion versus old, for laicist inspiration was really an antireligion with an ambition to replace traditional faiths.

As we can see, the two concepts, liberal and laical, were very dissimilar, one on the tolerant side, the other sectarian. One envisaged an impartial state and the other expected it to be the instrument of the extinction of beliefs. Though they differed substantially in their intentions and objectives, at the end of the nineteenth century the two philosophies found themselves allied against the intolerance of Roman catholicism and associated in the same undertaking of secularizing state and society. That is why the churches, the catholic more than the others, were unable at once to perceive the difference between the two trends; they saw them as a hostile coalition, taking the same initiatives aimed at driving the churches from the social area. The confusion lasted a long time; it would be generations before religious minds could realize the difference between the institutors of a secularity that was impartial and respectful of the choice of consciences and proponents of an intolerant laicism. It would also take time before the churches could bring themselves to see this difference as anything other than a mere divergence in strategy. When these two concurrent inspirations met, the process of secularization entered a third stage: after the acceptance of confessional pluralism, then of the disestablishment of state churches and recognition of the equality of denominations, came the time of a completely deconfessionalized state and the eviction of any reference of a religious kind from the public arena; not only from the state but also from civil society.

The Symbols

As the essential objective had already been won, since freedom of conscience was no longer contested, or fundamental rights threatened, arguments over the next phase of secularization were mainly concerned with symbols. Efforts were going to be made to see that every religious expression disappeared from public life and the social sphere. No longer must anything offend the sight of the non-believer. For some, it was also a means of working towards the disappearance of the churches.

In France, although the state kept its connections with the various cults and continued to subsidize their ministers, and maintained diplomatic relations with the Holy See, on the occasion of the review of constitutional laws in 1884, the republican majority decided to do away with the public prayers prescribed for the opening of each parliamentary session to call down divine blessing on the work of the assemblies. This was a measure obviously lacking much practical effect, but very symbolic.

It was less easy to efface the traces left by the faith of olden days on the monumental heritage. In the countries of western Europe, after the effects of revolutionary vandalism, no one thought any longer of razing religious buildings from ideological motives. It was profit-seeking and covetousness, combined with stupidity, that were responsible in the middle of the Restoration for the destruction of Cluny, the largest abbey left by the middle ages. If other large religious buildings survived, such as the palace of the popes at Avignon, Mont Saint-Michel, and the abbeys of Clair-vaux and Fontevraud, it was thanks to their appropriation for use by the army or prison administration: a fortunate outcome of the secularization of ecclesiastical property. Town planning in the Haussman style also brought about the destruction of numerous churches, razed to create new roads. In Paris, the reorganization of the Île de la Cité alone, and the clearing of the parvis in front of Notre Dame, resulted in the disappearance of several churches. In the twentieth century, it was in eastern Europe that hatred of religion prompted a furious wave of destruction. In Moscow, nine out of ten churches were destroyed to make way for swimming-pools, warehouses and collective facilities.

As it was not possible to eliminate from view the monuments, symbols of faith, erected by preceding generations, the spirit of secularization set about increasing the number of public buildings put to other uses: law courts, schools and university departments, and, in the France of the Fifth Republic, cultural centres, of which André Malraux would say at the time that they were the cathedrals of the twentieth century. Although these buildings simply met precise needs and their construction was free of all irreligious intent, animosity against religion took possession of certain edifices, turning them into the symbol of progress contrasted with the cathedrals and basilicas, monuments of the past and obscurantism. Thus the Eiffel Tower, erected for the Universal Exhibition in 1889, celebrating the centenary of the Revolution, was intended to be the monumental reply on the Paris skyline to the basilica of the Sacré Coeur on the summit of Montmartre. A riposte to the signs of atonement of penitent France, the metal edifice issued the challenge of science and technical engineering, inventions of the human intellect. Iron versus stone; a resolutely modern style contrasted with the Romano-Byzantine pastiche. In the same years, on the other side of the Alps, the monument built in the heart of the Eternal City in memory of king Victor-Emmanuel, started in 1885 and completed in 1911, contrasted the unity of modern Italy with the cupola of Saint Peter's, the symbol of pontifical Rome and the Counter-Reformation. The same thinking lay behind the construction, just beside Castel Sant'Angelo, of a huge law court, where the device carved on the pediment proclaimed national unity and civic liberty in the face of territorial division and pontifical authority: *Patriae unitati civium libertati*. Thumbing its nose at the catholic church, the Paris municipal council erected near the Sacré Coeur basilica a statue of the Chevalier de la Barre, the victim of intolerance, and gave his name to the street leading to the religious building.

Stemming from the same spirit and similarly proceeding from the desire to suppress every expression of the religious factor were the measures which restrictively regulated all external manifestations of forms of worship: limited bell-ringing, subjection to parsimoniously issued permits for processions on the public highway.

Secularization also affected the arrangement of the year's events. Of course, there was no longer a serious suggestion, as at the time of the Revolution, of replacing a religious with a lay calendar, but the institution of national festivals of purely secular origin deprived the churches of the monopoly of dividing time between work and leisure. One of the very first symbolic measures decreed in France by the Republicans was the institution of a national holiday for the anniversary of the taking of the Bastille. A section of catholics would for a long time consider the choice of 14 July as provocative. For the same reasons, in 1889 Crispi in Italy decreed a national holiday on the anniversary of the entry of Piedmontese troops into Rome on 20 September 1870, and one of the main Roman roads was named Venti Settembre.

The Issue of Schools

Among all the rest, one institution was most constantly at stake in the arguments over secularization: schools. The reasons were obvious: both sides believed they were taking an option on the future by ensuring the control of education of children and adolescents. The church pleaded the historical role it had played in the birth and development of education; had it not been at the origin of all educational institutions? The religious orders had created modern secondary schools and, in most countries in the nineteenth century, universities were still church institutions, some even by pontifical right. The churches also argued their special mission to teach. To those who objected that this teaching concerned knowledge of God and the transmission of revealed religion, and not secular sciences, the theologians replied that to acknowledge such a distinction would be already to enter the logic of secularization, as if the church's infallibility did not extend to every truth. The opposing party had just as good reasons for wanting to snatch education away from the clutches of the clergy; it was the only means of liberating intelligence, training the enquiring mind and founding democracy.

It was a long-standing debate that had opened well before the more radical phase of secularization, or even the first dissociation between society and religion. The question had already been raised in the time of the confessional state; it had set the *ancien régime* monarchies of France and Portugal against the Society of Jesus. In the nineteenth century the idea grew that the public authority had responsibilities in the matter of education. From then on the question became one of the place of religion in teaching; whether the church should be present in the public institution or create its own system alongside the public service. In France, under the Restoration, the liberals defended the monopoly of the state university and were opposed to the catholics who campaigned for freedom to teach: an argument in which the sides were reversed. Depending on country and period, the problem was to receive very varied solutions, ranging from tight control by ecclesiastical authorities over general education and compulsory religious education in state schools to complete separation of two concurrent systems. The argument raged in France, Belgium, Portugal, Spain, Italy – in short, all the catholic countries – but it did not leave the protestant countries indifferent. In England, too, it was a subject of discord. The methods adopted varied at the whim of changes in majority; liberal victories brought laws running counter to ecclesiastical demands, and a return to strength of conservative majorities unfailingly resulted in measures which gave satisfaction to the catholic church. For the past two hundred years or so, the history of relations between religion and the educational institution therefore followed the rhythms of political ups and downs, the progress of secularization keeping time with political developments.

In the countries which carried secularization to its extreme consequences, the 'laicization' of teaching meant the elimination of all religious reference. In France, the state Faculties of Theology disappeared at the beginning of the 1880s. It is true that the religious authorities did nothing to save them, for they had incurred the mistrust of Rome and the episcopate because of their attachment to Gallican doctrines. They taught a different ecclesiology from that of ultramontane catholicism. In 1858 the Holy See rejected a request from the imperial government that they should be granted canonical appointment. Suspect in the eyes of the church, ill-regarded by the laity, they disappeared without a voice being raised in their defence. Hence that French singularity which, with the exception of the protestant and catholic Faculties of Theology in Strasbourg which survived because of Germany's annexation of Alsace, makes France one of those rare countries where religious sciences are completely absent from official teaching, although it produced some of the century's greatest theologians. The secularization of education also meant the removal of any religious reference in training programmes and the 'laicization' of teachers, instituted in France in 1886, the principle of the incompatibility of belonging to a religious order, even a teaching one, and holding a teaching post in a state school. In 1904, it would even go as far as banning any member of a religious order from teaching, by a law which deprived members of congregations of a liberty acknowledged for all other citizens. By an unexpected reversal, but one which had its own logic, the movement for secularization, initially inspired by the desire to suppress every inequality arising from confessional reference and which had effectively erased all discrimination based on religion, ended up with an outcome that was contrary to its spirit, since it established a new kind of discrimination, this time against the church which had formerly exercised its dominion over society.

The Final Break

The last stage in this long process of dissociating religion and society could only be the snapping of the last links uniting state and churches; in a word, separation. On this point again, it was the French Republic which pushed the logic of secularization to its extreme limit, at the close of a series of vicissitudes in which circumstances perhaps played as important a role as the deliberate will of the participants. In December 1905, the French Parliament adopted a law proclaiming that henceforward the Republic neither recognized, subsidized nor paid ministers' salaries for any cult whatsoever. Without consulting the Holy See, France unilaterally annulled the treaty laboriously drawn up a century earlier between the papacy and the regime that had emerged from the Revolution. In little more than a hundred years France had thus tested nearly the whole gamut of conceivable forms of relationship, or absence of relationship, between religion and state, from the quasi-symbiosis of the *ancien régime* to total disregard.

The solution adopted satisfied the liberals; it was in keeping with their idea of religion as a private affair. Separation saved the state from clerical interference and guaranteed individual liberty. It also had the advantage of settling once and for all a tangle of disputes that were endlessly being reborn. However, the Law of Separation did not release the public authorities and administrative apparatus from all responsibility in the matter since, in its first article, the law of 9 December 1905 stipulated that the Republic guaranteed the liberty of forms of worship, which was a way of recognizing that religion was not a purely individual concern, as it was distinguished by its social aspect, the celebration of the act of worship.

The formula also suited the religious minorities who still feared, in a regime which recognized religious bodies, that the oldest and largest might be tempted to abuse their precedence and numerical superiority thereby reaping the benefit of preferential consideration on the part of the authorities. Protestants and Jews, therefore, were pleased about the suppression of relations between state and churches, as was the Waldensian church in Italy.

The separation also matched the ideas of a minority of catholics who attached greater value to the freedom of the church than to state protection and the honours it bestowed; they considered that the time had passed when religion needed the assistance of the civil authority. But although they were no less concerned than others about the interests of the church, they were not in its good graces and circumstances were scarcely in their favour. The climate of tension in which the separation law was adopted, and the ulterior motives ascribed to its authors, provoked the categorical opposition of the majority of the clergy and their flock, who gave unreserved approval to the condemnation of the law, issued by Pius X, which forbade anyone to be a party to its application. The cost was the loss of all the church's temporal powers. Another group who did not rejoice at such a radical measure were the heirs to the regalist tradition, who lost all chance of influencing episcopal appointments and keeping the clergy under the thumb of the state.

What followed will show that there were several ways of understanding the separation and putting it into practice. In the interpretation that prevailed at first, separation was synonymous with the total absence and even the prohibition of relations and apparently implied the public authorities' complete disregard of the religious element. Another version gradually emerged in which separation meant neither disregard nor total lack of relations; the distinction did not rule out the state's recognition, at least *de facto*, of the existence of communities based on a common faith, and even of institutions with which it could have dealings. In any case, in the eyes of the law the government of the Republic was deemed to be the guarantor of freedom of worship.

Morality and Legality

With this separation of the churches and state, one might have thought that secularization had attained its final goal and exhausted all its consequences, if another dissociation had not already commenced along a very different line, that is, between morality and the law or, to be more precise, between the morality laid down by the churches, to which Christians sometimes seemed to attach even more importance than to religion itself, and civil legislation. The problem was relatively new. Formerly, even at the time of the keenest confrontations between religious authorities and public powers, disagreements left aside questions of morality. With the exception of a few dogmatic cranks, considered to be a kind of lunatic fringe, people did not believe that there could be any other morality than the one taught and professed for centuries, of which the churches were the institutors and custodians. During the nineteenth century, however, following official recognition of individual choice in the matter of religion, the idea gradually dawned that the dominant church – catholic or protestant, depending on the country – was perhaps not entitled to impose the rules it had itself elaborated on those who did not share its faith. Why should agnostics model their personal conduct on the standards laid down by an institution whose authority they challenged and whose teachings they rejected?

Quite naturally, the divergences first revealed themselves over the subject of marriage, because marriage was an institution in which both church and society were equally interested. The churches, considering that the union of a man and a woman was of major concern to them, claimed that ecclesiastical jurisdiction should have full competence over the validity of marriages. But society also had an interest, if only from the aspect of the transmission of inheritances. So all governments without exception assumed the right to legislate on marriage. In Prussia, mixed marriages had been a serious subject of disagreement with the catholic episcopate. As we have seen, nearly all governments had had to institute a civil marriage alongside the religious ceremony for those who did not belong to any church. The problem was to know whether it would concern only the latter or whether the civil act would be imposed on all without exception, sometimes enjoying precedence.

The next stage had a much graver significance: was the state to adopt as its own the churches' position on the indissolubility of marriage? Their teaching was that marriage freely agreed committed the couple for the rest of their life; breaking the conjugal bond was to go against the will of God, and both the duty and interest of society lay in ensuring that this bond was respected. But for liberals there could be no authority higher than individual will; since marriage was based on agreement, if one of the spouses wished to break the contract, on what grounds could that right be refused? At the same time as it had banned monks and nuns from taking lifelong vows, the Revolution had granted married couples the right to divorce. For the first time, there was also divorce between morality as religion had decreed it for centuries and the legal aspect. For over a century divorce in France had been an issue in political arguments and, like the educational regulations, the variations in its status reflected the fluctuations in political life. When the regime was conservative, it annulled divorce or made its practice difficult. When it was liberal or democratic, divorce was re-established and its application made easier. The Restoration abolished it in 1816, the Republicans brought it back in 1884. The

Vichy government extended its time allowances and complicated its formalities. Later regimes made it more flexible.

Whether it was contagion from the French example or the logical outcome of the spread of liberal ideas, in the majority of European nations, the introduction of civil marriages was followed sooner or later by the legalization of divorce. In Great Britain, from 1857: the reform raised less opposition than on the other side of the Channel, the protestant churches being less uncompromising on the subject than the catholic church. Nevertheless, it was an initiative whose scope differed in importance from the confiscations of ecclesiastical possessions or the other recurring topics in the disputes between churches and public authorities. It contained in embryo the dissociation of personal conduct from the morality taught by the churches. In the next century the extensions of this initial fracture would become visible. The defence of the indissolubility of marriage and the battle against legislation that refuses to acknowledge it would be a subject of discord between the catholic church and governments up to the present day. The catholic church has lost the last battles on this ground. First in Italy, where the episcopate resorted to the possibility opened by the constitution to hold a referendum on annulling the law; the consultation thus unwisely sparked off resulted in the repudiation of the church and had the unforeseen consequence of conferring additional legitimacy on divorce with the ratification of the law by the sovereign people. In 1994 another referendum, this time in Ireland, which supporters of divorce won by a very slender majority, saw the disappearance of the last country where conformity to the law of catholic morality had survived. In this respect these two expressions of public opinion marked the end of the process of secularization.

Part IV

The Second Era of Secularization

The first decade of the twentieth century comes about half way through the history of secularization; one hundred and ten years on from the original break to 1900, nearly a hundred years still to come.

From One Century to the Next

On the eve of the war that was to rend the continent from 1914 to 1918, throwing into chaos institutional systems, together with the balance of power and trends of ideas, relations between religion and society presented the most varied examples: from the closest symbiosis, in Holy Russia, to the most radical separation, in republican France. Across this diversity, two principles were diametrically opposed throughout the continent: one asserted the submission of all social activity to religion; the other worked to liberate the state and society from the domination of any religious belief. But could this difference survive for long? If one of these two inimical movements were to triumph, it would surely be secularity. It had already begun to transform institutions and even private conduct in nearly all European societies. Inspired by liberal thinking, which continued the philosophy of the Enlightenment, making individual liberty the principle and foundation of social order, in 1914 the majority of states had already ceased to impose unity of faith by law; freedom of conscience was recognized, freedom of kinds of worship accepted or beginning to be tolerated. Though they had at first brought in special and derogatory regulations for religious minorities, governments had then taken a route more in keeping with the modern spirit, won over to the principles of the universality of the law and uniformity of status, and had removed a number of institutions from ecclesiastical jurisdiction: civil registry, education, citizenship and sometimes the legal administration of marriage and the family. The secularization movement appeared irresistible and bound to continue to the detriment of the churches.

Many thought the twentieth century would see the accomplishment of the development which had commenced with the French Revolution and would reach the inescapable conclusion, either amicably or in conflict, of complete separation between religion and society, to which the French Republic had already pointed the way. Certainly, the less advanced countries were still a long way behind. Moreover, the various countries, having very dissimilar histories, would not all proceed on the model of France. In protestant countries, where there was a less fundamental incompatibility between the interpretation of Christianity and modernity, and where it had taken a less disputatious turn than in the catholic countries, divorce could probably take place by mutual consent. With the catholic church, on the other hand, it seemed unthinkable; given the stand taken by the Roman pontiff against any expression of modernity, the break could not take place except at the expense of the church, as had been seen in France.

At the close of the twentieth century, although one realizes that general development, all in all, has been in the direction of an increasingly marked slackening of ties between religion and society, things have not happened quite as would have been imagined in the 1900s. The trend has not regularly followed the line which seemed to be taking shape, and of which some people had extrapolated the continuation.

In the first place, the history of the troubled twentieth century has far from progressed along straight lines; it has included all kinds of breaks, rebounds and even retrograde steps. Rarely can history have similarly belied every attempt at purely rational explanation. Since the start of the century several periods can be distinguished, characterized by events of the first magnitude which created many decisive breaks in the flow of time and thereby formed sequences that were different, if not altogether in the opposite direction. The two great European wars, the rise and subsequent fall of totalitarian regimes, the predominance and then the ebb of ideological systems, the movement of political unification which first affected the west before extending to the rest of Europe; all these events were not without a bearing on relations between religion and society.

Indeed, one of the clearest lessons to be learnt from a comparative study of this history is that relations between religion and society bore the full brunt of the impact of more general history, that of both political regimes and intellectual trends. Religious history is not aloof from the great events of civilization or the upheavals that affect society, whether the October revolution, the coming of the Third Reich or the crisis of 1968. The repercussions on religion and its relations with society overall are an indication that, even in societies said to be indifferent to religion, which people like to describe as secularized, religion continues to arouse attention, interest, sympathy, mistrust or revulsion – in short, impassioned feelings.

This fragmented history, with its consequent discontinuity, sets up an obstacle to any attempt to reduce its development to a simply explainable principle such as, for example, a generalized and irresistible movement towards ever-increasing secularization resulting in total dissociation between individual religious belief and society. This difficulty for the historian is redoubled by the differences in timespans between one people and another. In the supposition – something which needs to be demonstrated and is precisely the object of the question – that all countries were travelling towards the same distant goal, they did not all do so at the same speed or rhythm. History shows neither simultaneity nor parallelism; some advanced while others retreated.

However, one piece of evidence seems to stand out at the close of this century: a lessening of the differences that separate the various experiences. Before 1914 they were still considerable, for example between tsarist Russia and the French Republic; today they have noticeably shrunk. Contrasts are less distinct. Nowhere in Europe is there a sacral society or even, since the disappearance of Francoism in Spain, confessional societies where social life is still ruled by the churches and all activities are centred around religion. The states where the latter enjoyed a privileged regime, Franco's Spain and Salazar's Portugal, have today relaxed the ties, suppressed the privileges and limited the advantages. At the other extreme of the spectrum of possible systems, however, since the fall of the regimes that had declared war on religion and replaced the churches' teaching with an irreligious state philosophy, there is no longer any society that excludes religion. Religious freedom is recognized almost everywhere and its practice fundamentally observed. As for those states which had believed it possible to quash all relations with religious institutions, reality soon led them in pragmatic fashion to re-establish another type of relationship, at first unobtrusive, later formalized, which gradually by small touches mapped out a novel regime nearly as far removed from the orginal break as from the alliance of throne and altar. So the range of differing situations has narrowed considerably.

In this reduced area one nevertheless encounters almost all the trends of thought that have been seen before, working, fighting, growing closer to one another, from the one which postulated the need for as complete a symbiosis as possible between society and religion, fighting for its restoration where it had been dissolved, to the one that ceaselessly tried to eradicate all religious belief from hearts and consciences forever. To this day, none of these tendencies has completely disappeared and their traces can still be pinpointed. But their relative importance has greatly varied; some have lost their impetus, others have been strengthened. Thus we shall find the last embers of the state's regalist pretensions, nostalgia for Christendom, militant laicity, combative irreligiousness, together with the quest for conciliation between liberty and religion. Because of this complexity, several lines intersect that are sometimes at odds, and their interactions prevent the variety of developments from being reduced to a single principle, as well as imposing caution and humility on anyone trying to render this history intelligible.

10

Lasting Elements

First, there is the continuity which seems to prevail on either side in the respective positions of churches and states.

The Enduring Quality of Religious Intransigentism

Ecclesiastical institutions had not immediately accepted the upheaval brought about by the French Revolution in their relations with society. A century later, they were no more resigned to the progress of secularization, whether full steam ahead or dragging behind, that was gradually eroding their position in the state and society as a whole. Certain as they were that they held the truth in all matters, how could they have consented to lose the status that justified their eminent distinctiveness? They were all the less tempted because they reckoned that society also would have everything to lose; did the churches not know the principles of a harmonious organization of the social body? Secularization appeared to them to be both a moral failing and a mistake. It was a moral failing because both society and individuals have the duty to proclaim the existence of God and recognize His laws. The state that neglected to do so would be gravely lacking in its duty; as for one that expressly refused to do so by declaring itself religiously neutral, it would quite simply be committing the sin of apostasy. It was a mistake, too, because it would undermine the foundations of social order; indeed, there could not be a well regulated society unless its laws conformed to the Christian morality taught by the churches. Ignorance of these principles was the source of all the evils that afflicted society and threatened to lead to its downfall. This set of convictions naturally entails a certain overestimate of the moral dimension of problems and a corresponding underestimate of the other factors that make collective communities function. At the beginning of the twentieth century, therefore, the churches continued to oppose with all their might the measures that tended to dissociate society and religion, and called upon the faithful to mobilize to restore the traditional order.

From one faith to another the arguments differed according to the dominant theology, depending also on the legal situation in the state; if they were in the minority, they were less implacably hostile to a relaxing of relations, on which they were counting for a freedom refused to them by the dominant church's identification with nation. Thus in France the protestant churches could only be happy about the work of the Revolution and were not opposed to the secularization effected under the Third Republic. On the contrary, the orthodox churches in eastern and Danubian Europe, having become autonomous churches with national independence, played on their identification with the nation and their historical role in order to claim a privileged status.

That argument could not be invoked in quite the same fashion by the catholic church because of its universality; sometimes it even had to defend itself against the suspicion that it sacrificed national interests to the policies of a foreign state. The main consideration on which it based its right to inspire collective behaviour as well as individual conduct lay in the affirmation of its nature as a perfect society from which it derived an extensive definition of its mission: while recognizing, sometimes even more than others, the autonomy of political and civil society, it believed it had the authority to set forth the principles which ought to rule the government of societies and asserted that it was the church's business to judge and, if need be, condemn, the actions of the ruling power.

Imbued with the juridical tradition inherited from Rome, the catholic church attached great importance to an explicit recognition of its rights, written into laws, which obviously ruled out any separation. The pope continued to reaffirm as ideal a Christian state whose leaders made open reference to religion, made its teaching the rule of their actions and imposed on their nationals a respect for the obligations fixed by the church.

The American episcopate had a special position on this subject. In the United States catholicism had experienced the advantages of religious freedom, without which it would not have achieved its remarkable expansion. But in Europe the episcopates were uncompromising in their demand for official recognition of the privileged rights of the catholic church. In March 1925, in mid-crisis with the government of the left-wing cartel, the assembly of cardinals and archbishops in France adopted a solemn declaration, drawn up by a Dominican, Father Janvier, condemning the very concept of laicity and urging catholics to disobey its laws; the latter could not be imposed on consciences because they violated God's laws. In 1936, Cardinal Goma y Tomas blamed Spain's misfortunes on its neglect of these laws; it was the apostasy of the ruling powers since the proclamation of the Republic in 1931 that had caused the civil war bathing Spain in blood. Later, when the war was over, in 1942 the archbishop of Toledo, Cardinal Pla i Deniel, rejoiced that the Spanish government in its laws had recognized 'the church as a perfect society and re-established the catholic unity proclaimed by King Reccared'. Even in 1946, the Italian episcopate persisted in seeing no difference between state neutrality and atheism: Cardinal Schuster, archbishop of Milan, the largest diocese in Christendom, declared, in the firm belief that the other Italian bishops shared his view, 'God's wish was so great for Italy's political destiny to be linked with its religious convictions that after so many centuries it is impossible to undo this knot that was tied by the Almighty with His own hand: the idea of a secular state for us is a historical error and a national crime.' The archbishop was arguing on the particular history of the peninsula but he forgot that Italy's unification had been achieved in defiance of the church and the pope's temporal sovereignty.

In practice, clergy and faithful manifested this recognition which welded church and society in a common profession of faith by deeds of devotion and solemn acts of public piety: consecration to the Virgin or Sacred Heart. They put pressure on the authorities to associate themselves with these demonstrations or even take the initiative for them. Spain was solemnly consecrated to the Sacred Heart in 1919, and Belgium also dedicated an official denomination to it.

Categorical rejection of secularization and unfailing attachment to the closest union between religion and society remained the objective of the catholic church in the first decades of the twentieth century, even after it had distanced itself somewhat from nineteenth-century intransigentism. After 1918 the pope did not resume all the latter's arguments, but even a pontiff as open to the preoccupations of his own time, alert to intellectual trends and favourably disposed to a certain modernity as Pius XI, remained true to an integralist view which subordinated all human activities to the kingdom of God. The introduction into the liturgical calendar on the last Sunday of the religious cycle of a feast day dedicated to Christ the King bears witness to his desire to rechristianize society. Although the impetus given by him to Catholic Action put forward other objectives than the restoration of the *ancien régime*, it was certainly aimed at rebuilding a Christian society. In the diplomatic negotiations for the signing of Concordats the Holy See was careful to mention the special character of the catholic church; thus the Concordat signed in 1929 with the Italian government asserts the catholicity of the state and several articles infer the consequences of this: religious marriage has civil validity and priests who break with the church are liable to civil sanctions and lose part of their citizens' rights.

On the eve of the Second World War, therefore, the principles remained: the churches did not yield in their determination to preserve or regain their rights, even at the risk of seeing the gap widen between them and intellectual trends and mindsets.

Confessional State and Regalist Tradition

Regalist reflexes and the traditions of the confessional state also persisted on the governments' side.

In a number of countries the church enjoyed a standing which, as well as recognition of its special nature, brought it advantages of various kinds, honours and sinecures. In return, the government had the right to keep an eye on its management and activities. Such control seemed the natural counterpart of the advantages that were granted. Jurists also justified it by the responsibility incumbent on the church as the guardian of national cohesion and public order. Realization that religion had an influence over the minds of the populace was a reason for the ruling powers to ensure the docility and monitor the loyalty of the ministers in each denomination. On the other hand, every government was tempted to channel that influence in its own interests. Traditional administrative practices continued to be observed in the twentieth century, therefore, but aroused growing resistance on the part of the ecclesiastical authorities, who were less willing to accept government interference and grew more jealous of their autonomy. Because of this, disputes increased and tensions between ecclesiastical institutions and governments grew more intense.

In protestant countries, Lutheran or Calvinist, the church usually remained dependent upon public authorities without this subordination giving rise to confrontations; religious hierarchies made the best of a regime that contained great advantages and, for their part, governments took care not to abuse prerogatives that legislation conferred on them. In England, Parliament still had the right to legislate on religious matters although it included members of other faiths than the Church of England; in 1927 it opposed a revision of the Prayer Book. The queen, in theory, but in practice the prime minister, selects the primate of the church. Since 1978 the choice has been made from a list of applicants drawn up by the church authorities. This situation extends typically *ancien régime* customs to the end of the twentieth century, quite out of keeping with contemporary aspirations. It was to put an end to this contradiction that the heir to the throne suggested the idea of breaking the link between the crown and the Church of England and dissociating the royal office from headship of the church. The situation in the Scandinavian countries is fairly similar to that of England: there the Lutheran church is the state church and all citizens legally belong to it from birth, citizenship thus being inseparable from adherence to the church whose constitution, some four hundred years earlier, had been contemporary with and a component of the nation's birth. In Denmark the Lutheran church is within the state: it is responsible for the public records of births, marriages and deaths, and for funerals. It is the nation's church, but it has absolutely no independence; it does not have its own central organization or national management. It is run on behalf of the queen by the minister for ecclesiastical affairs. Parliament legislates for it and the Supreme Court is the legal authority in its regard.

The union of church and state continued into the second half of the twentieth century in the catholic countries of southern Europe, Spain, Portugal, Italy, but in these three countries the pretensions of authoritarian regimes were in opposition to the catholic church's determination to preserve or reinforce the autonomy of its institutions, and provoked conflicts that were all the more serious because they involved a third partner – the Holy See.

At the inauguration of the Estado Novo in Portugal in 1926, everything conspired to secure excellent relations between the state and the church. The head of the government, Oliveira Salazar, was a fervent catholic, and the patriarch of Lisbon, head of the Portuguese church, had been his childhood friend. Above all, the regime explicitly referred to the teaching of the church and claimed that the corporative order it had instituted was the faithful application of the social encyclicals, affirming its desire to assist in restoring religion. As for the church, it was only too happy about the fall of the Republic which, since its establishment in 1910, had been animated by a keen anticlerical feeling and could find no more pressing matter than to imitate the French Republic by declaring a radical separation. Yet, even in such a well-disposed regime, in which the church had so many reasons to be satisfied, disagreements emerged. The status of Catholic Action proved to be the cause of discord, as the state could not accept that a sphere of influence could escape its control. In 1933 Cardinal Cerejeira sent his former school fellow a personal letter denouncing the resurgence of what he called the mentality of 5 October (the date of the proclamation of the Republic in 1910). He continued, 'the mental attitude of the Republic confused church and monarchy, this attitude confuses church and dictatorship'. Thus a new tendency took shape, striving to avoid any subservience by the church to the state.

The same causes produced similar effects in neighbouring Spain. The Spanish episcopate en bloc had sided with the Burgos government and had legitimized the nationalist uprising. Only two months after the end of the war the archbishops, assembled at a conference in Toledo, were already wondering about ways of resisting the state's totalitarian pressures and restraining the pernicious influence of the national trades unionist Falange, one of the elements of the national movement, whose inspiration was akin to that of the fascist regimes. The church certainly agreed to support the regime but only in so far as the latter would acknowledge its authority. Although unobtrusive, the tension became sufficiently sharp for the Minister of the Interior in September 1939 to forbid the circulation of a pastoral letter from the cardinal archbishop of Toledo on the lessons of war and the duties of peace.

It was the same in fascist Italy. It is true that the beginnings had been less fortunate: the regime did not have the same sources of inspiration as Salazar's Portugal or Franco's Spain; Mussolini would never have thought of quoting the catholic church's social doctrine as his authority. But the signing of the Lateran agreements in 1929, crowning a long and laborious negotiation, had brought an end to sixty years of wrangling and settled all outstanding questions. Now, barely two years after the signing, a grave crisis hit relations between church and state. As in Portugal, the status of Catholic Action was at its heart. The dispute set the will of the regime to control youth against a church determined to preserve the liberty of its own organizations. The battle grew so intense that it prompted the composition, in Italian, of an encyclical specially written on the subject, *Non abbiamo bisogno*, dated 29 June 1931, condemning pagan worship of the state and asserting the incompatibility of the fascist conception of society with catholic doctrine and natural law. The accusation of paganism was one which the Vatican habitually addressed to adverse ideologies; as for the reference to natural law, it was a classic argument in the thinking of catholic theologians.

To these three instances of catholic nations where an authoritarian state, professing to be inspired by a certain conformity with the catholic church's teaching, came into conflict with the Vatican because of antagonistic claims on young people, the case of Vichy France may be compared. Just as in Portugal and Spain, relations between the hierarchy and the new regime were at first excellent; the episcopate had hardly any reason to lament the disappearance of a Republic which had, in its view, adopted a discriminatory legislation and which it held partly responsible for both de-christianization and France's defeat. For its part, the new regime placed itself ostentatiously under the flag of moral values and granted the church substantial benefits, treating it with great consideration. Between the edifying language of the national Revolution and the habitual moral discourse of the church there appeared to be complete harmony. Nevertheless, the Assembly of cardinals and archbishops did not intend to become too closely linked with the regime, defining its attitude towards the government as 'loyalism without subservience'. On several points the hierarchy actually disagreed with the government, in particular on the subject of youth movements, as in the preceding countries. The episcopate was prepared to do battle to oppose plans for a single movement that would enroll all young people. This lofty defence of the freedom of movements, and indirectly pluralism, was by and large only a continuation of the battle that had been waged for over a century for the freedom of schools versus state controlled monopoly.

So four catholic countries, all authoritarian regimes, well disposed towards religion (through sincere conviction or shrewd calculation), had at the outset been unstinting with honours and advantages, and had worked to restore it, but their ambition to dictate everything had led them into conflict with a claim for independence on the part of a church less willing than in the past to let itself be subjugated or used by the state for other than religious ends.

11
Factors of Renewal

The Churches and Totalitarianism

From the time of the Revolution which, starting with France, had shaken the traditional structure of relations between religion and state, the Christian churches in Europe had had one major enemy: the rationalism that had given birth to liberalism, which initiated the separation of personal beliefs from social existence. Catholicism itself recognized no other enemy, for in its view it was the heresy of modern times, the source of all error. For intransigentism the three Rs – Reformation, Renaissance and Revolution – were in direct line of descent from the spirit of free enquiry. Although certain of the protestant churches did not rule out a compromise with rationalism and adapted themselves to making concessions to liberalism, catholicism stiffened its sinews in an unconditional resistance to the liberal spirit and all its political applications. Its sympathy went by natural inclination and logical reasoning to the regimes which ran counter to liberal assumptions. An inveterate mistrust of the ill-considered uses to which man would not fail to put his freedom, and denunciation of the misdeeds of individualism, naturally put most of the Christian churches on the side of conservative philosophies and authoritarian regimes.

This total opposition to liberalism explains why the churches were unable immediately to perceive the new threat being formed by the emergence in several large European countries of regimes which differed in nature from traditional and conservative ones, taking their inspiration from antichristian philosophies and intending to wield an undivided power over consciences and society in general; in short, regimes which today, using the name that was later applied to them, we would call totalitarian. Why should these churches, which believed they had suffered from liberalism, regret the suppression of the freedoms that had been invoked against them? As a whole they were slow to discern the perverse nature of the doctrines by which these regimes were inspired; even when charging them with being pagan, it is clear that the churches had not recognized their specific character. They were embarrassed in the face of these governments which presented themselves as the champions of a conservative revolution, breaking with liberalism, denouncing individualism, exalting the values of order and authority and showing the churches great consideration. At the outset, the Third Reich affected animosity only towards political catholicism, and proposed the signing of a concordat with the Holy See. The Vatican unhesitatingly sacrificed the Zentrum, as it had the Italian People's Party, upon obtaining a satisfactory settlement of outstanding matters and guarantees for the clergy's freedom of action; it acted in the belief that it was dealing with a partner who would honour agreements, and trusted in the strength of treaties.

A section of German protestantism had thought a synthesis between Christianity and national socialism possible, and had lent itself to an attempt at syncretism which sacralized the idea of race and expurgated the heritage of Judaism from religious teaching. This form of dissent took over the running of the church in several of the states which still made up Germany, notably Prussia where the principal official, Müller, became the head of the German Christian church for the whole Reich. Others made the opposite choice, of resistance to the infiltration of racism into the church; this was the case in Bavaria, at Württemberg and Hanover. At the Synod of Barmen in 1934, under the influence of the great theologian of Basle, Karl Barth, who was then teaching in Germany, one tendency adopted resolutions affirming the strong rejection of paganism; that was the birth certificate of the confessing church, which would pay a dear price for its spiritual resistance. Martin Niemöller, pastor of Dahlem, hero of the Great War, was arrested in 1937 and sent to a concentration camp; Dietrich Bonhoeffer, a remarkable theologian, was arrested after 20 July 1944 for having been connected with the conspirators, and executed.

As much for their historical antecedents as for their adherence to a church that was open to the outside world and their loyalty to Rome, German catholics were less likely to let themselves be seduced by national socialist arguments; in their ranks there would be nothing comparable to the German Christians. Until Hitler's arrival in the Chancellery, on 30 January 1933, the German Episcopate had upheld its ban on the faithful belonging to the national socialist party; the ban was lifted in March 1933, the national socialists being now in control, having attained office legally by virtue of the traditional doctrine of recognition of the established power. The Zentrum, the political expression of German catholicism, granted Hitler full authority; it did not foresee that this vote would be followed by its being banned. The signing of a concordat with the Holy See in July 1933 gave the regime a legitimacy. But relations swiftly deteriorated; the regime brought legal actions against numerous ecclesiastics on various pretexts. It was the *Kirchenkampf*. In March 1937 the publication of an encyclical written in German, *Mit brennender Sorge*, in the com-position of which several German prelates had co-operated, without actually naming national socialism, levelled irrevocable condemnation against its racist arguments and declared them un-acceptable to the Christian conscience. Brought into Germany clandestinely, it was read from the pulpit in the 15,000 catholic parishes. The Vatican at that time awoke from the illusion that had presided over the negotiation of the concordat on the possibility of an honest understanding with that type of regime. Numerous priests and monks were sent to concentration camps; at the liber-ation in 1945, the Allied soldiers would find some 800 priests in Dachau. More than one catholic personally reaped the con-sequences of the incompatibility between his faith and paganism: for example Dean Lichtenberg, priest in charge of Saint Hedwig's cathedral in Berlin – recently beatified by John Paul II – who publicly invited the faithful to pray for the Jews in the aftermath of the pogrom of Kristallnacht (1938), or Hans and Sophie Scholl, young Munich students who founded a clandestine movement, the White Rose, and were beheaded.

The difficult cohabitation with these regimes of oppression and violence certainly had an influence on the catholic hierarchy's atti-tude and their relations with the political power; they became aware of the danger that the totalitarian regimes constituted for both religious freedoms and the rights of man. Experience led them to temper the harshness of their judgements of liberalism. For the church and the truth that it taught there could therefore be erroneous doctrines other than that of the Enlightenment's philosophy. At the same time it discovered the soundness of the movement which proclaimed the rights of man; instead of seeing it only as the negation of God's laws and a manifestation of human pride, came the realization that it preserved values which were not necessarily in contradiction with the Gospel. Christians found themselves alongside liberals and democrats in the defence of certain principles against a common and far more fearsome enemy. The perception of the consequences of totalitarianism was a decisive factor in the gradual rallying of the churches to secularity, and especially the one that for a century and a half had been the most determined adversary of democracy, the Roman catholic church. Comparison between national socialism and fascism on the one hand, and liberal democracies on the other, turned to the latter's advantage as their practice presented fewer risks but also because of certain convergences revealed by history. In that long history circumstances had played a major role at every turn; not without good cause had those surrounding the proclamation of the Declaration of the Rights of Man and the Citizen figured in the Holy See's condemnation in 1791; a century and a half later, the opposite situation contributed not a little to healing the rift. In this regard, Pius XII's radio messages at Christmas 1944, praising democracy, was major evidence of this reversal. The way was clear for the establishment of cordial relations between religion and the state in liberal democracies.

Christians and Communism

When Christianity distanced itself from the totalitarian regimes it opened a path to a rapprochement with liberally inspired democracy. Resistance to communism completed this evolution by reconciling the church's teaching with the philosophy of the Rights of Man.

In March 1937, within a few days of each other, Pius XI issued two encylicals, one condemning racism, which had become a legal fact in the German state, and the other communism, and established an appearance of symmetry between the two systems. In fact the balance was not entirely equal; the first text did not condemn the regime, but denounced the most glaring aspect of its inspiration and policies, while the second declared communism to be 'intrinsically perverse' and damned it in its entirety. So the catholic authorities were not tempted to look for any compromise arrangement with regimes boasting of Leninist-Marxism.

But although the Vatican was never inclined to show any understanding with regard to doctrine, Christians were not unanimous about the conduct to adopt towards communism. First, because of an initial fundamental difference, which was a consequence of the war; the end of fighting left the continent divided and Christians to the east of the Iron Curtain subject to communist domination with no hope of freeing themselves from it in the foreseeable future. Although there was scarcely any attempt at synthesis between Christianity and dialectic materialism, the state ideology, clergy and laity in democratic Germany, Czechoslovakia, Hungary and Poland, differed over the attitude to assume. As citizens, it was their duty to contribute to the rebuilding of the country and the creation of a society that would share resources and costs more equitably. They should show themselves to be outstanding sons of the fatherland, and its most devoted citizens. On the other hand if, as official propaganda did its utmost to persuade them, peace was effectively threatened by United States imperialism, surely Christians belonged in the camp of the supporters of peace, of which Moscow was the leader. This issue of a peace to be preserved against the atomic threat was probably the most decisive factor in the people's democracies in the rallying of many Christians and their joining satellite organizations of the communist party, such as the PAX movement in Poland or Pacem in terris in Czechoslovakia, the party which excelled at making use of religious references to enroll Christians in the service of its political aims.

As for the orthodox churches under communist rule, a long tradition of submission to government had not prepared them for resistance. Accustomed to being subservient to the state, with a few exceptions, they withdrew into their religion. Their only public stands on questions other than those relevant to their faith concerned their participation in the battle for peace as advocated by official propaganda: denunciation of American imperialism and a campaign for the banning of nuclear weapons, as long as the Soviet Union possessed none of its own.

The situation in the west of the continent was quite different, in countries with a liberal democracy, where more than one Christian wondered about social inequalities; some refused to see the expression of Christian civilization in the Atlantic bloc led by the United States. Minorities of intellectuals, clerics, militant trade unionists devoted themselves to keeping a balance between the two worlds or even advocated an alliance with the communist party, the expression of the working classes and vanguard of the mass of the people for whom Christians ought to have greater sympathy because of their poverty.

However, the intervention of the Christian churches carried an overall weight against communism and played an important role in the battle to contain, and then overthrow, it. In particular, the Vatican exerted all its spiritual authority against communism. A decree of the Roman Congregation of the Holy Office, dated 1 July 1949, threatened with excommunication any catholic giving any support whatsoever to communism. Even if that ban was mainly dictated by the Vatican's fear of seeing the Italian communist party attain power in Italy, the decision did not fail to have repercussions in all countries where catholics were numerous and active, whether or not those countries were in the hands of communists. The resistance of Christians and the resoluteness of episcopates played a part in the collapse of communist regimes. This was especially so in Poland, where the stand taken by the primate, Cardinal Wyszynski, was carried on by the laity, intellectuals and militant workers. If the catholics were not the only ones to oppose the regime, it was certainly the catholic church which gathered the Polish people together and spoke for civil society, totally isolating the regime and the party.

In the German Democratic Republic, resistance to the official ideology and the communist government gradually crystallized around the evangelical church, the majority faith. Opposition first focused on an initiative by the political authorities: wanting to remove young people from the church's influence, they had instituted a secular ceremony of dedication for adolescents entering the official youth movement, including the taking of an oath. This aping of confirmation, a substitute for the religious rite, brought protests from the evangelical authorities. They too set in motion the movement which was to sweep the regime away: on the occasion of a service, celebrated for peace every Monday in Leipzig, rather similar to the masses for the homeland celebrated by Father Popieluszko in his Warsaw parish. It is therefore no exaggeration to ascribe to the churches a share in the responsibility for the downfall of the system and the collapse of communist authority.

But it was *only* a share; in fact, the churches behaved differently from one country, and also from one faith, to another. In the Czech Republic, an ancient tradition of mistrust with regard to Rome and of anticlericalism, which had prevailed at its foundation in 1919, restricted the role of Christians. Although there were some who joined the Charter 77 movement, unlike Poland they had neither the initiative nor the main responsibility. As for the orthodox churches, with the exception of a few heroic personalities, they practised an inglorious docility towards the government. If the revolution sort of stopped half-way in Romania and marked time for six years, if Bulgaria was slower to shake off the communist yoke, if the party managed to maintain itself in Serbia, it was partly because in these three countries orthodoxy was the majority religion and churches there had no tradition of autonomy.

Coming after the disastrous experience of totalitarian regimes, the Christian churches' confrontation with communism managed to convince them of the harmful nature of any regime that did not give freedom its necessary place or make personal liberty the principle of its organization. On the contrary, experience had shown the positive nature of recognition of the rights of man. It is perhaps because he himself had lived under communist rule and in the exercise of his pastoral duties experienced the wickedness of this sort of regime that John Paul II became their defender. At all events, throughout his pontificate he has never ceased to assert that religious freedom cannot be dissociated from other liberties. It was then that the fracture which had been open between catholicism and the rights of man since the French Revolution was healed. That was a considerable event if its historical bearing is measured against the long duration of the conflict and the extent of the consequences of the rupture between Rome and the principles of 1789. The major obstacle to an understanding between one of the main Christian confessions and modern society was erased. However, although John Paul II has played a major role, by the firmness of the stands he has taken, the clarity of his statements and the universal interest conferred upon them by his charismatic personality, his intervention was the crowning point in a development that had begun long before.

The Catholic Church Rallies to the Cause of Religious Freedom

From the Revolution onwards there appeared to be an unshakeable opposition between the steady movement of European societies towards secularization and the intransigence of ecclesiastical institutions boldly insisting on their claim for recognition of their religious and moral teaching as the truth of society. This opposition seemed even greater in the case of the catholic church which condemned absolutely the very idea of secularity in the state. There had probably always been some catholics who thought that Christianity was not incompatible with liberty and hoped that the conflict which set them at odds was nothing more than a temporary misunderstanding. Their conviction was that liberty itself needed the support of Christians and that in a liberated society the church would find a climate more favourable to its spiritual mission. Did not the example of the United States, after that of Belgium, confirm the soundness of their intuition? In 1863 at a catholic congress in Malines, Montalembert had formulated the idea of a free church in a free state. But those views clashed with the announcement that, as only the truth had rights and error none, the state was not free to remain neutral between one and the other. Now, what was secularity if not a neutrality that was indifferent to truth? If the catholic church made its decision because the public authorities in this or that country conceded a certain freedom to other confessions, or was resigned to sharing the government's favour with others, it was essentially for a circumstantial reason – the impossibility of winning automatic acceptance for its position. To resume the distinction conceived by inventive theologians after the promulgation of the Syllabus in 1864, it was not in the name of the thesis which alone had the merit of consistency, but by virtue of the hypothesis, that is to say, in consideration of the frailty of human nature, with regard to the misfortunes of the times, by a dispensation conceded with bad grace.

However, after 1945 the catholic church did better than become more flexible; it accepted the very principle of religious freedom and did so solemnly in a major document adopted by the Fathers of the Vatican II Council. The decision was all the more remarkable because it was effected by the denomination that had always most systematically stood against development and opposed all secularization. There is no better illustration than one borrowed from the country that had gone farthest in secularization – France. In March 1925, the Assembly of cardinals and archbishops had adopted a declaration condemning the laws of laicity as contrary to God's law and the rights of the church. Now the new text recognized the legitimacy of religious freedom.

The change was so complete and so unexpected that some people were tempted to doubt its sincerity and ascribe such rallying to tactical motives: the church forced to take heed of the irresistible nature of secularization, making the best of a bad job, was trying to arrange the possibility of surviving in an irrevocably secularized society. They did not believe the catholic church capable of surrendering its domination over consciences; a change of strategy, perhaps, but not of doctrine. The fact was that they had not picked up certain signs indicating a possible change. For example, that same Assembly of French cardinals and archbishops who had fulminated anathema in 1925 against the idea of laicity, exactly twenty years later in 1945, had adopted another declaration on the same subject, differentiating between laicity, the juridical regime, and laicism, the ideology, and distinguished no less than four interpretations of the concept of laicity, two of which no longer posed any problem to the Christian conscience.

The sceptics were not wrong, however, in ascribing a share of the responsibility for this development to events; the experience of confronting totalitarianism had led to a revision of the judgement formerly passed on liberalism and liberty. Nevertheless, the declaration on religious freedom proceeded from an entirely new kind of reasoning, which no longer justified it by the poor excuse of the hypothesis and considerations of simple opportuneness, but by reasons of the same kind as those on which the opposing position had traditionally been based. Faith, the personal step that concerned the most intimate part of the being and engages the conscience, could not be the object of any constraint whatsoever, whether of social pressure or political power. The church, which not long before had still required the state's assistance to propagate the truth and impede the spread of error, henceforward declared it incompetent in religious affairs: it was not qualified to interfere in choices of conscience. This was a desertion of the traditional position, a reversal of the viewpoint. It was no longer only civil society that brought about deconfessionalization, but the catholic church itself. A new chapter was opening in relations between religion and society.

One may wonder if this revolution, in the geometrical sense of the word, was not the result of a characteristic peculiar to Christianity whose singularity is startingly revealed by a comparison with other religions which built nation or state on the foundation of religious reference. Christ made the distinction between what belonged to God and what to Caesar; that could perhaps have been the origin of the idea of secularity. It was not unrelated to the myth of Antigone contrasting unwritten laws that compel conscience with state laws that may be iniquitous. Christianity held the seeds of freedom of conscience; indeed, by refusing through loyalty to their faith to sacrifice to the imperial cult, were not the early Christians its first martyrs and witnesses? At all events, certain thinkers unhesitatingly maintained that the idea of secularity was a Christian one and that, if it blossomed chiefly in the Christian west, it was probably not mere coincidence, even though the churches had taken so many centuries to recognize its inspiration.

The catholic church's acquiescence in the principle of religious freedom, was not, as obstinate upholders of the traditional argument suspected and accused, a desertion of the truth or surrender to indifference; it was not even the repudiation of the idea that society needed religion and that the latter should inspire individual and collective behaviour. To use recent concepts, if the catholic church had thus renounced the intransigentism that characterized the preceding era, it remained attached to an integralist view. The change showed only that all integralism is not necessarily intransigent, that it can come to terms with confessional pluralism and the recognition of freedom of conscience. In other words, the unchanged conviction of being custodian of the truth was not necessarily bound up with a reactionary system of thinking.

This change of view began to be seen in the Holy See's relations with states, especially in the drawing up of concordats. Thus the Vatican accepted a review of the Concordat with Italy. In 1946 the Lateran Agreements had been integrated into the Constitution of the Republic at the express request of the Secretariat of State, under pressure from the Christian Democrats and with the agreement of the communist party. The constitutionalization did not close the door to modifications, some of which had become inevitable. For example, it was not really possible to maintain the measures planned against apostate priests, which violated the principle of equality for all citizens in access to public office. As early as 1965, the Italian Parliament was seeking to open negotiations; these lasted nearly twenty years. The accession of a pope from the east probably helped them to a conclusion in February 1984. The new concordat took its inspiration from the declaration on religious freedom and aimed to harmonize the principles of Italian democracy with the demands of the Vatican. The consent of individuals became the rule, including for the financing of the church. The state no longer subsidized it directly; it was up to the citizens to decide whether they wanted a portion of their income tax, which would not exceed 0.8 per cent, to be allocated to the church. Religious marriage would preserve its legal features if such was the wish of the spouses.

Not all the episcopates, however, followed the same path; some did not completely give up trying to regain positions that had been lost or to reconsider certain effects of secularization. In the countries recently liberated from the grip of communism, some of the clergy simply demanded the restitution of confiscated ecclesiastical possessions or, as in Poland, made efforts to have moral law become civil law, notably in the matters of divorce or banning abortion. In the Council itself, a minority of bishops had voted against the declaration on religious freedom. The traditional position still found determined supporters; for centuries it had benefited from the authority of the Vatican and could refer to the laws of truth. For minds which had been raised in a rejection of any autonomy for civil society, confirmed in their prejudice against liberty by the spectacle of the modern world and the course of history, it was not easy to break out of a system which regarded any change as the sign of error and any deviation from tradition as a betrayal. Not by chance was it precisely about religious liberty and the church's relations with the world that the break occurred between the Council's tendency and the minority which was called integrist, but which would more aptly be designated by the word intransigent, for it was plainly the heir to the intransigentist way of thinking. One of its most representative spokesmen, Mgr Lefebvre, who had in fact voted against the bill on religious freedom, later used the very language of the Counter-Revolution's doctrinarians without altering one iota, and continued to defend the order of things in which religion and society were completely interwoven. This fracture which gave birth to a schism, in the literal sense, and would be consummated by the initiative of the prelate when, ignoring Rome's prohibition, he consecrated four bishops, was certainly at first an internal affair for the catholic church, but was not unconnected with or lacking influence on the church's relations with society. On the contrary, the rupture emphasized the historical importance of the change brought about by the principal Christian denomination's rallying to the idea of secularity.

12

The Other Aspect of Secularization: the Churches' Independence

Dwelling too much on the negative consequences for religion of the advances of secularization sometimes causes us to lose sight of the opposite aspect: the regaining by confessional institutions of an autonomy that had been lost or perhaps never possessed. If, in the wake of the French Revolution, the disappearance of the traditional regime that closely linked monarchy and religion had resulted in the early days in tightening the state's control over the churches, in a second phase secularization had loosened links with the political power, although that had clearly not been the government's intention. By secularizing, the ruling power no longer wished to derive its legitimacy from consecration by religious institutions as in the time of sacral society, but in doing so lost its right to meddle in their internal affairs. The church, whether catholic or protestant, which previously had accepted government supervision as long as it was the only one recognized, no longer had any reason to admit the interference of a state which henceforth extended its recognition to other denominations and increasingly tended to declare itself neutral in religious matters. If it no longer professed any religious conviction, what right did it have to interfere in the church's affairs? So those who had previously been most prompt to call upon the state to assist in the church's mission were not slow to challenge its right to intervene and to declare its claims unacceptable as soon as it ceased to make itself the docile instrument of the church. This reversal in position is illustrated in the intellectual route followed by La Mennais, who in the early stages of the Restoration had set out the programme of a modern theocratic government but who, his hopes dashed in the last years of the same regime by the Gallicanism of ministers, came to advocate a complete separation of church and state.

In most countries both protestant and catholic churches – the latter perhaps more than the former – gradually recovered all or part of the autonomy of which they had allowed themselves to be stripped. This reconquest began with the exercise of a liberty that was fundamental to communities whose organization rested on a certain collegiality – the freedom of their leaders to hold meetings and reach agreements. Nearly all the *ancien régime* governments, fearing they would be faced by a counter-power that might hold them in check, had banned bishops from meeting together. In France, when the clergy ceased to constitute an order, they had lost their Assemblies, and in the restrictive framework of the Concordat governments forbade bishops to act in concert and to meet other than on occasions of purely religious ceremonies. The Holy See was no keener than governments on the formation of national episcopates, especially in France, towards which Rome maintained a persistent mistrust because of its Gallican ambitions. A tacit understanding thus existed between the sovereigns and the papacy. In the protestant states, notably Germany, the principle of the *Landeskirche*, which traced church organization on the pattern of political division, subjected each local church to the government and prevented any dialogue or consultation in a broader territorial framework.

During the nineteenth century the resistance of the civil powers gradually weakened; less jealous of their authority, or less sure of their rights, or having become more indifferent to religious matters, governments tolerated what they had previously prohibited. The churches also took advantage of the crises that shook the state's authority. In France, the Second Republic permitted episcopal conferences to take place. At the same time, the bishops of all Germany met at Würzburg, instituting a tradition that would be uninterrupted after 1867; each year they would meet at Fulda at the tomb of St Boniface, the Apostle of Germania. In 1871, following the defeat, answering the longstanding prayer of part of French protestantism, a first national synod of the Reformed church was held. After the dislocation of the Double Monarchy in

1919, the episcopates would hold regular meetings in most of the successor states: Hungary, Czechoslovakia, Poland. In Great Britain, an Act of Parliament in 1919 curtailed the patronage of the gentry regarding the allocation of vicarships, and created a sort of Church of England Parliament, comprising two chambers, one of bishops and the other whose members were chosen by a system of election by several stages.

Similarly, Rome's old mistrust of national episcopates lost some of its virulence; the code of canon law promulgated in 1917 made provision for national episcopal conferences. In France, where the Vatican had not allowed Assemblies to be held other than those known as la Muette, the convocation of which had been imposed by the decisions to be taken regarding the Law of Separation, a first meeting of cardinals and archbishops was held in 1919 to examine current problems raised by the end of the war and, in particular, the reintegration of Alsace and Moselle. This assembly quickly became an institution and acquired great moral authority; it was held quarterly and its agenda continued to expand until it included every question concerning the church in France. From 1951, in addition to the Assembly of cardinals and archbishops, every three years a Conference was held, attended by all the bishops. Rome authorized the Italian episcopate to do the same, starting in 1954. The Vatican II Council, applying the principle of collegiality to which it restored its dignity, instituted episcopal conferences in each country.

The autonomy of the catholic church in every country drew support from the change which the Holy See brought to its relations with states. Since the birth of the modern states, partly to limit the attraction of the Reformation and spare catholic rulers any dilemma between loyalty to Rome and freedom of action, the popes had generally granted them the most important right, that of appointing bishops, the Holy See confining itself to conferring canonical institution on those whom the sovereign had chosen to guide the church. From the middle of the nineteenth century the Holy See endeavoured to regain this power by an effort of perseverance that continued for more than a hundred years. In the view of the Holy See, the reasons that had formerly justified such a serious concession had disappeared; states were no longer confessional or inspired the same confidence. The danger formed by liberalism now eclipsed that of schism and crossing over to the protestant churches. In fact, things had started badly in the aftermath of the Revolution. The concordat with France brought back the previous rules for the appointment of bishops and after the Congress of Vienna the Holy See was not in a position to refuse the states with which it was dealing the re-establishment of measures that were so advantageous to them. This was the case, for instance, of the Concordat signed with Bavaria in 1817, which confirmed the regalist tradition. But patiently, sometimes by dint of long and delicate negotiations and sometimes because of revolutionary situations that suddenly opened up unexpected opportunities, the Holy See gradually regained the appointment of bishops. Paradoxically, the change in relations with governments, and still more their severance, accelerated this development. The Law of Separation of churches and the state in France destroyed at one fell swoop the entire administrative edifice that had been built during the centuries by successive regimes to exercise close control over the life of the catholic church. Now the latter would answer to one authority only, that of the pope who was completely free to choose the incumbents of dioceses as he pleased. There was no longer any need to negotiate with the government of the Republic; the same applied to the unified Italy.

The collapse of the empires in 1919, bringing in its wake the disappearance of several of the Holy See's historical partners, was an opportunity for it to declare null and void the agreements which no longer suited it because they reintroduced measures imposed by the regalist tradition. At the Consistory of 21 November 1919, Benedict XV stated that in his view these Concordats had become completely worthless. His successor Pius XI, together with his Secretary of State, Cardinal Gasparri, negotiated texts more in keeping with the views of the Holy See, and granting more liberty to local churches, as in Rome. In the numerous treaties signed during his pontificate – ten Concordats, plus a certain number of conventions that were more limited in scope – papal diplomacy made sure that the right of the state to appoint bishops was replaced by their appointment by Rome. It was the end of the system known as patronage, which left to civil authorities the choice of the Apostles' successors. In parallel, the growth of pontifical power was at the expense of the traditional freedoms of the chapters.

One country was for a long time the exception to this Vatican strategy – Spain. For centuries it had enjoyed special privileges, even extending to the observance of some of the church's commandments; the faithful were absolved from the obligatory Friday fast, in recognition of the part played by Philip II in the victory at Lepanto over the Turks in 1571. The Concordat of 1753 had confirmed the king of Spain's right to appoint bishops. In the nineteenth century, the Holy See had maintained that right in return for the constitutional acts making catholicism the state religion, and the fact that they continued to deny freedom of worship to other Christian faiths. In 1875, after the short republican experience, Rome had confirmed the right that had been started by the 1851 Concordat. In 1931, after the founding of the Republic, Pius XI agreed on the need to adjust the concordat to bring it into line with the new regime's legislation, but the civil war resulted in the restoration of a typically old regime situation. Barely six months after the nationalists' victory, a law repealed divorce, in 1941 a decree instituted compulsory religious marriage for all Spaniards. Other laws made the teaching of the catholic religion obligatory in all schools and granted the religious authorities the right to monitor education as a whole. In May 1942, the archbishop of Toledo, Cardinal Pla i Deniel, took pride in the fact that the Spanish state had recognized the church as the perfect society and re-established catholic unity in Spain. In this climate of the restoration of the confessional state, it is not surprising that in June 1941 General Franco obtained the privilege of the right of nomination to the episcopate, a right that was confirmed twelve years later after laborious negotiations by a new Concordat which neither the Spanish government nor the Holy See had seemed in any hurry to conclude. The application of this right swiftly aroused tensions which continued to worsen, Rome increasingly having reservations about the government's choices, and becoming more and more reluctant to give its approval. As the text of the Concordat alluded only to the titular bishops of their dioceses, the Holy See increased the appointments of auxiliary bishops. After the fall of Francoism, Rome's most urgent task was to regain the right it had conceded. Since the re-establishment of democracy in Spain, relations between the state and the Holy See have again become more as they used to be. The Spanish exception was over.

While it thus strove to free national churches from the domination of the state, the Holy See disengaged itself from its dependence on governments. By not conforming to the traditional custom of inviting rulers' representatives to councils at the time of the first Vatican Council, Pius IX had already initiated the movement. Some thirty years later, following his election, which he owed indirectly to the use of the right of debarment made by Austria against Cardinal Rampolla, Pius X repealed that right and, on pain of excommunication, forbade cardinals to transmit a debarment formulated by a state. The settlement of the Roman question by the Lateran Agreements and the guarantees given for the sovereignty of the Vatican State completed the founding of the Holy See's total independence. Recognition of the pope as head of a state, even symbolic, nowadays allows representatives of the Holy See to have a presence in international relations, to be observers in the specialized institutions of UNO, to take part in certain diplomatic conferences, and today to be a party to the Organization for Security and Co-Operation in Europe (OSCE); all positions which bear witness to an independence gained as the counterpart of secularization.

In the national protestant churches also, a movement has recently taken shape to loosen the links connecting them with the state. Since 1997 in Sweden, the newborn are no longer automatically enrolled in the Lutheran church, and the government, which still appointed the last archbishop of Uppsala, the highest religious authority in the country, has given him the task of concluding the separation of church and state for the year 2000. Since 1 January 1997 in Finland, bringing to a close four centuries of connection, the government has ceased to intervene in the administration of the eight chapters of the national Lutheran church. In England the idea has been put forward of dissociating the office of monarch from the headship of the church.

Thanks to the Revolution of October 1917, the orthodox church too was given the hope of freeing itself from the domination of the tsar's government; for the first time in its history it had a brief taste of freedom with the patriarch Tikhon at its head. At the same time the Holy See cherished a similar illusion, imagining that the end of the imperial caesaro-papism would open opportunities, which had always been denied to it, for catholicism to penetrate that immense empire. For both the illusion was short lived; the longest and most systematic persecution in history suppressed all religious freedom. In 1927, the Metropolitan Sergii of Nizhni-Novgorod made a declaration of unconditional submission to the Soviet government. Seventy years later, the fall of the communist regime and rejection of its ideology emancipated the church and it was the government that earnestly requested its support and sought its backing. Provided one takes into account the difference in situation and ideology, it is not really so absurd to compare the position of Pius XII in 1945 after the defeat of Italy and the fall of fascism, when it was said of him that he was the uncrowned king of the peninsula, and that in present-day Russia of the patriarch Alexis II, whose blessing was requested by Boris Yeltsin during the ceremony that installed him as President of the Republic.

If a more clearly perceived recognition of the distinction between religion and politics resulted in the governments' allowing greater freedom to the churches in their own organization, in return the churches distanced themselves to some extent from politics. In particular, the instances became much rarer of clerics simultaneously exercising an ecclesiastical ministry and a political office. Under the *ancien régime*, especially in catholic countries, it was a frequent practice to entrust important political posts to priests, prelates, or even cardinals. The kingdom of France, one of the most obstinate nations about the merging of roles and the most stubbornly resistant to any kind of clericalism, entrusted the management of its affairs to a whole prestigious series of members of the college of cardinals. Pastoral functions formed one of the best training grounds for the exercise of power, and the clergy provided a pool of talents from which rulers could draw their loyal servants; at the same time a path to advancement was opened to men of modest condition, as long as class consciousness did not retain access to the episcopate for the nobility.

In the nineteenth century the conditions under which clerics could get into government were different; it was no longer a matter for the prince or ruler, but by election through institutions and in connection with the birth of modern party systems. Representatives of the higher clergy sat by law in certain assemblies. The British upper house had twenty-six spiritual lords; under the constitution of 1852, French cardinals were by right members of the imperial senate. The Spanish senate today numbers nineteen prelates in its ranks. Voters also delegate clerics to sit in the lower chambers. In Belgium, after the revolution of 1830, twelve priests were present in the national congress whose task was to draw up a constitution; a just consequence of the part played by catholics in the conquest of independence. The first in Europe to be elected by manhood suffrage, the French Constituent Assembly in 1848 had no fewer than some fifteen priests and members of religious orders; among others, Lacordaire, who had just re-established the Dominican order and took his seat wearing a white vestment.

It is not surprising that clerics were particularly numerous in confessional parties, as these were formed precisely with the aim of obtaining equality of rights in favour of the catholic minority. There were no fewer than ninety-one ecclesiastics out of the 483 members sitting on the benches of the Zentrum in the German Reichstag between 1871 and 1914. In France too priests canvassed and obtained the votes of their fellow-citizens with the aim of reconciling the church and the Republic; the democratic abbés, Lemire, Garnier, and Gayraud before 1914; Abbé Bergey and Canons Desgranges and Polimann between the wars, and after the Second World War, Canon Kir and the abbés Gau and Pierre.

Between the wars, the prevalence of the political priest was at its greatest in central Europe, especially in the new states that emerged from the dismemberment of Austria-Hungary. Mgr Seipel was Chancellor of Austria, Mgr Ludwig Kaas president of the German Zentrum between 1928 and 1933. In Czechoslovakia Mgr Hlinka played an important role in the new Republic, and it was yet another prelate, Mgr Tiso, who personified the nationalism of his native Slovakia until he became an accomplice of the Third Reich.

This long tradition no longer survives, unless as an exception, for example in Ulster with the Reverend Paisley. Religious authorities, especially those of the catholic church, are very cautious about the involvement of priests in politics. The new code of canon law, drawn up following the Vatican II Council, makes a provision that priests or monks thinking of offering themselves as candidates for election must request authorization from their superior, and this is usually refused. Such a change in attitude is dictated by a concern not to be dragged into conflicts in which religion would have more to lose than to gain, and the desire to forestall any suspicion of clericalism. But it is inspired even more by the wish to mark the distinction between religion and politics; it is the corollary to the church's claim for independence with regard to governments. Vatican II confirmed the distance assumed by the ecclesiastical institution when it stated that involvement in the responsibilities of society, especially politics, was a matter for the laity and not the clergy. Thus the division and allocation of responsibilities became clearer, and was not without a bearing on relations between religion and political society.

13

An Amicable Secularization

In two hundred years secularization has made immense progress throughout Europe. There is no longer any sacral state combining government and religion, and hardly a confessional state left. With one or two exceptions, in countries where orthodoxy is the historical religion – Greece, Serbia or the Scandinavian democracies – the state everywhere has ceased to maintain a privileged relationship, still less an exclusive one, with one church in preference to others. Even in England, where for four hundred years the church has been part of the establishment and is one of the symbols of national identity, the heir to the throne reveals his intention to treat all faiths, including Islam, on an equal footing, and the queen contemplates renouncing her position as head of the church. The state now belongs to all citizens; it practises equality of treatment between all faiths and leaves everyone free to decide his or her belief without that choice having any effect on personal status, exercise of rights and access to responsible positions and offices of all kinds.

The churches themselves took the side of secularization; they were convinced that it was irreversible and admitted that the distinction between political society and religion was not of itself contrary to the interests or even the principles of Christianity. If by doing so they lost authority and perhaps in prestige, they learned to value what they had gained: independence. Indeed there is hardly any country where the political power still assumes the right to interfere in their internal affairs. Religion is sometimes freer than justice, despite the affirmation in all constitutions of the independence of the judiciary.

During the second half of the twentieth century, a change of direction has taken place in secularization that was unexpected and has altered its spirit and practice. At first, and also later, secularization was put into effect against religious institutions and was imposed upon them in an atmosphere of conflict from a position of strength that was unfavourable to them. It was doubtless inevitable that the churches, accustomed for centuries to laying down the law quite literally, to being honoured and benefiting from privileged status, resented all acts that did away with their age-old advantages as nothing less than attacks on their dignity, denouncing as iniquitous every measure taken against their special liberties. All the more so since the transition of a privileged regime to common law was sometimes accompanied by highly discriminatory measures, notably in countries with a majority of catholics. Thus in France the law which in 1901 established for every association the most liberal set of rules that could be conceived in that era also included much harsher regulations for congregations. Another law, passed in 1904, deprived those in religious orders, simply because they belonged to a congregation, of a right recognized for all other citizens – the right to teach. At that time secularization was synonymous with marginalization of religion, and the neutrality of both state and education meant total disregard of and absolute silence about the existence of the churches. It is hardly any wonder that this rupture was experienced by churches and faithful as persecution, and for a long time left a raw wound.

Starting from principles that were far apart, whether from a confessionalism that had long been hegemonic or, on the contrary, from an intolerant secularization, the majority of states made their way towards establishing amicable relations with institutional religions and a certain recognition of the religious factor. In place of a refusal to acknowledge that the majority of citizens belonged to religious communities, experience led the political power *de facto* to recognize religion as an integral element of civil society.

Arranging Separation, French-style

Nowhere was this evolution more wide-ranging than in the country that had gone farthest in secularization: France. In 1905 legislation adopted a law which not only brought to a close centuries of relations based on concordats but categorically asserted a refusal to recognize all cults thenceforward. Since then an interpretation that was fairly far removed from the initial application has gradually prevailed. This evolution came about in empirical fashion rather than by the revenge of one camp over another, except perhaps at the time of the Vichy regime. Politicians had to yield to the evidence; it was neither reasonable nor even opportune for a government to pay no heed to religion. Experience made short work of the liberal premise that reduced it to something strictly individual and purely private; although it was true that faith was a fundamentally personal choice concerning conscience, that was not *all* it was.

It necessarily contained a collective dimension and social expressions. First, because every conviction, not only religious, informs judgement, guides behaviour and thus indirectly has consequences for life in society and relations with others. Then, every religion gives birth to communities; faith is communicated, transmitted, is the subject of a catechesis. Furthermore, it is celebrated, it creates a liturgy. Administrative terminology took note of it, usually designating religion by types of cult; the Law of Separation itself knew no religions or churches except by the denomination of forms of worship or religious bodies. The management of these bodies – with their minister, budget and freedom – all underlined the naturally collective nature of the religious factor. In addition, these communities were organized, endowed themselves with institutions and had at their head authorities whose existence could not be completely disregarded by the political power, which must also ensure that they did not exceed their rights. Lastly, most churches would not accept that their role was reduced to dispensing the sacraments or assuring individual salvation; they believed it their duty to set forth general principles, define a collective morality, and did not refrain from passing judgements on society. They thus possessed an influence that could not leave any government indifferent. In any case, why should separation be synonymous with an absence of any relationship, or imply a refusal to recognize the existence of a certain religious reality? The separation of the authorities did not prevent them from maintaining relations; it was even one of the principal objectives of constitutional texts to regulate those relations.

Relations were gradually established, especially in France, between the public authorities and the principal denominations.

The re-establishment came about through settlement of the dispute inherited from the Law of Separation and the circumstances of its application. When Rome prohibited catholics in France from forming religious associations, to which the legislation had made provision to transfer ecclesiastical possessions, it had prevented the planned system from coming into force and deprived the government of partners to negotiation. The Republic's authorities had to open dealings with the Holy See and accept some of its demands. If Pius X was categorically opposed to the application of the law, it was chiefly because the formation of religious associations as envisaged by the law, associations of laymen in the framework of the parish, taking no account of the church's hierarchical structure, seemed to him to conceal the fatal seed of a free democracy of the faithful. In his view parliament was repeating the error of the Civil Constitution of the Clergy which, a century earlier, had triggered the process of the break between church and state. After 1918, the government agreed to replace these democratic basic units with diocesan associations which recognized the specific nature of ecclesiastical organization. When all was said and done, it was only the application of an article of the Law of Separation laying down that private associations should conform 'to the organizational rules of the religious body whose practice they propose to ensure'. For seventy-five years the jurisprudence of the Council of State, which had the task of defining the practice, has never swerved from respect for this special condition. The significance of this situation is perhaps not always appreciated; an undeniably secular state agreed to accept the principles of the catholic church as the rule for the relations between them, although they were far removed from those regulating political society. The state conceded that the bishop should be the sole negotiator for his diocese and that priests accredited by him should be the only ones qualified.

Gradually relations were set up by sectors or types of activity. In any case, the Law of Separation which stated in its article 1 that the Republic guaranteed freedom of forms of worship, had made special provisions for all closed communities; there had to be chaplaincies for boarding schools, prisons, hospitals and the army. After the victory of 1918, in order to avoid the military occupying the left bank of the Rhine and civil servants posted to Germany being obliged to resort to the German clergy to satisfy their religious duties, the French government negotiated with the Holy See for the creation of a military chaplaincy with clergy paid from public funds and at their head a bishop in authority over this original diocese. This experiment came to an end with the early evacuation of the Rhineland in 1930. But fifteen years later, for the same reasons, at the time of a second occupation, a military chaplaincy was reconstituted. In 1949, a decree guaranteed it a lasting legal existence, confirmed on the ecclesiastical side by the creation in 1952 of a vicarate for the army. The other recognized denominations also had their chaplaincy.

From the early 1970s, the French administration granted those religious communities who asked for it the legal status of congregation or group of monasteries; some two hundred communities obtained it at that time. Its application was even extended to religions which, quite justifiably, had not entered the legislator's mind, for example, Buddhist communities.

It was also necessary to think up solutions inspired by the same spirit of conciliation to deal with the unprecedented problems resulting from the way society was developing. Thus the institution of a system of social protection for wage-earners could not, as it stood, be applied to the ministers of the various denominations; for them a special system was created which in this way indirectly recognized both the existence of their ministry and the particular conditions of their station. The arrival of new media, first radio then television, functioning within a state organ and for a long time having a monopoly, posed another problem, of freedom of expression and religious beliefs. At the time of the separation the question had not arisen because, as rules governing the press which was then the only means of expression were very liberal, the state had not had to worry about it. In the early days a strict interpretation of secularity in the polemical spirit that reigned during its initial stages, had led a left-wing majority in 1932 to suppress any religious broadcast in the schedule of state radio stations. Today an interpretation that is more respectful of freedom of expression and the diversity of religious groupings has won acceptance for an opposite practice: the articles and conditions imposed on public radio and television companies by the administrative authority obliges them to ensure religious broadcasts. These involve no threat to secularity as they are open to all recognized religious bodies and even to others such as Islam and Buddhism.

The Recognition of Communities

Whatever may be said and whatever justification is given to these sector-based arrangements, they provided an outline of legal status and implied a certain recognition of the religious factor. It has been asserted that they were a violation of the separation that became the law of the Republic in 1905 on which no regime, not even that of Vichy, has since reneged. It has also been said that they contravened the secularity which the constitution has made a characteristic and attribute of the state since 1958. When the term 'recognition' is applied to relations between state and churches, it is loaded with ambiguity. Historical circumstances had conferred on it a meaning which went far beyond the simple recording of the existence of the churches and the establishment of ordinary relations with them; more than a legal act, it was a profession of faith acceding to the demand of the majority religion to hold a privileged status in society. But merely to recognize groups founded on a common faith is not necessarily to cleave to their convictions, any more than when a government grants recognition to a trade union or professional organization but does not have to embrace its point of view. Between the confessional state of former days and the state which refused to admit that churches exist, there was room for a new type of relationship: a state which takes care not to express its opinions on the main issue, defends without concessions both its independence and the right of every citizen to make a free choice of belief, and which also maintains cordial and confident relations with the various religious communities. Between the merging of the political and the religious which exposes the government to the risk of falling into the clutches of clericalism, and the antagonistic breach, a great variety of permutations is imaginable. If one compares what most European societies have experienced for some decades, the difference – fundamental in comparison with *ancien régime* societies – is that today governments treat all the major religions on an equal footing, without preference or exclusivity, in full acceptance of the plurality of beliefs.

By agreeing to consider the churches as partners in dialogue, the state acknowledges that citizens may belong to intermediate communities. Formerly their membership was imposed on them by the collective society, as still happened recently in certain Scandinavian countries where every child was enrolled in the national church from birth. Today, the state leaves it to citizens to make their own choice; it is they who fix the amount of the community's aid to the church. That is the mechanism of the ecclesiastical tax as it has been functioning in Germany since the Weimar Republic. When filling out an income tax statement, the taxpayer indicates which church he wishes to receive the share of his tax that the finance law plans to allocate to religious categories. He is equally at liberty to disaffiliate himself, and every year several tens of thousands of Germans do so. The system set a fashion and several large democracies have adopted a similar arrangement, or are preparing to, for example, Italy and Spain. Since 1987 French taxpayers have been offered the opportunity, when working out their tax dues, of obtaining a deduction of the amounts paid as the church's portion, which happens to be a form of indirect aid to the churches; this is surely a version of the ecclesiastical tax. The expression of personal choice thus maps out in society the contours of communities whose existence is recognized in public law and to whom it grants allowances. It is another way of recognizing the religious factor, though in an original form very different from that of earlier times.

Nowhere has this system been taken quite so far as in the Netherlands, the perfect example of the structuring of civil society around communities of believers that have been set up as equal partners. The system known as 'pillarization' has profoundly influenced Netherlands society, which was organized on denominational lines. From schools it has expanded into the audio-visual sphere; each denomination has its own radio network. It is rather like the party-rule regime in post-war Italy when each large political formation controlled a television channel. The system was so effective in the Netherlands that it was necessary to create a third pillar out of nothing for those Netherlanders who did not belong to the major confessions, catholic or protestant, this one called humanist, to cover the agnostics.

If the Netherlands pushed the principle to its farthest limits, to the point of making it an institution, other countries have taken large strides along the same road. Belgium was almost predisposed to do so at the outset by the circumstances of its independence, which was snatched through the union of liberals and catholics. The pact ending the schools war which had split the country for over a century sanctioned the existence of several networks which received state aid in proportion to the number of children attending. Here too, alongside the major denominations, a humanist alternative has become established: the free University of Brussels (ULB) – and the adjective 'free' is to be understood in its original sense as the affirmation of the spirit of free enquiry versus dogmatic teaching – is the summit of the pyramid raised to confront the catholic Universities of Louvain. Belgian society rests on three pillars: catholic, socialist and liberal. A constitutional review in 1970 allowed the state to recognize non-confessional philosophical communities. Since 1981 secularist institutions have received some public funding, and in 1991 alongside the chaplaincies for the recognized religious bodies, a corps of moral counsellors was created in the army.

France itself, which is not only the paradigm of the most advanced secularization, but also home to the people who founded relations between politics and society on the concept of a citizenship shunning everything that differentiated between individuals, did not remain completely outside this evolution towards a certain recognition of the plurality of denominational communities. Was it not on this basis that the education dispute, which had for so long divided France into two antagonistic camps, found a solution with the Debré law in 1959? This opened the right to public aid to private teaching establishments (of which nine-tenths are catholic) in a framework of contracts comprising, in return for the government bearing the costs, a set of obligations that brought them closer to the state school service. Still more significant of the advance made along this route of a certain tendency to divide civil society into communities was the measure taken in 1983 on government initiative when a consultative committee of bioethics was created with the task of throwing light on government decisions and the legislator's deliberations on these matters: the constitutive document made provision for the presence of representatives of the principal 'sensibilities', this being the euphemism used to designate the spiritual groupings and perhaps conceal the possible snag of a rigid definition of secularity. Since its creation, therefore, a catholic, a protestant, a Jew, a Muslim and generally a Marxist on the same footing as the spiritual groups, have sat on this committee. A significant distribution which enlarges and actualizes the range of cults that have been traditionally recognized since the time of the Organic Articles.

This search for a way of relating the political power and the religious communities that are recognized as part of civil society today seems a meeting point for most European societies. Recognition is directed more to communities than to religions. It is in harmony with the evolution of our idea of democracy which increasingly tends to emphasize the acceptance of diversity and acknowledgement of the right to be different, as a reaction against the abuses of a certain interpretation of unity. Reference to pluralism is perhaps the most commonly invoked criterion today to define the essence of democracy and underline the specific nature of liberal experiences in western Europe.

Indubitably, this conception diverges from the vision that reigned over the first stages of secularization. Indeed one, if not the main, reason motivating its originators almost as much as the desire to establish freedom of conscience and preserve state independence, was the passion for unity and a concern to preserve a cohesive body of society. In the sacral or confessional societies of the *ancien régime*, religion was the principle of unity; that was based on community of faith as much as on loyalty to the monarch and a single legislation: one faith, one law, one king. As soon as the philosophy of the rights of man acknowledged that everyone had the right to choose his or her religion, and as a result the state dissociated itself from adherence to religion, the religious factor could no longer be the principle of national unity or the cement of the social fabric. When diversity of confessions became the rule, religion was henceforward a cause of division. Preoccupation with the unity of the homeland, like concern for civil concord, led logically to parenthesizing all religious references, so to speak. In France's case, in the aftermath of the disaster of 1870–1, the passion for unity which inspired the republican founders of the new order was a determining factor in the achievement of a secularity that completely ousted religion from the social sphere, and especially from state schools pledged to be the sanctuary of the fatherland. But today national unity seems strong enough not to have to fear the recognition of diversity. The revolution brought about in general administration in 1982 by the laws of decentralization, which set up regional district communities in partnership with the state, and the generalization of contractual procedures in relations between ministries and their partners, have transformed the conception of administrative law.

Moreover, relations between the public authorities and civil society have undergone a profound transformation. The French Revolution, which had been even more vehemently against intermediate bodies than against monarchic absolutism, had left only the mass of the citizenry opposite the state. Between the two there was a vacuum; not until the early twentieth century would forming associations cease to be a punishable practice. In this empty space, recognition of the churches represented an excessive privilege of common law. At the end of the twentieth century, which has seen the reconstitution of all kinds of groups, the burgeoning of organizations of every sort and their recognition by the state, obstinate refusal to take religious organizations into consideration would be a discriminatory exclusion.

The choice of this other way of regulating relationships between society and religion still raises difficulties, however. It naturally encounters resistance from those who cling to the original concept of secularity, ruling out any invasion of the social area and public discourse by religious beliefs. The persistence of this way of thinking in contradiction to the development of the practice explains the recurrent nature of the controversies about the idea of secularity. There is also the impact of events, which renew traditional problematics or bring old concepts to the surface again. This is the case in several European states where there are large Muslim populations.

Islam and Secularity

Islam is not an unknown quantity for European nations. Europe has shared a history with it for some fifteen hundred years, more often one of conflict than cordiality. For centuries Islam was a major threat and for Christendom the number one enemy, the infidel. Several nations in Europe were formed or became independent only after fighting and repulsing the Muslims; from the Spain of the Reconquista to the Christian populations of the Balkans. The tables were turned subsequently and Europe established its domination over Islam. Large nations, principally England and France, but also Italy later on, claimed the privilege of having Muslim dependencies. Relations were peripheral, superimposing a colonial society on native populations, and the parent countries had only a distant acquaintance with Islam. Today this situation is very different; in Europe itself millions of Muslims share the life of the native inhabitants, work alongside them, dwell in the same housing blocks. The three countries which have the greatest number of them, Germany, France and Great Britain, alone have no fewer than twelve million, many of whom are citizens of the country where they live and have no intention of returning to their native land which many, having been born in Europe, have never actually known. These millions of men and women expect to be treated like the others but many intend to remain loyal to their culture and to practise their religion. They therefore demand to benefit from the same rights and liberties which states afford to Christian faiths.

There is no apparent reason why this request should not be granted, since the relations with religions in European societies are established on the basis of equality between the denominations and the liberty of each individual to choose his or her own belief. Recognition of this right, however, encounters two kinds of difficulty. The first is that, unlike the other confessions with responsible institutions, Islam has no hierarchy; governments work unceasingly to find spokespeople who are qualified to communicate on behalf of their co-religionists and to negotiate. The other obstacle is more fundamental: contrary to Christianity which, even if it sometimes rejects the consequences, admits a natural distinction between religious community and civil and political society, Islam is presented as a unified whole. The confusion goes far beyond what it was in the so-called sacral societies of the *ancien régime*; it knows one law only, the religious law imposed on society and all its members. Laws pertaining to family, laws of inheritance, property ownership, penal and fiscal, are all derived, no matter what the country, from this set of religious rules. The fundamentalist revival of Islam fuels the demand to make the *sharia* the civil and political law. Nothing could contrast more with secularization. In addition, their customs, authorized or laid down by Islam, deviate from European traditions on several far from minor points; often they are even in direct contradiction, for example on the subject of marriage, and we have seen to what extent anything concerning marriage could be a subject of discord between the Christian churches and political powers. Islam authorizes polygamy; all European countries condemn bigamy. Can a government forbid indigenous citizens what it allows for others, and vice versa? Throughout Europe, partly inspired by Christianity and in the wake of Roman law, it is an absolute principle that there can be no valid marriage unless it is based on mutual consent of the two spouses; on that point churches and states are at one. This freedom of contract, however is not a condition *sine qua non* in Islamic tradition. Is it possible for two different laws to be observed in the same territory? In other words, the presence of Islam once again calls into question the civil heritage of Christianity and what has been gained by secularization. Denial of the distinction between religion and civil society reopens the debate on secularity that one might have hoped was over, and provides an unexpected argument to the supporters of a secularization driven to the point of a radical separation and a laicity identified with resolute disregard of anything concerning religion.

14
A Latent Secularization: The Secularization of Customs – the Divorce is Complete

The way in which the successive phases of secularization have followed on from one another raises an unavoidable question: has the process reached its final goal or will it still continue and to what extent? Step by step it has re-examined the most ancient practices and the most soundly established certainties. But for the future of religion in society there is perhaps something more formidable than the discontinuance of the religious budget or the abandonment of external symbols. True secularization could still be to come. This would be a total separation between the values revered by religions and those of civil society, between the moral principles taught by the churches and personal codes of conduct. The dissociation initiated between them by the progressive legalization of divorce, which is at present allowed in almost all European states – today only Malta's legislation conforms to the teaching of the catholic church – had opened a breach which has since grown steadily wider.

In the majority of European countries, until the 1960s, legislation on other matters of morality had been strictly in keeping with the teaching dispensed by the churches; what they defined as sin was, in the eyes of the law, misdemeanour or crime. The penal code was modelled on the moral code. Thus adultery was punishable and guilty parties caught in *flagrante delicto*, duly noted by a police officer, had penalties imposed on them. The civil code similarly reproduced the moral code; children born out of wedlock, and with even greater justification, those that were the fruit of a union regarded as reprehensible, adulterine children, suffered in their identity and their rights, the results of measures punishing infractions of rules that had a double validity – moral and legal.

A similar situation today seems unacceptable to many, owing to the way in which people's attitudes have evolved. Since the beginning of the 1960s a movement has taken shape and then asserted itself with the aim of liberating personal conduct from the judgements of any institution, whether state or religious. This change expresses a profound demand for individual autonomy. The movement was born in northern Europe, the Scandinavian democracies and the British Isles, in other words, countries which had for centuries been the most rigid moralists: Denmark, Sweden, Victorian England. In 1960, a law in England abolished restrictions on betting and gambling. In 1968, another banned all censorship on written works. The movement then extended to the rest of Europe, sparing no nation, and the catholic countries of Mediterranean Europe have not been left behind today. The archbishop of Canterbury, Doctor Carey, came up with a striking phrase to describe this phenomenon: he called it 'the privatization of the ten commandments'. It is indeed a privatization through rejection of an imposed rule and through the will to make morality a personal matter. Until recently the Decalogue was still the reference to which governments and laws conformed; it enjoyed universal assent. The moral and the legal coincided; today they diverge. This is probably the newest and most radical aspect of secularization. After religion, it is morality that ceases to be a matter for society, to become only a question of individual conscience. As there is no longer any official truth in beliefs, so there is none in the way people behave. It is the ultimate triumph of liberalism; the state ceases to give the backing of its authority to moral teaching. It makes a point of staying neutral in this area as well. Codes are seeing the gradual disappearance of measures inspired by moral considerations, which were themselves drawn from religious reference. In this way discriminatory measures against children born outside marriage have disappeared from common law. The same applies to the differences between families formed by a legitimate couple who have contracted a marriage before society and other forms of cohabitation.

The contradiction between the churches' moral teaching and legislation is even more pronounced on the issue of the transmission of life. In 1967 the French Parliament adopted a law authorizing contraception. In the same year Great Britain legalized voluntary abortion, copied by France seven years later. In its turn, Belgium has more recently decriminalized abortion. There is scarcely a country left in western Europe, with the exception of Ireland – and for how long? – that maintains the old condemnation of abortion. Voters recently consulted on this matter repudiated the *status quo* and gave a vote that may well be taken to presage a forthcoming review of the penal code. Confirming its precedence on the road to a permissive society, the England that imprisoned Oscar Wilde for homosexuality decriminalized this count of indictment in 1967. Even Russia, in its new penal code, has stopped regarding homosexuality as a crime.

At the same time that scientific discoveries have conferred on humankind an unforeseen power over the transmission of life, the moral teaching of the catholic supreme pontiff has become more definite and more restrictive in an unconditional defence of life; the contrast is sharper than ever between the position of the catholic church and the development of mindsets, customs and legislations. As a portion of public opinion is inclined to make the liberation of mores the criterion of modernity and opening out to the world, by this yardstick Roman catholicism is reputed to be incurably archaic. The misunderstanding is aggravated by the fact that the pope does not refrain from passing censure on governments that think it their duty to legalize abortion, and urges the faithful to put pressure on the public authorities to alter the legislation.

The 'Profanation' of the Era

There is one feature that is common to all the aspects of secularization I have mentioned up to now: the role of politics. All the successive phases of the process that have been retraced were clearly deliberate, decided in full knowledge of the facts; the measures taken did not always produce the anticipated results, and their application sometimes underwent delays and even deviations, but they were all the expression of a plan for society and imposed by law in conformity with the view of what relations between religion and society ought to be.

This inventory already contains a fairly wide variety of forms and fields of application, but it is not complete: there is one missing, which owes little to political will even if the latter was able indirectly to facilitate its insidious progress. To designate it and highlight its originality, perhaps a specific term should be sought. If 'dereligionization' were not so clumsy, it would probably be the least inadequate term. The result of this process is in fact no longer the separation of religion from society, but its gradual marginalization which might lead to its total disappearance.

When I say that this evolution owes hardly anything to political will, I mean that it has not been the object of an explicit plan or concerted action; it is, rather, the consequence – as well as the indication – of increased indifference towards religion, which records but does not react to the withdrawal of its presence and the effacement of the symbols that give evidence of its presence in society. Religion is less and less the reality around which life in society is organized. The *ancien régime* societies that have been termed 'sacral' were not defined only by the close intertwining of government and church, but just as much by the osmosis between religion and society, attested by the universal and constant presence of the religious element in collective life.

The secular world was punctuated by the cycle of religious festivals: the alternation of periods of work and amusement, the feast days which ensured that social existence kept breathing were wedded to the liturgical calendar. This situation has not been entirely abolished and even today in the majority of European countries public holidays perpetuate religious festivals, but the origins have often been lost to sight. For example: in most university systems the year was geared to religious feast days, apart from the summer vacation; All Saints, Christmas and Easter marked the rhythm of the academic year. Today the calendar of school holidays is dissociated from the religious cycle; when governments decide on holiday dates, they consider the demands of the hotel and tourist industry, compute the logistical possibilities of means of transport, sometimes even take account of the interests of children, but a concern to respect religious festivals and make attendance at services easier is the least of their worries. And all this happens without any malevolent intention on the part of the authorities or any desire to attack religious freedom. This area of preoccupation has simply disappeared from the consciousness of rulers and ruled alike.

Another example concerning the passing of the days of the week also affected the educational system. In the early 1880s, opening a new phase in the secularization of French society, the republican party undertook to secularize state schools and instituted a separation between the lay teaching dispensed by the school and the religious instruction provided by the parish priest; and Jules Ferry, in order to respect the liberty which had been the motivation of the first phase of the process, freed one whole day, Thursday, to allow children to attend catechism lessons: a remarkable measure of deliberate secularization. Today, under pressure from social demands, parents, and teachers too, who want to avail themselves of a completely uncommitted weekend, lessons increasingly tend to be compressed into four or five days, causing the Thursday interval to disappear and thereby compromising the chance of receiving religious instruction. The paradox is evident: at the time when politicians were crossing swords with the church, a place had been set aside for religion in the week's organization; this does not happen now that those in authority no longer have any designs against religion. This inversion of intentions and attitudes emphasizes the difference in nature between deliberate and concealed secularization, the insidious consequence of the way in which collective behaviours have developed and the enfeeblement of religious adherence.

This 'profanation' of the era, obviously imparting a different sense to the word than its customary meaning, is to be found in every collective activity. If public holidays with a religious origin continue to be observed, and perhaps more than ever, it is not for religious motives; commercial preoccupations combine with a desire for relaxation and the need to introduce some respite into the monotonous daily grind. If Christmas today is celebrated more than ever, it is less and less to honour the birth of Christ. The same applies to respect for Sundays. For centuries the observance of Sunday as a day of rest was a commandment to which the churches attached the greatest importance. It was a subject for sermons, and examinations of conscience mentioned it as one of the points on which penitents should question themselves. The churches made the authorities ensure that Sundays were respected; in France, on the Restoration, a law of 1814 forbade people to work on Sundays and feast days. Probably nowhere was the Sunday day of rest better respected than in England, where it was a symbol of the Victorian era. All activity ceased at mid-day on Saturday, and regulations banned any public celebration; there was nothing else to do but stay at home with the family or go to church. The rule began to be relaxed at the end of the nineteenth century; in 1896 a law authorized the opening of museums on Sundays, with the justification that these were institutions where attendance was likely to elevate the soul, and a National Sunday League was created, which organized Sunday train excursions. The legislative machinery that coerced society into a strict respect for Sunday rest was gradually dismantled. In France, where the law banning Sunday work had been repealed in 1880 when the republicans came to power, religious motives were superseded in the early twentieth century by philanthropic arguments; it was a matter of ensuring a day of rest for the workers. Catholic associations then campaigned in favour of a law re-establishing Sunday rest; their members pledged themselves not to make purchases on Sundays, and to do their buying from tradesmen who closed on that day. The development of social legislation consolidated the system which today is the subject of a counter-campaign to obtain the repeal of these laws. If the measure still survives in essence, it is certainly not from reference to the commandments of the church or from a religious motive, but on the initiative of trade unions in the name of the defence of rights that have been won.

This marginalization of religion is the sign that it no longer plays the central role it enjoyed for so long in European societies. Its effacement contributes in its turn to reducing still further the presence of the religious element. Even the collective customs and rites that had their origins in a reference to Christianity have today become detached from their roots and for this reason no longer fulfil the function of regular reminder for which they had been instituted. Thus religion no longer regulates social activities or private conduct; it no longer inspires collective beliefs or dictates common values.

Is This the End of Religion?

Does this apparently irreversible marginalization, this trivialization that puts religion on a level with other activities, whereas for centuries it occupied an unparalleled place even in a secularized Christian Europe, mark the final stage in its evolution, heralding its disappearance in a fairly near future? Has the moment come when the prediction formulated by Ernest Renan over a century ago in the preface to his *Souvenirs of Childhood and Youth*, 'religion has irrevocably become a matter of personal taste', will come true? Some people believe they can announce the end of

Christianity; Emmanuel Todd prophesies that catholicism has entered its terminal phase.

Historians have no appropriate answer to such a question; they possess no special revelation about the future, but their experience forewarns against making extrapolations and teaches them to be cautious. They are reminded, among other things, that it is not the first time such prophecies have been made but events have not confirmed them. In 1825, Jouffroy entitled an article that caused a great stir 'How dogmas die'. A few years earlier, La Mennais had devoted an essay to *indifference in matters of religion*. And since then how many times have there been predictions of the imminent obliteration of faith in the face of science, and the triumph of reason over religion! This reminder of the recurrent nature of such questions does not, however, give more latitude to affirm that religion will preserve or regain its position and role in society.

This long and detailed description of the progress of secularization for the last two hundred years has nevertheless been able to describe only part of the landscape; it says nothing of the other forms of the presence and enduring qualities of religion. To keep only to the one aspect would be to forget that, even in the most secularized societies, the religious factor assessed statistically is still clearly in the majority, and is by far the most massive social element of a voluntary nature. The history of secularization reveals, quite rightly, the gradual eviction of religion from the positions of power it formerly occupied, but does not take into account the other ways in which its presence persists in the heart of societies. As a moral example it is all the more sought these days, and perhaps the more heeded since the disappearance of most of the institutions which fulfilled that function, and because there is no longer an implicit agreement on common values being passed from one generation to the next. At the same time, as if they felt freer to take a stance since they have been removed from the exercise as well as the temptation of power, the churches intervene more in the problems of society. There are no longer any issues, however burning, on which the religious authorities do not assume a position. As for the papacy, never in the past has it held such a place in the world. The churches no longer hesitate to act like a critical tribunal: though Christians were certainly not the only ones to stand up to totalitarian regimes, and cannot claim the monopoly in the fall of communism, they nevertheless played a determining role. In international relations, for the reconciliation of former enemies as in the establishment of relations replacing those of colonizer and colonized the action of religious forces has been important. Lastly, as a source of unstinting devotion and active solidarity the role of religious communities is probably unequalled. But it is true that these new forms of action belong in an environment that is totally different from the time when religion directly inspired the public authorities. They operate in a context of secularization that relies more on the initiative of individuals and free institutions in civil society.

15

Today and Tomorrow

If there is one thing that becomes obvious from both this historical survey and observation of the present, it is the discovery that the question of relations between religion and society is neither resolved nor over, and that the time has not yet come to write 'the end' at the foot of this history.

Resurgence of the Debates, Durability of the Issues

Although there was a sincere belief at the start of this century that the definitive solution had been found, recent events generally give the lie to this conviction. In fact, in most European countries – the old liberal democracies just as much as the nations recently emancipated from totalitarian regimes – the matter relaunches controversy. From Ireland to Poland and from Germany to Portugal, relations between religion and society continue to arouse passions and enliven political life. And in the few countries where the problem has not raised a storm, questions are being asked about the validity of the rules that are in force and their relevance challenged. The list of issues at stake seems like a summary of the successive stages of secularization; all the strata of its history run through the subjects of the arguments. Traditional problems resurface, without prejudice to the new questions which stem from its evolution.

Examples of the most traditional disputes, those which correspond to the first phase of secularization, are the demands of the ecclesiastical authorities for reparation for the losses inflicted by spoliation, especially for the restitution of confiscated property. This matter arises today in the majority of countries of central eastern Europe after the collapse of the regimes of popular democracy which had nationalized all the possessions of the churches, generally great landowning powers. In Czechoslovakia, Hungary and Poland, they are seeking the restitution of what has been taken from them; the feeling of having been unjustly despoiled urges them on, and also they need to have their property available to them. These churches, whose destitution is extreme, need to recover the buildings that they previously used as seminaries or clergy houses. So at the end of the twentieth century we have the reappearance of the problem that was raised two hundred years earlier in western Europe after the French Revolution. There is one difference between the two situations: the attitude of the ecclesiastical institution. It may be recalled that in negotiating with the French Republic, Pope Pius VII, yielding to the demands of the other parties, had agreed in the interests of harmony not to challenge the sale of the church's possessions. The religions of eastern Europe are today far more exacting. It is true that, as the French Revolution was of liberal inspiration, the church's property had been sold to private purchasers: its restitution to religious orders or dioceses would have been to dispossess the new owners. In communist countries, the church's property was seized by the application of a policy of general collectivization; its return to religious orders or episcopal revenues would not have had the same disadvantages with regard to public peace. Even today the problem is no less a source of discord, especially in the Czech Republic where the catholic church is demanding the return of some five hundred buildings and 700,000 hectares of forests, which are the subject of delicate bargaining between the episcopal congress and the Czech government. Settlement has been obstructed for five years.

In Prague the status of St Vitus's cathedral is another contentious matter, dividing political parties themselves over to whom it belongs. In 1954 the communist government decided to nationalize it on the grounds that it was part of the Czech nation's cultural heritage and must therefore belong to the people. Since the Velvet Revolution, the church, and especially the cathedral chapter, have been demanding its restitution, offering the plea of a bull of Charles IV which bestowed it upon them. In December 1994, the Prague tribunal gave judgement recognizing the rights of the church, but this created a wave of protests demanding that it be kept as a national monument. The question was complicated by the fact that the monument is situated in the heart of the castle which has for centuries been the seat of government and the symbol of the Czech nation. The passions aroused by this issue bear witness to the persistence in Bohemia of a keen anticlerical feeling, which has endured from the time of the Hussite wars and the defeat of the White Mountain. The same question of restitution is posed in Russia, where the government is gradually returning religious buildings to the orthodox church. It is even participating in the rebuilding in Moscow of the basilica of the Holy Saviour, which was destroyed in Stalin's time. But the material problems are not completely settled by restitution; will the churches have the wherewithal to maintain the buildings in the absence of a financial allocation from the religious budget?

Poland provides both an extreme and intermediate example. The former because of the role that the catholic church played in resisting the government and then in the fall of the communist regime. The second because relations between church and society have become, here as in other countries, a subject of discord since the institution of democracy, essentially because of the claims of some of the clergy who are resuming the traditional demands regardless of the experiences in other countries. The church intends to re-establish an even tighter control than in the past over Polish society, on the grounds that catholicism should be part of the identity of the Polish nation. The church is militating for the signing of a Concordat in which the measures would be closer to those of past Concordats signed between the wars than to the agreements concluded since Vatican II. It is fighting for religious instruction to be made compulsory in state education. But the point that has raised the deepest reservations concerns the legal ban on abortion which the hierarchy is demanding, unaware that these claims are interpreted by a public opinion tired of the heavy hand of the state as a presumptuous desire to take the place of the abolished regime. These traditional-style demands have had something to do with the defeat of candidates and parties backed by the church in recent electoral consultations, and have contributed not a little to bringing the former communists back to power. Thus the Polish instance combines issues from several generations of secularization, from the oldest to the most recent, concerning the disagreements between catholic morality and the legislation.

In the west of Europe the old lands of Christendom are engaged in the last phase of secularization. In Italy, the combat waged by the catholic church to put obstacles in the way of divorce ended in failure; a majority of the electorate confirmed its legalization. In its turn Ireland, where the legislation on sexual matters was still closely modelled on the moral prescriptions of the catholic church, has followed the same path; consulted on an alteration to the constitution authorizing divorce under certain conditions, the voters pronounced themselves in favour of the government plan. In another consultation they similarly rejected a resolution banning Irish women from going abroad to have an abortion. As noted, Belgium has decriminalized voluntary termination of pregnancy.

Germany's case is one of the most interesting; this country, with a long-standing practice of confessional pluralism and a supreme example of a relatively peaceful coexistence of religions, is today experiencing a certain resurgence of religious quarrels. Reunification has had quite a lot to do with it; the division of the two Germanies more or less followed the historic dividing line between the denominations. Moreover, the two Germanies had adopted very different legislations, especially on matters with ethical implications. On the question of abortion, therefore, the German Democratic Republic had a far more liberal set of rules than the Federal Republic. Consequently, on either side of the wall dividing Berlin the problem had different solutions. Once reunification had taken place, the question of which regime to follow naturally arose: for a while the difference of opinion almost held up the actual reunification. East Germany, of protestant tradition but having undergone over forty years of a policy that aimed to eradicate religion, is today much farther than the former Bonn Republic from recognizing pluralism; 70 per cent of those under twenty-five state that they belong to no church at all. This disparity in religious attitudes is a source of tension between the new Länder and the federal government. The Land of Brandenburg decided in 1996 to do away with all religious instruction in state schools and thereby came into conflict with the federal authorities.

The gulf between the east and west is cross-cut again by another, setting north against south. Germany is experiencing a second point of difference with exactly the opposite causes, between Bavaria and the federal institutions on two subjects that correspond to two distinct phases in the process of secularization. In both cases, the Bavarian state, which was defined as a kingdom, intends to have the difference recognized; its special identity is partly the result of its belonging to the catholicism of the Counter-Reformation. The first subject in dispute is symbolic: a complaint was laid by a couple of anthroposophist parents against the presence of the crucifix in Bavarian schools, on the grounds that it contravened the state's neutrality regarding religion, and after it had been nonsuited by the Bavarian administrative legal authorities, the constitutional court of Karlsruhe found for the plaintiffs in August 1995, consequently ordering the Land of Bavaria to withdraw the crucifixes from public buildings and annulling the school regulation requiring them to be affixed to the walls. The constitutional jurisdiction thus settled the question in the same way as the French Republic a century earlier. But in Bavaria the decision provoked a protest movement by the churches, catholic and protestant alike, all kinds of demonstrations and petitions, and finally a categorical refusal by the Land authorities, who in September adopted a bill to keep the crucifixes. The controversy quickly overflowed the Bavarian boundries and took on a national political dimension with the intervention of Chancellor Kohl, criticizing the conclusions of the tribunal which he censured as endangering Germany's Christian tradition. The controversy had repercussions even outside Germany. In Austria, an argument started up almost immediately on the legitimacy of the presence of the crucifix in all state schools.

The second point of difference between Bavaria and the federal courts was added to the first, on the subject of abortion. In July 1996 the Landtag of Bavaria adopted measures on the termination of pregnancy that were clearly more restrictive than those of the federal legislation, and cast doubt on the compromise solution adopted by the Bundestag in January 1995 to bring the legislations of the two parts of Germany into harmony: women wanting abortion would now be obliged to justify their reasons and no doctors performing abortions could obtain more than a quarter of their income from this practice. Application to appeal was made by its opponents to the constitutional tribunal of Karlsruhe with the aim of obtaining the quashing of the regional law.

No country illustrates as well as France the enduring quality of the arguments and the permanence of the issues at stake. It may well have been the first to go to the furthest limit of the process of secularization and have since developed a concept of secularity and tried out a practice which could lead one to believe in a definitive peacemaking, but recent events have rudely revealed that passions were merely dormant and that a combination of circumstances was enough to bring problems thought to have been resolved back to the heart of the political debate.

Of course, one may regard as insignificant the protests of the splinter groups who remain the punctilious guardians of the intransigent interpretation of secularity: for them any emergence of religion into the public arena is an interference that the state should not tolerate. They militate for the suppression of diplomatic relations with the Holy See, demand the abolition of the Concordat in Alsace-Moselle and the introduction of secular laws in these three *départements*. Their campaigns no longer receive much sympathy in public opinion; with the abatement of the religious dispute, the growth of indifference and the enfeeblement of religious institutions, the argument about the danger of clericalism is no longer true. That traditional mistrust is not totally extinct, however, and it takes very little, a mere conjunction of circumstances, to breathe on the embers and rekindle the blaze. The old rule that the left wing can find no greater cement to unite it than the fight against the church has not yet lost all its validity. Moreover, the new and extremely delicate problem presented to the authorities and public opinion by the presence of Islam, the fears it inspires both for secularity and for democracy and the national identity, restore a certain immediacy to the denunciation of religion. Although the religions are very dissimilar and differ in particular over their conception of relations with society, mindsets that are most alien or hostile to religious feeling lump them all together under the common title of fundamentalism. They suspect them all of wanting to seize power and restore domination over minds. There is no other recourse, in their view, than to combat every religious expression without exception by a literal application of secularity.

Three subjects have recently relaunched the controversies. In first place, naturally, is the schools question. It is the oldest issue in the disputes between church and state, and today remains the only institution likely to raise tensions even in periods of quiet. Yet the point of the disagreements has constantly dwindled, the catholics having stopped challenging the authorities for responsibility in teaching matters, and the vast majority of the laity no longer questioning the principle of freedom of education. In 1959 the Debré law had in essence settled the question of the funding of private schools. The matter cropped up again in 1981 with the election of François Mitterrand to the presidency; his programme included 'the institution of a great unified and secular teaching service'. This commitment seemed to threaten the existence of catholic education. The mobilization of parents and staff, supported by a section of the political forces and having the sympathy of a public opinion that was in favour of pluralism and saw a guarantee of freedom in the maintenance of education distinct from the state's provision, caused the failure of the plan in 1984. The problem re-emerged at the end of 1995 in connection with a government initiative seeking to rescind a clause of a law adopted in 1850 by a conservative majority, the Falloux law. This clause, which limited the tax contribution of communities to 10 per cent of the investment expenditure pledged by the private establishments, seemed contrary to both the spirit of the Debré legislation and the policy of decentralization adopted by the left in 1982. There seemed no good reason why members of parliament should be prohibited from granting teaching institutions the financial facilities which they had the right to grant to any other social activity, unless it were in the name of a concept of secularity which imposes a discriminatory ruling on religious matters. But the way in which the matter was conducted, the absence of any prior consultation, wording that did not give sufficient guarantees about the allocation of money and the status of investments provoked an upsurge of passion culminating in a huge street demonstration, on 16 January 1994, replicating the one which, ten years earlier, had brought about the abandonment of the plan to unify the educational system. The success of this demonstration is partly explained by the chance provided to the left to mobilize against a right-wing government suspected of over-eagerness to please the church. But it also revealed the permanence of a problem and the enduring quality of a state of mind which continued resolutely to oppose any kind of recognition of religion by the state and the establishment of relations between society and religion. A tendency persists in the public mind to challenge the right of religious forces to public expression and denies them what is accepted for every other element of society; every statement by a catholic dignitary is immediately denounced as meddling in the life of society and a proof of clericalism.

Another event also reawoke passions that were believed dead, revealing disagreement over the relationship between Christianity and the French nation: the commemoration in 1996 of the fifteenth centenary of the presumed date of the baptism in Reims of the Frankish leader Clovis by St Rémi. As a retort to the suspicion of a desire to take over the celebration by the integrist catholic and counter-revolutionary right wing, for whom catholic France is the only France and who wanted to turn it into a counter-symbol of the bicentenary of the Revolution, a section of lay France mobilized, disputing that the event had the slightest significance for national history, refusing to accept that France had begun before 1789. This was an outlook significant of the refusal to identify the national community with a religion, and even considering that secularity prohibited the recall of an event if it was of a religious nature. If this campaign did not in the end awaken many echoes, it was because the church of France, unlike the Polish episcopate, was very careful not to lay claim to a privileged right over national identity.

The third subject of dissent concerns private morality, and comes about through the clash between the teachings of the Vatican and the legislation. If the religious authorities, at least in France, no longer call into question the law on divorce, legislation on the transmission of life has reopened the controversy. John Paul II's insistence, under all circumstances, on categorically recalling the church's traditional teaching on sexuality, his repeated condemnation of contraception and abortion, his denunciation of these practices as signs of a 'culture of death', all reverberated through the media, help to deepen the gap with a public opinion inclined to view the liberalization of customs as the criterion of modernity. In the name of a certain concept of secularity, some people denounce the reminder of these principles as a desire to re-establish the church's dominance over personal conduct and restore a moral order. On this point, too, we again meet the great problem of harmonizing intervention by religious institutions in the public area with respect for laicity in a secularized society.

New Subjects for Examination

The permanence of the most classic issues is no obstacle to the emergence of new subjects for examination and possible dissent. As already mentioned, there are the quite unprecedented problems resulting from the presence in Europe of several million Muslims, some of whom already hold the status of citizenship of their country of residence, where many of them have been born, and who wish to enjoy all the rights conferred upon them by belonging to a European nation but also to preserve their habits and customs. This is the great question of the compatibility with Islam of the idea of secularity as it has gradually grown and become clarified in Europe in the last two hundred years. The recent penetration into the continent by religions from Asia poses fewer questions to governments and public opinion, and doubtless not only because their followers are less numerous. They obtained recognition of their religious communities far more quickly than Islam.

Another phenomenon which affects fewer people but arouses more worries would on its own suffice to show that the time has not yet come when governments can totally lose interest in religious matters and refrain from intervening: the proliferation of those splinter groups known as sects, whose common characteristic is to maintain secrecy or at least great discretion about their activities and rites, and to demand unconditional obedience from their followers. In France their pursuits were the subject of two parliamentary reports, in 1983 and 1986. There is the question of whether they should be accorded the benefits of the freedom that legislation grants to traditional religions in European countries. There are no real objective reasons why a harsher set of rules should be applied to them, as once was done to catholic religious orders. It is not easy to trace the boundary between religious institutions that deserve esteem and consideration and those which the authorities are justified in mistrusting. Where do churches stop and sects begin? Some are suspected of taking away their followers' freedom; that is the main ground for complaint expressed by families whose children slip away from their affection. But that was the reproach commonly voiced against religious vocations by the anticlericals and the argument once invoked to prohibit monastic vows.

Yet governments cannot remain passive. They are the guardians of the freedom of worship, and it falls within their competence to see that laws are respected. Not all beliefs are equally worthy in their consequences; there are some that flout the law and whose teaching provokes behaviour which goes against the values recognized by society. But how is it possible to avoid relapsing into the abuses of the times when the state operated an arbitrary choice between confessions? The solution to the dilemma lies in reference to the law: each time a sect contravenes common rules of financial management, advocates behaviour contrary to morality or compromises personal liberty, then applying the full force of the law is the only recourse. In any case this is what several governments already do. In France, for instance, the Social Affairs Department denies Jehovah's Witnesses the opportunity to adopt children. Not because of their beliefs, but since they refused to submit to vaccinations or blood transfusions, at a time when these did not yet raise suspicion, the government considered that it would be subjecting children to too great a risk if they were entrusted to homes which did not fulfil legal obligations. Even in societies that have gone as far as possible in dissociation between individual beliefs and public life, the necessarily collective nature of all religious convictions and the consequences that result oblige governments to take an interest in them, recognize them and, if need be, intervene.

The question of knowing whether it is legitimate for religion to have a social dimension is thus resolved positively by what actually happens. Experience has brought us up against the illusory nature of the liberal idea that it was possible to enclose religion in the sphere of the private and individual. It also emphasizes the mistakenly simplistic nature of a dichotomy that would reduce the whole range of happenings to two categories only, the private and the public, roughly corresponding to another distinction, between the individual and the collective. The entire evolution of contemporary society has revealed the existence of a middle sector which has considerably expanded, of the collective private, and a mixed domain in which private initiative and intervention by the authorities intermingle; religion is part of it and therefore has a public expression recognized to benefit from the liberties acknowledged for all components of civil society. If the distinction between religion and politics has continued to become clearer and deeper, to the point of expressing itself as an extreme mutual reserve, the same cannot be said of relations between religion and society.

A European Model of Relations between Religion and Society

This study does not include a conclusion because the history whose first chapters it retraces has not yet come to an end. Contrary to what might have been thought, the last word has not yet been uttered and cannot therefore be written. The most classic problems resurface here and there; new issues emerge that call previously accepted solutions into question. Countries which have preserved their state church for four and a half centuries have recently queried the relevance of the formula or have begun to modify it. On the contrary, those who had opted for a radical separation have been guided by good sense and real life experience to re-establish relations. The evolution is therefore far from being complete and there remains uncertainty on what it may become; even the eventuality of a step backwards cannot be ruled out.

Failing a conclusion, perhaps a few observations may not come amiss, starting with some reflections inspired by a review of this history. Rereading these pages which gradually took shape, I suddenly became aware of the space occupied by catholicism. It was neither sought for nor deliberate, and is not the expression of a preference. It is not due mainly to an imbalance of interest, and I should like to think it does not reflect an inequality of capabilities between religions and countries. The cause does not lie in any numerical superiority. Fundamentally, it has to do with two features which make catholicism singular among Christian confessions, and which both have direct bearings on its relations with society: its unity and its special conception of relations between faith and human activities. Rather than its unity, it would be more accurate to say its universality. Of course, the other Christian confessions are also universalist, or at least incline that way. A church such as the Church of England is spread all over the globe and is at the head of some sixty million followers scattered throughout the world. The primacy of the Patriarch of Constantinople is recognized by all orthodox churches, even the independent ones. However, between the other denominations and catholicism there is one irreducible difference, which has a determining effect on relations with states. That is the pontifical institution, the unity surrounding the pope, who exercises the government of the churches and intervenes as a third party between local churches and secular governments. The other confessions are all contained in an exclusively national framework; territorial division generally coincides with confessional distribution. Because of this the relations between catholicism and the states form a particularly rich history.

On the other hand, the Roman pontificate has always expressed the claim to dispense moral teaching, to define a doctrine on the organization of society and to set forth the effects of faith on community life. For a century this teaching has continued to grow richer; the popes increasingly intervene in all questions concerning the life of men and women in society and the relations between peoples. It is therefore not surprising that a study on relations between regime and society is led, out of respect for reality, to make more frequent mention of catholicism.

There is also the fact that the lion's share of the discussion has focused on France. Contrary to what may be imagined, I do not in the slightest share the conviction of certain of my compatriots that the experience of France is an example for the world, the model of a harmonious settlement of the inevitable differences of opinion between religion and society. But without embracing this naive illusion, which is all the stronger because it is sustained by lack of knowledge of their status in other countries, it is a historical fact that France, before any other country, posed the problem in its most radical form; it cannot be robbed of the privilege of precedence. France was also the first country to infer the logical consequences of the premises and carry the effects to their furthest limits. Moreover, France is no exception to the rule; nowadays, secularization is no longer a special field, and most other countries have adopted the fundamentals. If there must be an exception for France, it would lie in its precedence and also the conflictive character that often accompanied it, even though other catholic countries have hardly been left behind when it comes to the dramatic intensity of confrontations and the violence of controversies; anticlericalism was no less strong in Belgium, Italy or Spain. The real difference in this regard is between catholic and protestant countries. It is less a case of French exception than of catholic singularity. The explanation for this difference is not unrelated to the one mentioned earlier regarding internal organization, discipline and ecclesiology between Roman catholicism and the other Christian denominations.

Between countries the distances are less pronounced than is thought. Above all, they are tending to diminish; although they still offer a wide variety in the forms they take, among them all exists a fairly general agreement on fundamentals which enables one to say that today there is a way, both common to all European peoples and original as regards the rest of the world, of regulating religion – society relations. All admit the natural distinction, which imposes an absolute separation, between personal religious convictions and citizenship. The state can no longer be confessional; belonging to everyone, it must be neutral and practise a strict equality between denominations. Even if not all states – far from it – like the French Republic since the constitutions of 1946 and 1958, make secularity an attribute and foundation of the state, and almost the fourth term of the republican slogan. Secularity is one of the elements of the entente between the members of the European Union; in the same way as the separation of powers, the independence of justice or the control of constitutionality, it forms a part of the *corpus* that defines the law-based state and gives a direction to the European nations' common will to live. It is a safe bet that in the next century secularity and the arguments about it will continue to occupy an important place in the political life of the European nations. That is why this book could not have a conclusion. May it at least contribute to throwing some light on the sense of the controversies and the significance of the issues at stake!

Bibliography

General

Bauberot, Jean (ed.), *Religions et laïcité dans l'Europe des douze*, Paris, Syros, 1994, 298 pp.

Davis, Grace and Hervieu-Léger, Danièle, *Identités religieuses en Europe*, Paris, La Découverte, 1996, 335 pp.

Gadille, Jacques (ed.), *Les Catholiques libéraux au 19ème siècle*, Grenoble, Presses universitaires de Grenoble, 1974, 595 pp.

Léonard, Émile G., *Histoire générale du protestantisme*; Vol. 3, *Déclin et renouveau (XVIIIe–XXe siècle)*, Paris, PUF, 1964, 787 pp.

Mayeur, Jean-Marie, Pietri, Charles, Vauchez, André and Venard, Marc, *Histoire générale du christianisme*, Paris, Desclée and Fayard, Vol. 11, *Libéralisme, industrialisation, expansion européenne (1830–1914)*, 1995, 1,172 pp.: Vol. 12, *Guerres mondiales et totalitarismes (1914–1958)*, 1990, 1,149 pp.

Schmidt, M. and Schwaiger, G., *Kirchen und Liberalismus im XIX Jahrhundert*. Gottingen, 1976.

Belgium and the Netherlands

Un siècle de l'église en Belgique (1830–1930), Brussels, 1930, 2 vols.

Aubert, Roger, *150 ans . . . des Églises*, Brussels, 1980.

Brachin, Pierre and Rogier, Ludovicus Jacobus, *Histoire du catholicisme hollandais depuis le 16ème siècle*, Paris, Aubier-Montaigne, 1974, 263 pp.

Courtois, L. and Pirotte, J., *Foi, gestes et institutions religieuses aux 19ème et 20ème siècles*, specially Malevez, G., 'La "bonne mort" ou la "mort libre"? La municipalisation des inhumations à Bruxelles-Ville', pp. 41–54, Louvain-la-Neuve, 1991.
Post, H., *Pillarization. An analysis of Dutch and Belgian society*, Gower, 1989.

British Isles

Bédarida, François, *La société anglaise du milieu du 19ème siècle à nos jours*, Paris, Le Seuil, 1990, 540 pp.
Bedouelle, Guy, *L'Église d'Angleterre et la société politique contemporaine*, Paris, 1966, 445 pp.
Burleigh, J. H. S., *A Church History of Scotland*, London, 1960.
Chadwick, Owen, *The Victorian Church*, Vol. 2, London, 1972.
Charlot, Monica, *Religion et politique en Grande-Bretagne*, Paris, Presses de la Sorbonne nouvelle, 1994, 190 pp.
Gilbert, Alan D., *The Making of Postchristian Britain: a history of the secularization of modern society*, London, Longman Group, 1980, 173 pp.
Haussy, Christiane d', Mews, Stuart and McLeod, Hugh (eds), *Histoire religieuse de la Grande-Bretagne*, Paris, Le Cerf, 1997.
Lesourd, Jean-Alain, *Les Catholiques dans la société anglaise (1765–1865)*, Lille.
Machin, Georges I. T., *Politics and the Churches in Great Britain*, Oxford, Vol. 1, *1830–1868*, 1977; Vol. 2, *1869–1921*, 1987.
Marx, Roland, *Religion et société en Angleterre, de la Réforme à nos jours*, Paris, PUF, 1978, 208 pp.
Norman, Edward Robert, *Anticatholicism in Victorian England*, London, G. Allen & Unwin, 1968, 240 pp.
Norman, Edward Robert, *Church and Society in England, 1770–1970. A historical study*, Oxford, 1976.
Routley, E., *English Religious Dissent*, Cambridge, 1960.
Slack, K., *The British Churches Today*, London, 1961.
Spinks, G. S., *Religion in Britain since 1900*, London, 1952.
Thompson, K. A., *Bureaucracy and Church Reform: the organizational response of the Church of England in social change, 1800–1965*, Oxford, Clarendon Press, 1970, 264 pp.
Tracy, G. M., *Le Catholicisme britannique sous la deuxième Elizabeth*, Paris, Grasset, 1956, 256 pp.

Danubian Europe or the Habsburg Empire

Nemec, L., *Church and State in Czechoslovackia*, New York, Vantage Press, 1955, Vol. 14, 577 pp.

Seibt, Ferdinand (ed.), *Bohemia Sacra. Das Christentum in Bohmen (973–1973)*, Düsseldorf, 1974.

Wandruska, A. and Urbanitsch, P. (ed.), *Die Konfessionen. Die Habsburgermonarchie*, Vol. 4, *1848–1918*, Vienna, 1985.

Weinzierl, E. (ed.), *Kirche in Österreich (1918–1965)*, 2 vols, Vienna, 1967.

France

Barbier, Maurice, *La Laïcité*, Paris, L'Harmattan, 1995, 311 pp.

Basdevant-Gaudemet, Brigitte, *Le Jeu concordataire dans la France du XIXème siècle: le clergé devant le Conseil d'État*, Paris, PUF, 1988, 298 pp.

Baubérot, Jean, *Vers un nouveau pacte laïque?* Paris, Le Seuil, 1990, 266 pp.

Bedouelle, Guy and Costa, Jean-Louis, *Les laïcités*, Paris, PUF, 1998, 266 pp.

Benoist, Jacques, *Le Sacré-Coeur de Montmartre. De 1870 à nos jours*, 2 vols, Paris, Editions ouvrieres, 1992.

Boussinesq, Jean, *La Laïcité française. Memento juridique*, Paris, Le Seuil, 1994, 212 pp.

Boyer, Alain, *Le Droit des religions en France*, Paris, PUF, 1993, 260 pp.

Caperan, Louis, *Histoire contemporaine de la laïcité française*, Vol. 1, *La Crise du 16 mai et la Revanche républicaine*, Paris, M. Rivière et Cie, 1957, 297 pp. Vol. 2, *La Révolution scolaire*, Paris, M. Rivière et Cie, 1960, 291 pp; Vol. 3, *La laïcité en marche*, Paris, Nouvelles Éditions latines, 1961, 328 pp.

Cholvy, Gérard and Hilaire, Yves-Marie, *Histoire religieuse de la France contemporaine*, Toulouse, Privat, Vol. 1 *1800–1880*, 1985, 351 pp.; Vol. 2, *1880–1930*, 1986, 457 pp.; Vol. 3, *1930–1988*, 1988, 569 pp.

Costa-Lascoux, Jacqueline, *Les Trois Âges de la laïcité*, Paris, Hachette, 1996, 140 pp.

Coq, Guy, *Laïcité et République*, Paris, Éditions du Félin, 1995, 335 pp.

Coutrot, Aline, and Dreyfus, Françoise-Georges, *Les Forces religieuses dans la société française*, Paris, Colin, 1966, 344 pp.

Durand-Prinborgne, Claude, *La Laïcité*, Paris, Dalloz, 1966.

Encrevé, André, *Les Protestants en France de 1800 à nos jours: histoire d'une réintégration*, Paris, Stock, 1985, 281 pp.

Jeuffroy, Bernard, and Tricard, François (ed.), *Liberté religieuse et régime des cultes en droit français. Textes, pratique administrative, jurisprudence*, Paris, Le Cerf, 1996.

Haarscher, Guy, *La Laïcité*, Paris, PUF, 1996, 127 pp.

Lafon, Jacques, *Les Prêtres, les fidèles et l'état: le ménage à trois du XIXe siècle*, Paris, Beauchesne, 1987, 372 pp.

Lagree, Michel, *Religion et cultures en Bretagne: 1850–1950*, Paris, Fayard, 1992, 601 pp.

Lalouette, Jacqueline, *La Libre-Pensée en France (1848–1940)*, Paris, Albin Michel, 1997, 636 pp.

Larkin, Maurice, *Church and State after the Dreyfus Affair. The Separation Issue in France*, London, 1974.

Latreille, André, *De Gaulle, la Libération et l'Église catholique*, Paris, Le Cerf, 1978, 146 pp.

Launay, Marcel, *L'Église et l'école en France (XIXe–XXe siècles)*, Paris, Desclée, 1988, 172 pp.

Le Goff, Jacques and Rémond, René, *Histoire de la France religieuse*, Paris, Le Seuil, Vol. 3, *Du roi très chrétien à la laïcité républicaine: XVIIIe–XIXe siècles*, 1991, 556 pp; Vol. 4, *Société sécularisée et Renouveaux religieux: XXe siècle*, 1992, 476 pp.

Leniaud, J.-M., *L'Administration des cultes pendant la période concordataire*, Paris, Nouvelles Éditions latines, 1988.

Léonard, Yves (ed.), *Religions et société*, Paris, La Documentation française, Cahiers français series, No. 273, 1995.

Marchese, Stelio, *Francia e Santa Sede (1914–1924)*, Naples, 1969.

Maurain, Jean, *La Politique ecclésiastique du Second Empire, de 1852 à 1869*, Paris, F. Alcan, 1930, 991 pp.

Mayeur, Jean-Marie, *La Séparation des Églises et de l'État*, Paris, Éditions ouvrières, 1991, 188 pp.

Mayeur, Jean-Marie, *La Question laïque, XIXe–XXe siècles*, Paris, Fayard, 1997, 236 pp.

Méjan, Violette, *La Séparation des églises et de l'état. L'oeuvre de Louis Méjan*, Paris, PUF, 1959, 573 pp.

Metz, René, *Églises et état en France. Situation juridique actuelle*, Paris, Le Cerf, 1977, 146 pp.

Noël, Léon, *Le Statut de l'église en France après la séparation: l'affaire des associations diocésaines*, Auxerre, 1978.

Pelletier, Denis, *Les Catholiques en France depuis 1815*, Paris, La Découverte, 1997.

Portier, Philippe, *Église et politique en France au XXe siècle*, Paris, Montchrestien, 1993, 160 pp.

Poulat, Émile, *Liberté, laïcité. La guerre des deux France et le principe de la modernité*, Paris, Le Cerf, 1988, 439 pp.

Poulat, Émile, *La solution laïque et ses problèmes. Fausses certitudes, vraies inconnues*, Paris, Berg international, 1997, 230 pp.

Rémond, René (ed.), *Forces religieuses et Attitudes politiques dans la France contemporaine*, Paris, Colin, 1965, 397 pp.

Rémond, René, *L'Anticléricalisme en France de 1815 à nos jours*, Brussels, Complexe, 1985, 388 pp.

The Germanies

Besier, Gerhard, *Preussische Kirchenpolitik in der Bismarckära*, 1980.

Besier, Gerhard, *Religion, Nation, Kultur. Die geschichte de christlichen Kirchen in den Gesellschaftlichen Umbrucken des 19 Jahrhunderts*, Neukirchen, Vluyn, 1992.

Gotto, Klaus and Repgen, Konrad, *Kirche, Katholiken und National Sozialismus*, Mainz, Matthias-Grünewald-Verlag, 1980, 155 pp.

Goyau, Georges, *L'Allemagne religieuse. Le protestantisme*, Paris, Perrin, 1906, 360 pp.

Harcourt, Robert d', *Catholiques d'Allemagne*, Paris, Plon, 1938, 357 pp.

Lill, Rudolf, *Die ersten deutschen Birchofskionfernenz*, Freiburg, 1964.

Lindt, Andreas, *Protestanten-Katholiken-Kulturkampf. Études sur l'histoire des églises et des mentalités du 19ème siècle*, Zurich, 1963.

Montclos, Xavier de, *Les Chrétiens face au nazisme et au stalinisme. L'épreuve totalitaire, 1939–1945*, Paris, Plon, 1983, 303 pp.

Morsey, Rudolf, *Der soziale und politische Katholizismus. Entwickhungslinien in Deutschland (1803–1963)*, Munich, 1981.

Reymond, Bernard, *Une église à croix gammée? Le protestantisme allemand au début du régime nazi (1932–1935)*, Lausanne, L'Âge d'homme, 1980, 313 pp.

Rovan, Joseph, *Histoire de la démocratie chrétienne*, vol. 2: *Le catholicisme politique en Allemagne*, Le Seuil, 1956, 295 pp.

Schatz, K., *Zwischen Säkularisation und zweiten Vatikanum. Der Weg des deutschen Katholicizismus im 19 und 20 Jahrhundert*, Frankfurt, 1986.

Spotts, Frederic, *The Churches and Politics in Germany*, Middletown, Wesleyan University Press, 1973, 419 pp.

Thalmann, Rita, *Protestantisme et nationalisme en Allemagne de 1900 à 1945*, Paris, Klincksieck, 1976, 482 pp.

Ireland

Miller, D. W., *Church, State and Nation in Ireland (1898–1921)*, Dublin, Gill and MacMillan, 1973.

Whyte, J., *Church and State in Modern Ireland (1923–1979)*, Dublin, Barnes and Noble, 1980, 491 pp.

Italy

Jemolo, Arturo-Carlo, *Chiesa e Stato in Italia dalla unificazione a Giovanni XXIII*, Turin, Einaudi, 1965, 496 pp.

Jemolo, Arturo-Carlo, *Chiesa e Stato in Italia negli ultimi cento anni*, Turin, Einaudi, 1971, 754 pp.

Jemolo, Arturo-Carlo, _Chiesa e religiosità in Italia dopo l'Unità (1861–1878), Relazioni_, Milan, 1973.

Menozzi, Daniele, _La Chiesa cattolica e la secolarizzazione_, Turin, 1993.

Miccoli, G., _Fra mito della cristianità e secolarizzazione. Studi sul rapporto Chiesa-società nell'età contemporanea_, Casale Monferrato, 1985.

Rosa, Gabriele de, _Il movimento cattolico in Italia. Dalla restaurazione all'età Giolittana_, Rome, Bari, Laterza, 1970, 402 pp.

Scoppola, Pietro, _Chiesa e Stato nella storia d'Italia_, Rome, Bari, Laterza, 1967, 862 pp.

Spadolini, Giovanni, _Le due Roma. Chiesa e Stato fra '800 e '900_, Florence, Le Monnier, 1973, 554 pp.

Spadolini, Giovanni, _L'opposizione cattolica da Porta Pia al 98_, Milan, Mondadori, 1994, 551 pp.

Vaussard, Maurice, _Jansenisme et Gallicanisme aux origines religieuses du Risorgimento_, Paris, Letouzey et Ané, 1959, 144 pp.

Poland

Castellan, Georges, _'Dieu garde la Pologne!' Histoire du catholicisme polonais (1795–1980)_, Paris, R. Laffont, 1981, 302 pp.

Davies, Norman, _Histoire de la Pologne_, Paris, Fayard, 1986, 542 pp.

Kloczowski, Jerzy, _Histoire du catholicisme polonais (1795–1980)_, Paris, Centurion, 1981.

Kloczowski, Jerzy (ed.), _Histoire religieuse de la Pologne_, Paris, Centurion, 1987, 639 pp.

Tollet, Daniel, _Histoire des juifs en Pologne du XVIᵉ siècle à nos jours_, Paris, PUF, 1992, 331 pp.

Rome and the Papacy: the Roman question

Alix, Christine, _Le Saint-Siège et les nationalismes en Europe (1870–1960)_, Paris, Sirey, 369 pp.

Aubert, Roger, _Le Pontificat de Pie IX (1846–1878)_, Paris, Bloud et Gay, 1952, 510 pp.

Boutry, Philippe, 'La Restauration de Rome. La sacralité de la ville, tradition des croyances et recomposition de la Curie à l'âge de Léon XII et Gregoire XVI (1814–1846)', viva given at Paris IV, 1993.

Levillain, Philippe (ed.), _Dictionnaire historique de la papauté_, Paris, Fayard, 1994, 1,759 pp.

Minnerath, Roland, _L'Église et les états concordataires (1846–1981)_, Paris, Le Cerf, 1983, 510 pp.

Mollat, Guillaume, _La Question romaine de Pie VI à Pie XI_, Paris, J. Gabalda, 1932, 469 pp.

Vaussard, Maurice, *La Fin du pouvoir temporel des papes*, Paris, Spes, 1964, 228 pp.

Scandinavia

Hunter, L., *Scandinavian Churches*, London, 1963.

Spain and Portugal

Almeida, F. de, *Historia da Igreja en Portugal*, Vol. 4, *1750–1910*, Porto-Lisbon, 1970.
Andres-Gallego, José, *La Politica Religiosa en España (1889–1913)*, Madrid, 1975.
Carcel, Orty, V., *Historia de la Iglesia en España*, Vol. 5, *La Iglesia en España contemporanea (1808–1975)*, Madrid, 1979.
Diaz-Salazar, Rafael, *Iglesia, Dictatura y Democracia. Catolicismo y Sociedad en España (1953–1979)*, Madrid, 1981.
Ebenstein, William, G., *Church and State in Franco's Spain*, Princeton, Princeton University, 1960, 53 pp.
Hermet, Guy, *Les Catholiques dans l'Espagne franquiste*, 2 vols, Paris, Presses de la FNSP, 1980–1981.
Petschen, S. *La Iglesia en la España de Franco*, Madrid, 1977.
Ruitz Gimenez, Joaquin, *Iglesia, Estado y Sociedad en España (1930–1982)*, Barcelona, 1984.
Vidal Baraquer A., *Iglesia y Estato durante la Segunda Republica española (1913–1936)*, 2 vols, Monserrat, 1971.

Switzerland

Pfister, Rudolf, *Kirchengeschichte der Schweiz*, Vol. 3, *1720–1950*, Zurich, 1984.
Stadler, P., *Der Kulturkampf in der Schweiz; Eidgenessenschaft und Katholische Kirche in europäischen Umkreis (1848–1988)*, Frauenfeld, 1984.

Tsarist Russia and the Soviet Union

Leroy-Beaulieu, Anatole, *L'Empire des tzars et des Russes*, Paris, 1890–1989, re-ed. R. Laffont, 1991, 1,392 pp.
Smolitsch, Igor, *Geschichte der russischen Kirche (1700–1917)*, Leyden, E. J. Brill, 1964.

Suggestions for Further
Reading (in English)

General

Bruce, Steve, *Religion in the Modern World*, Oxford, 1995.

Chadwick, Owen, *The Secularization of the European Mind in the Nineteenth Century*, Cambridge, 1975.

Chadwick, Owen, *The Christian Churches in the Cold War*, Oxford, 1992.

McLeod, Hugh (ed.), *European Religion in the Age of Great Cities 1830–1930*, London, 1995.

McLeod, Hugh, *Piety and Poverty: working class religion in Berlin, London and New York 1870–1914*, New York, 1996.

McLeod, Hugh, *Religion and the People of Western Europe 1789–1989*, Oxford, 1997.

Martin, David, *A General Theory of Secularization*, London, 1978.

Mol, Hans, *Western Religion*, The Hague, 1972.

Tallett, Frank, and Atkin, Nicholas (eds), *Catholicism in Britain and France since 1789*, London, 1996.

Belgium and the Netherlands

Strikwerda, Carl, *A House Divided: catholics, socialists and Flemish nationalists in nineteenth century Belgium*, Lanham, 1997.

Wintle, Michael, *Pillars of Piety: religion in the Netherlands in the nine-teenth century 1813–1901*, Hull, 1987.

France

Charlton, D. G., *Secular Religions in France 1815–1870*, Oxford, 1963.
Gibson, Ralph, *A Social History of French Catholicism*, London, 1989.
Gough, Austin, *Paris and Rome: the Gallican church and the ultramon-tane campaign, 1848–1853*, Oxford, 1986.
Kselman, Thomas, *Death and the Afterlife in Nineteenth-century France*, Princeton, 1993.
Tallett, Frank, and Atkin, Nicholas (eds), *Religion, Society and Politics in France since 1789*, London, 1991.
Weber, Eugen, *Peasants into Frenchmen*, London, 1977.
Zeldin, Theodore (ed.), *Conflicts in French Society*, London, 1970.

Germany

Bergen, Doris, *Twisted Cross: The German Christian Movement in the Third Reich*, Chapel Hill, 1996.
Bigler, Robert M., *The Politics of German Protestantism*, Los Angeles, 1972.
Conway, J. S., *The Nazi Persecution of the Churches*, London, 1968.
Goeckel, Robert, *The Lutheran Church and the East German State*, Ithaca, 1990.
Hope, Nicholas, *German and Scandinavian Protestantism 1700 to 1918*, Oxford, 1995.
Ross, Ronald, *The Failure of Bismarck's Kulturkampf*, Washington, DC, 1998.
Scholder, Klaus, *The Churches and the Third Reich*, 2 vols, London, 1987–8.
Sperber, Jonathan, *Popular Catholicism in Nineteenth-Century Germany*, Princeton, 1984.

Great Britain

Badham, Paul (ed.), *Religion, State and Society in Modern Britain*, Lampeter, 1989.
Brown, Callum, *Religion and Society in Scotland since 1707*, Edinburgh, 1997.
Cox, Jeffrey, *English Churches in a Secular Society: Lambeth 1870–1930*, Oxford, 1982.
Davie, Grace, *Religion in Britain since 1945: believing without belonging*, Oxford, 1994.

Davies, E. T., *Religion in the Industrial Revolution in South Wales*, Cardiff, 1965.

Gilbert, A. D., *Religion and Society in Industrial England: Church, Chapel and Social Change, 1740–1914*, London, 1976.

Gilley, Sheridan, and Sheils, W. J., *Religious History of Britain*, Oxford, 1994.

Green, S. J. D., *Religion in the Age of Decline: organisation and experience in industrial Yorkshire 1870–1920*, Cambridge, 1996.

Hastings, Adrian, *A History of English Christianity 1920–1990*, London, 1991.

Hempton, David, *Religion and Political Culture in Britain and Ireland: from the Glorious Revolution to the decline of empire*, Cambridge, 1996.

Machin, G. I. T., *The Church and Social Issues in the Twentieth Century*, Oxford, 1997.

McLeod, Hugh, *Religion and Society in England 1850–1914*, London, 1996.

Parsons, Gerald, and Wolffe, John, *Religion in Victorian Britain*, 5 vols, Manchester, 1988–96.

Parsons, Gerald, *The Growth of Religious Diversity: Britain since 1945*, 2 vols, London, 1993–4.

Wolffe, John, *God and Greater Britain 1843–1945*, London, 1994.

Ireland

Bruce, Steve, *God save Ulster! The religion and politics of Paisleyism*, Oxford, 1989.

Connolly, Sean, *Religion and Society in Nineteenth Century Ireland*, Dundalk, 1985.

Hempton, David, and Hill, Myrtle, *Evangelical Protestantism in Ulster Society, 1740–1890*, London, 1992.

Italy

Jemolo, A. C., *Church and State in Italy 1850–1950*, Oxford, 1960.

Kertzer, David, *Comrades and Christians: Religion and Political Struggle in Communist Italy*, Cambridge, 1980.

Poland

Szajkowski, Bogdan, *Next to God . . . Poland*, London, 1983.

Rome and the Papacy

Chadwick, Owen, *A History of the Popes 1830–1914*, Oxford, 1998.

Hastings, Adrian (ed.), *Modern Catholicism*, London 1991.

Luxmoore, Jonathan, and Babiuch, Jolanta, *The Vatican and the Red Flag*, London, 1999

Pollard, John, *The Vatican and Italian Fascism, 1929–32*, Cambridge, 1985.

Russia and the Soviet Union

Davis, Nathaniel, *A Long Walk to Church*, Boulder, 1995.

Freeze, G. L., *The Parish Clergy in Nineteenth-century Russia*, Princeton, 1983.

Hosking, Geoffrey, *Church, Nation and State in Russia and Ukraine*, London, 1991.

Pospielovsky, D., *The Russian Church under the Soviet Regime 1917–1982*, 2 vols, New York, 1984.

Ramet, P. (ed.), *Eastern Christianity and Politics in the Twentieth Century*, Durham, NC, 1988.

Scandinavia

Brohed, Ingmar (ed.), *Church and People in Britain and Scandinavia*, Lund, 1996.

Hope, Nicholas, *German and Scandinavian Protestantism 1700 to 1918*, Oxford, 1995.

Spain and Portugal

Callahan, William J., *Church, Society and Politics in Spain 1750–1874*, Cambridge, MA, 1984.

Lannon, Frances, *Privilege, Persecution and Prophecy: the Catholic Church in Spain 1875–1975*, Oxford, 1987.

Vincent, Mary, *Catholicism in the Second Republic*, Oxford, 1996.

Switzerland

Steinberg, Jonathan, *Why Switzerland?*, Cambridge, 1995.

Index